KING ALFRED'S C
WINCHESTE DRAMA:
y and Method of Analysis

THEORY AND
METHOD OF ANALYSIS

BERNARD
BECKERMAN

Dynamics of Drama

DRAMA BOOK SPECIALISTS (PUBLISHERS)
NEW YORK

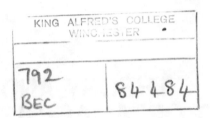
First published in 1970 by Alfred A. Knopf, Inc.

Library of Congress Catalog Card No.: 79-65301
ISBN 0-89676-019-7

Manufactured in the United States of America

10 9 8 7 6 5 4 3 2 1   9 9 0 0 1 1 2 2 3 3 4 4 5 5 6 6 7 7 8 8 9 9

TO GLORIA BRIM BECKERMAN

FOREWORD

Drama is an ancient art, one of the most ancient. Writings on drama are almost as ancient and far more voluminous. Yet despite heritage and volume, drama lacks a system of practical aesthetics. Reliable tools for the analysis of dramatic form as it manifests itself in the theater are simply not available. It is true that the principles of acting, as developed by Constantine Stanislavski, are invaluable, and the concepts of dramatic form, as enunciated by Aristotle and transmitted by successive generations of critics and scholars, are indispensable. But these principles and concepts are not comprehensive; they do not encompass classic and nonclassic, oriental and occidental, traditional and avant-garde theater. Because of this deficiency, theater artists, critics, and teachers are severely handicapped in their efforts to deal with a play's kinetic elements, which are, after all, the essential elements of drama. A comparison of drama's analytic resources with those of music and the fine arts reveals how paltry are drama's means for artistically grasping and manipulating its materials. In an art that is temporal as well as spatial, we have hardly any terms for designating the sequential features of a play, let alone the subtle interactions of the presentation itself. Our vocabulary is inadequate, our descriptions of the theatrical process imprecise, and our definitions of what constitutes the art of the drama virtually nonexistent. Perhaps at an earlier time, when a tradition or style of theater was passed down from generation to generation, this inarticulateness was not so crucial. Immediate example made elaborate definition unnecessary. Now, however, that we are in the midst of fundamental social and theatrical changes, we need to undertake an equally fundamental reexamination of the nature of theatrical art. In this book my purposes are theoretical and practical. I propose a theory of dramatic form and illustrate a method of descriptive analysis. These proposals emerge from my encounter with the ideas and presentations of others filtered through my own experience in theatrical production. I proffer them, not as definitive conclusions but, hopefully, as provocative contributions toward a new dramaturgy.

Acknowledgments

The concepts and methods of this book emerge from years of teaching and stage directing. For all the students and actors who patiently, and sometimes not so patiently, encountered this material in its formative states, I have the most profound gratitude. Their responses appreciably influenced the course that this work has taken. Also influential was the late John Gassner, who provided salutary advice upon seeing the first chapter in an early draft. The entire text received the conscientious and detailed criticism of my colleague Albert Bermel, to whom I am deeply indebted, and from whose astute judgment I have benefited immensely. I owe much appreciation to David Dushkin for his confidence in this analytical study, to Carol Green for her thoughtful advice, and to Claire Adams for her editorial assistance. Throughout the entire period of conceptualization and composition, I have imposed repeatedly upon my wife. She listened patiently to my ideas and proofread the typescript valiantly. Her insight as an individual and her experience as a teacher of literature transformed our continuous dialogue into a collaboratory exchange.

CONTENTS

DYNAMICS OF DRAMA:
Theory and Method of Analysis

Definitions

⊚ Each time a reader takes up a copy of a play, he also puts on a pair of spectacles. The frame of these spectacles is not plastic or horn but history. The lenses are not optical glass but accumulated dramatic practice and theory. Fashioned by generations of creative and critical theater artists, these glasses are compacted of preconceptions about what constitutes drama and how it produces its effects. Each scene and each act is filtered through these invisible panes before reaching the imagination. Though similar intermediaries lie between the reader and the novel, their influence is not so decisive because the novel is a finished work. A play, however, is a mere skeleton; performance fleshes out the bones. Reading an "unfinished" play script depends upon the governing vision of one's spectacles.

Within the past century drama has undergone a revolution in form and content. During the same period of time, concepts of dramatic form have changed little. What we expect of a play and how we identify its salient features are still refractions of *The Poetics* of Aristotle and its many historical offspring. Ideas of climax, of dramatic progression, and tragedy come directly and indirectly from Aristotle. Even where serious dramatic theorists depart from the substance of his theories, they usually observe the Aristotelian mode of analysis. Drama is regarded as a branch of poesis; its subdivisions include tragedy, comedy, and related genres; its structure is arranged into linear patterns of plot, character, language, and thought.

A scientist by temperament, Aristotle brilliantly codified the distinguishing characteristics of a specific type of drama. His aim was to identify, describe, and catalogue the species. Although he alludes to the emotional impact of tragedy, Aristotle does not attempt to examine the total experiential process itself. In fact, he mentions the much debated term "catharsis" only once. We may compare his work to a model of the human heart. The model itself is a static representation of a living entity and, in gross features, is faithful to reality. But in depicting the functioning heart either additional description is required or modern technological aids, such as the motion picture, must be utilized. Similarly, dramatic analysis requires finer analytic tools than are now available in order to describe how those plays which belong to the Aristotelian species function. In addition, there are types of drama that do not fit into that scheme of classification. Long after it was evident that Shakespeare's plays were distorted when seen through Aristotelian lenses, scholars and critics and, therefore, producers and readers persisted in evaluating and studying the plays as part of the classical dramatic tradition. Only in the last decade have studies in Shakespearean dramatic form, benefiting from sixty years of research in Elizabethan poetry, theater, and printing practices, begun to provide us with a fresh understanding of Shakespeare's artistry.

The modification of the Aristotelian image of drama is underway though still incomplete. Strindberg, Brecht, Meyerhold, Piscator, Peter Brook, and Genet have delivered blow after blow against conventional dramatic form and so have transformed our eyesight. As artists they have acted independently of any prevailing dramatic theory, though almost all of them, at one time or another, have tried to give conscious expression to their artistic views. What they have actually given us, however, is not theory but astonishing and disconcerting experience. At the very least they have demonstrated that our vision of drama has been limited indeed. Thus, they have challenged, if not replaced, the Aristotelian outlook, thereby opening the way to a new theory of dramaturgy.

And yet so many people distrust theory. Theatrical performers are among the first to express contempt for generalized ideas about theater. But unthinking practice does not avoid theory. It merely acts upon old-fashioned "theory," even though such "theory" may be no more than a residue of unexamined premises and reflex habits. Theory is inescapable because fundamental propositions always underlie accumulated artistic practice. Such practice, in order to be fully explored, appreciated, assimilated, and utilized as a historical and active art, must be given theoretical formulation.[1] It is never a question of whether or not theory shall interpret experience. Rather, it is only a question of which theoretical outlook shall prevail.

In the present state of dramatic ferment the scraps of ancient theory that we have inherited are not very useful, because they confine our understanding and analysis of the plays we read. This is particularly the case when understanding and analysis are part of an organized program of study. Drama-studied-as-literature usually ignores the very artistic basis upon which the work is constructed. Drama-studied-as-theatrical-score often fails to examine adequately the artistic form that the actor and director seek to project. To penetrate works of the past as well as works to come, a new way of dealing with the drama is necessary. It must be equally useful in dealing with traditional European plays, less familiar non-Western drama, and the inchoate forms emerging from the present state of theatrical chaos. The refinement of socio-aesthetic attitudes and the formation of analytic techniques must accompany any efforts to develop comprehensive views of the art of the drama. Already that necessity has been recognized by a number of dramatic theorists, such as Kenneth Burke, Francis Fergusson, Suzanne Langer, Ronald Peacock, J. L. Styan, Elder Olson, and Eric Bentley.[2] In the *Tulane Drama Review* Richard Schechner has attempted to broaden the scope of outlook by introducing related, but nontheatrical insights drawn from the sociology of everyday life.[3] What is common to most of these writers, and will be repeated in this book, is the practice of beginning at the beginning. Like them, I have found that preconceptions about the nature or dynamics of drama can be untrustworthy, for they ultimately prove to be narrow or misleading within present circumstances. To retrace the obvious pathways of theatrical analysis may seem gratuitous, but how else can one be sure that the route has been properly followed? In the very use of the fundamental terms "theater" and "drama," for example, there are misconceptions. I am therefore compelled to start with the simplest definitions and the most basic examination of theatrical materials.

THEATER

Definitions are hazardous enterprises. Like sands in the desert they may shift when they seem most firm. Yet we cannot do without them. They are the referents by which we gauge our understanding. They are also tools with which we do our work. To comprehend the relation of drama to theater, consequently, we need to agree on what is meant by theater.

DEFINITION: Theater . . . What shall the verb be? Shall we write "Theater is . . ."? But theater is not a thing. Theater is not an object to be manipulated. It does not have the solidity of a physical form which one can touch, like sculpture, or the permanence of a printed form to which one can return, like poetry. We cannot write, "Theater is . . ." Instead we might write, "Theater occurs . . ." Theater does not exist except when it is occurring. The building may exist. The performers may exist individually. The script may exist as well as the scenery. A poem is a thing made. Theater is not. It is something happening.

Thus, *theater occurs when one or more human beings* . . . The occurrence of theater is dependent upon human presence. Eliminate the actuality of man and eliminate theater. Such a definition excludes cinema from the boundaries of theater. Immediately, there will be objections. Cinema, it will be asserted, is clearly a form of theater. Is it not shown in theaters? Does not the cinema present dramatizations of events through the medium of characters? No, it does not. Cinema presents a sequence of visual images which can be used to tell a story or describe a place or record an event. It makes use of actors, but they are subordinate to the images. It is the work of the man who arranges the images not the work of the actors themselves that reaches us, the viewers.

The unbridgeable gap between the film and theater arises from the fact that the medium of film is celluloid and of theater, man. One can argue that this difference is not essential to the meaning of life that can be conveyed by these media. But meaning is not the end of art; experience and impact of experience are. And the experience of seeing human beings battling time and space cannot be the same as seeing visual images upon a screen. Without the living presence of beings assuring us that what is offered is not a thing made, but an event occurring, we do not have theater.

Is puppetry a theater art? After all, the puppets or marionettes are not human. They are media, but no more alive than the film image. Yet puppetry belongs in the theater. Like every subdivision of the theater, it involves human presence, though that presence may very well be screened. In the Bunraku doll theater the human performers who sing or manage the dolls are visible as well as audible. In the typical Punch and Judy show the human performer is seen through the effects he produces and is heard through his characterizing of the puppets. In both, the puppet play occurs, and therefore allows room for communal interplay. Though partially veiled, the human presence is felt throughout the presentation.

Theater occurs when one or more human beings present themselves . . . People make theater occur. What are they doing? Not pursuing tasks or activities oblivious of others. They are consciously displaying themselves. Man is not only the creator but also the means. This, then, is perhaps the most unique aspect of theater. The performers manipulate the media for expressive purposes, while they themselves are the media being manipulated. Through their skills, personalities, sensibilities, they make an offering. What is the nature of the offering? When we think of theater, we assume that the offering is a fictitious story, which we call drama. But that assumption divorces one part of theater from its close ties with other parts. Theater includes men performing a story. It also includes men performing tricks (gymnastic or illusionary), dances, songs, demonstrations, even rites under certain conditions. The lecturer, too, as *Our Town* has so affectionately shown, may operate within a theatrical context.

The act of conscious self-presentation distinguishes theater-as-a-socio-aesthetic experience from games or madness. Imagine a game of cops and robbers. When played by children, it is an imaginative form of play; when played by adults who believe their roles, it becomes a form of delusion. Presented by children or adults to others, it is a form of theater. As game its purpose is to provide pleasure for the participants. As theater its purpose is to affect spectators.

The act of presentation implies another or others to whom the presentation is being offered. In primitive cultures there are instances where an entire social unit presents itself to the gods thus giving us the archetypal form of theater. The spectator is a god or becomes god-endowed. Witnessing is an act of godhood though the temptation does arise in every age for the spectator to abandon his godhood and descend, whether to the dancing circle or to the stage, in order to participate in the presentation.

Our definition then becomes: *Theater occurs when one or more human beings present themselves to another or others.* But does not such a definition include too much? It includes the circus, dancing, and may even include sporting events. Exactly. Theater is potpourri. It can contain anything that man offers to others in his person. Its vital image might be most truly reflected by those omnibus vaudeville programs which toured the United States fifty years ago. On a single bill were included singers, dancers, dog acts, and comic sketches, notorious or celebrated figures as well as world famous actors or actresses appearing in scenes from Shakespeare. In microcosm, such bills sum up the authority and province of theater.

One observation must be made about sporting events. Although Brecht found theatrical possibilities in prizefighting, sporting events are not strictly theatrical events or, at the very least, are on the outer fringes of theater. In a sporting event one or more individuals engage one or more opponents in a contest of some sort. The basic act is challenge, not presentation. The validity of the contest is not certified by the spectators, but is inherent in the contest itself. It may be uneconomic, but not unusual, for sporting events to be held without the presence of spectators. Their absence in no way invalidates the occurrence but does remove sporting events from the province of theater.

By definition I state that the presentation can be to one person as well as to others. Presentation to a single person is rare though not completely unknown. In recent years performances have been given at the White House before the President with dignitaries of various rank also attending. Yet, it is the Presidential presence that is crucial and, in this respect, faintly reminiscent of the Court performances of the Renaissance, when the monarch, seated in state, served as *the* essential spectator. Primitive communities, as we have already seen, presented themselves to the gods. The more advanced civilization of Athens preserved this relationship by placing the statue of Dionysos as a symbolic spectator in the theater named for this god. Later ages brought other gods to life. Elizabeth I and Louis XIV were terrestrial deities who viewed from their seats of state the theater, which existed by their sufferance and for their glory.

The definition is almost complete. Only one final qualification need be added. Theater occurs when one or more human beings *isolated in time and space* present themselves to another or others. The performers and spectators must be separated from each other so that the spectators can observe what is happening. But this isolation is not merely utilitarian; it is both physical and psychological. A sacred grove may be selected, a dancing circle may be circumscribed, a platform may be erected. Somehow, an area is defined, which then becomes the servant of the performer. It is manipulable, both as actual and imaginative space; it is the place where presentations can be made. Recently, in drama, we have had instances, in productions such as *The Connection* and *The Blacks,* in the work of Jerzy Grotowski, and in novelties such as Happenings, where a breakdown of isolation is sought. Frequently, roles are reversed, and the spectator, instead of being god, becomes scapegoat. Such attempts to erase the line between presenter and presentee only define it more sharply. The auditor becomes acutely aware not only of the performers but of himself, thereby sensing that he has been cast in the role of a particular kind of spectator. Isolation is not eliminated, merely recharacterized. Demarcation is crucial in theater if the oscillation of stimulus and response between presenter and presentee is to occur.[4]

The degree of isolation varies considerably from one kind of theater to another. During the same historical period, for example, the Elizabethan theater observed three different degrees of audience intimacy. In the public playhouse, the separation between stage and audience was sharply marked. In the private theaters, there were constant encroachments upon the stage by cavaliers eager to share the glory of the performers. Despite the efforts of the actors, the gallants would thrust their stools upon the platform, even to the very rushes, or reeds, upon which the actors played. Not the performers but the spectators sought to break down the separation of presentation space from viewing space. In the Court theaters, during the performance of the masque, the presentation space remained isolated during the first part of the presentation, the anti-masque. But then, as the dance began, the performers invited certain of the spectators to enter the dancing circle, become participants and, in effect, performers. Nonetheless, in this theater as in the private theaters, the principle of isolated performer persisted. In fact, only the special aura of the playing area lent piquancy to the spectators' incursions.

Just as space is defined for presentation, so is time. Ritual drama observed set days for performance. The five days of the Greek tragic contests and the nine days of the Hopi Snake dance were equally sacred periods of presentation. Only through the knowledge and the power to conclude a showing do the performers have the capacity to begin one. They divorce themselves from actual life and enter into imaginative existence. Without isolation and temporal control presentation is merely life.

Theater, then, occurs when one or more human beings, isolated in time and/or space, present themselves to another or others. Such a definition is not an attempt to limit the nature of theater, but to distinguish the quintessential conditions that govern its character. The breadth of the definition should remind us that the ease with which one type of performance, the circus, for example, can slip into another, such as the burlesque, arises from the common bond linking these diverse forms. Dancing and singing readily become dramatic, because, although they are not necessarily theatrical, they can be easily utilized in the theater. Theater is a glutton. It will swallow any kind of material and experience that can be turned into performance.

THEATER ACTIVITY

Thus defined, the distinguishing characteristic of theater is conscious self-presentation. It is not the presentation of a painting or of a film, but of one's very being. Yet *being*, that wholeness of life in a person, cannot actually be presented in a time-bound medium, because, when observed over a span of time, *being* becomes *doing*. One of the first lessons Stanislavski taught was that even if a person sits absolutely still, he is doing something. The observer may not be able to interpret the meaning of this "doing" without an illuminating context; nevertheless, he witnesses not being but doing.

All presentation, then, is doing. From the observer's point of view doing consists of a sequence of perceptible, and therefore external, signs of motion produced by the performer. These external signs are purely physical. They include bodily and vocal signs, which are normally divided into gross movement and specific gesture or speech. Such signs may actually compose a language, as most vocal signs do, or may emerge in forms that can only be interpreted within a particular context. Also included in these signs are those motions which arise from the manipulation of or contact with objects and people. Lifting a cup or gazing at a person are external signs effected by physical means.

In witnessing motion, a person does not perceive signs discretely but contextually. As he observes someone going through a sequence of moves, he usually perceives not the individual motions but the sequence itself. A man stands and walks to the window. The observer does not "see" the straightening of the back, the extension of the knees, the shift of weight, and the stride as autonomous phenomena. Instead he sees the sequence as "going to the window." Only when he encounters a sequence that does not readily convey familiar behavior does he become aware of the individual motions as motions. Imagine that A has never seen a game of baseball. He comes upon B swinging a length of wood and stops to watch him. As B goes through the motions, A "sees" the separate flexures of shoulder, hip, knee, and wrist. Only if A were familiar with the game, would he identify these motions as "batting" and see them as the "swing" of the batter.

Both the performer and the spectator contribute to the proper identification of discrete motions. By the way he accents his motions and directs his energies, the performer relates his moves to one another in order to compose a coherent sequence. Simultaneously the spectator, taking his clues from the performer, strives to differentiate one related sequence from another. As students of visual perception have shown, people tend to generalize what they see so that they perceive a totality rather than its parts.[5] That same tendency in a performing art means that a spectator tends to divide the presentation of phenomena into a sequence of related activities rather than individual motions.

Motion refers to the actual physical moves, activity to the way motions relate or are related to each other. Hence an activity is a coherent sequence of motions. The coherence arises from the way in which the motions are done, the way they are perceived, or both. One complication arises from the fact that coherence can be seen in the briefest of sequences as well as the lengthiest. That is why the term activity, though it has a temporal character, cannot designate any set duration. Antony at Caesar's funeral is engaged in the activity "delivering an oration." As part of that activity, he performs the sub-activity "reading the will." In distinguishing activity, therefore, we need to discriminate between an extended activity and the sub-activities which compose it.

Identifying certain motions as an activity is one phase, the descriptive phase, of an extended differential process. Most people's lives are conducted at this level. The daily routine of preservation and play depends upon recognition of the descriptive meaning of other people's motions and only intermittently does a person probe for other meanings. Yet every activity can potentially lead to a further stage of identification, namely, the interpretive, which involves the use of the constituent motions as clues to the unearthing of more generalized or more subtle implications. There is thus a continuity of phenomena from motion to underlying purpose through the accurate perception of activity. The more critically an individual observes the *how* of an activity, in effect, its form and quality, the more he can penetrate its purpose and origin.

Customarily, activity receives scant consideration in the study of theater. Instead critics concentrate upon the term "action," by which they mean the underlying purpose of motion. They tend to see motion as superficial, action as fundamental. Kenneth Burke illustrates the distinction between action and motion by citing an example of two men engaged in identical operations. "Yet they are performing radically different acts if one is working for charitable purposes and the other to the ends of vengeance. They are performing the same motions but different acts." [6] But are they? In a gross sense, they may seem to perform identical operations, but in a critical sense they do not, for their purposes affect *how* they act. Within the broad framework of similar motions, the individual performs unique activity distinguished not only by the content but also by the rhythm, accent, and pace of the motions. Unfortunately, dramatic theory has not sufficiently addressed itself to a close analysis of theatrical activity, primarily because it has seen theater as a composition of words rather than of activities. It has tended to split motion from action, and then to concentrate upon the discussion of action. This seems to be a serious error, because, in failing to concern itself fully with activity before examining the concept of action, dramatic criticism and theory are ignoring the foundation of theatrical art. (For further discussion of action see p. 51.)

Activity is the basic medium of theater. It is the only channel through which presentational ideas can be projected, and so the art of the theater is the art of manipulating activity. To understand theater, one must focus attention on that activity: its texture, its nature, its symbolic power. A playscript merely gives the hint of the activity intended. Presentation gives it concrete expression. For example, one of the simplest dramatic devices is the soliloquy. In a playscript, its activity is suggested in the most general terms: a person, though alone, speaks aloud. Only in production is one forced to decide upon the specific nature of the activity. Is the person speaking to himself? If so, to what part of himself? Or is he speaking to the audience? Each choice leads to quite different effects. The present fashion of directly addressing the audience has sacrificed, in many cases, the activity of self-contemplation for that of confiding in the audience though the true dramatic values may lie in the former and not the latter activity. This is nowhere so evident as in Benedick's soliloquy in the garden (*Much Ado About Nothing*, II, iii). Benedick, the professed woman-hater, has just overheard his friends vow that Beatrice, the principal object of his scorn, is deeply in love with him. Alone, he argues himself into taking their words as truth. What is amusing is to witness how Benedick justifies his about-face to himself. If the actor confides in the audience, he stresses Benedick's foolishness at the expense of his vanity. The activity of self-disputation seems to be richer in possibilities, for it allows the audience to see Benedick wriggle out of his professed opinions for the flimsiest of reasons. Whichever activity is presented, each will project its own distinct experience, even though the identical lines are spoken.

Traditionally, European dramatic theory has thought of theatrical activity as essentially mimetic. Theater historians assume that imitation preceded presentation, that the source of peformance arose from the human impulse to copy animals and men.[7] In accordance with historical habit, audiences tend to expect lifelike behavior in the theater, a behavior measured in terms of its adherence to observable experience. As a result, this tradition, especially as manifested in the nineteenth and twentieth centuries, has obscured the purely presentational side of theater.

But there are other kinds of activities, such as juggling, tap dancing, acrobatics, that are so distinctive in character and so specialized in form that they cannot be recognized as stemming from familiar patterns of behavior. They exist wholly for the purpose of presentation as activities devised and practiced by men to astonish and delight others. They are indeed artificial activities, artificial referring to artifice in the original sense of being "made by human skill." [8]

Occasionally, as in the circus on one hand or in radical forms of documentary drama on the other, performers present relatively pure examples of artificial or natural activity. Normally, however, the theater utilizes mixed types. Natural behavior is theatricalized and artificial constructs humanized. But, though the types are mixed, the resultant activity is not uniform. Theatrical activity is composed of natural and artificial elements in differing proportions to produce different modes of presentation. Natural and artificial behavior each have distinctive effects upon an audience, and that is why failure to be sensitive to the artificial elements in theatrical activity excludes a vital factor in the study of dramatic form.

As an example of the artificial type, the acrobatic act of walking the high wire is particularly instructive. It is a purely presentational activity that requires a high degree of skill. At its most basic level of proficiency, it may merely consist of one person walking upon a taut wire. But since such a simple presentation would not hold an audience's attention, more challenging varieties of the high-wire act are usually devised. The true virtuoso might tread a slack wire, ascend a diagonal wire and slide down it, or carry two, three, or more people on his shoulders as he traverses the wire. Each of these activities involves skills not normally possessed by the spectator. In fact, the degree of excitement in the spectator depends upon the unusualness of the acrobat's skill. The activity produces mounting tension capped by a burst of admiration as the feat is accomplished.

Such an activity, and this applies to all those activities that are mainly artificial, is not abstracted from life but constructed. Constructed, in this sense, designates an activity determined by its own logic. Its "rules" do not emerge from nature, but are imposed upon nature by human contrivance. Consequently, it does not represent a natural life activity but possesses its own life activity. Music is an illustration of a constructed art. Constructed activity is characterized by limited, but extraordinary physical skill and is directed toward producing wonder and delight.

In a vague way, the spectator may carry over the excitement of acrobatic performance into his own life, but, by and large, the experience is nonevocative. That is, the high-wire act is self-justified. It exists for itself and does not produce emotional-intellectual overtones in the individual. Rather than relate the spectator to other experiences, it isolates him in the thrill of the moment. For one thing, this activity exists wholly on the surface. It has no inner life. And without an inner life it is restricted in its capacity to project generalized meaning. For another thing, the activity is actual. What the acrobat purports to be doing, he is actually doing. He is not pretending to be skillful; he *is* skillful. He is not pretending that danger exists; danger does exist, unless, of course, the activity is mere hoax.

Among the most completely "artificial" presentations are other forms of acrobatics and gymnastics as well as specialized forms of dance, such as tap dancing. But characteristics of artificial activity are not confined to such presentations and may appear in other theatrical forms. Not infrequently, within a variety revue or a musical comedy, a performer will insert an act that exhibits a particularly unique skill. The lingual dexterity of Danny Kaye or the dancing of Ray Bolger is precisely of that order. Though in their purest expression the distinguishing marks of artificial activity can be best seen in acrobatics, they may be found in all forms of theater. Exhibiting and witnessing performing skills are related pleasures of presentation and play-going.

Prestidigitation and other "magic" acts move one step away from such artificial activity. As in the high-wire act, the performance of sawing a woman in half is an activity devised for the theater alone. It produces a personal, visceral response, similar to but more intense than the fearful titillation that spectators enjoy as they witness a particularly hazardous acrobatic act. Skill, though less apparent, is still extraordinary, being a skill equally of suggestion and execution. Just as with the high-wire act, the magician's act exists for itself. It too lacks inner life, although it has hidden features. These hidden features, however, are the masked aspects of the magician's skill, not an evocative power. But magical acts depart in one important way from acrobatic acts. The activity is not actual. The magician purports to be sawing a woman in half, and, although our eyes seem to support his claim, we know he cannot be doing so. In a sense he is creating "an image of the act," a phrase Sartre has used to define the drama.[9] As "an image of the act," the magician's trick creates a visual illusion that we accept as actual though, in fact, it is "virtual."

I have adopted Suzanne Langer's term here, applying it to the entire realm of theatrical activity. "An image, something that exists only for perception, abstracted from the physical and causal order," Langer writes, "is the artist's creation." Through the artist's efforts, "a new appearance has superseded [the] natural aspect" of the raw materials, and the resulting image "is, indeed, a purely virtual 'object.' " [10] An object, enlarged here to include activity, is virtual, not because it does not exist, but because the center of its existence is appearance. Miss Langer makes it quite clear that she is not restricting the term "image" to the class of visual phenomena. It is applicable to all forms of creative practice, regardless of the sense to which it appeals. Thus, the magician's act is virtual while the acrobat's act is actual. The first does one thing while trying to create the illusion that he is doing another; the second is actually doing what he appears to be doing.

Of all forms of theatrical activity, dramatic activity seems to be furthest removed from artifice. Yet, it would be a mistake to place drama at one end of the theater spectrum and acrobatics at another. When viewed in historical and geographic perspective, drama reveals that it makes rich use of the entire range of theater activities. It absorbs and transforms the broadest variety of life-like and constructed acts to its own uses. That is why the breadth of the definition of drama must match the breadth of the definition of theater.

DRAMA

It is my contention that drama is *organically* connected with theater and is, in truth, but a special form of the art of presentation. This standpoint is a departure from the conventional use of the term "drama" as the verbal or literary basis of theatrical presentation. In *The Theatre and Dramatic Theory* Allardyce Nicoll defines drama as "a literary work written, by an author or by several authors in collaboration, in a form suitable for stage presentation." [11] In similar fashion, Northrop Frye asserts that "drama is a mimesis of dialogue or conversation," [12] and even Suzanne Langer sees drama as an art of poesis. "Drama is essentially an enacted poem," she claims, though she tries to throw emphasis upon the enactment. She recognizes that drama is more than lines and that "speeches are only some of the acts that make drama," but she does not uncover the formula for relating the speaking act to the act of presentation.[13] Such points of view, still too common, no longer go unchallenged. Elder Olson warns that "a play is *not* a literary composition," [14] and Francis Fergusson states that "drama, as distinguished from a lyric, is not primarily a composition in the verbal medium." But he then goes on to qualify that negation of the literary, not by making clear the essential element of drama but by explaining that "the words [of drama] result, as one might put it, from the underlying structure of incident and character." [15] Unfortunately, the literary bias of such writers as Nicoll and Frye and the equivocal observations of Langer and Fergusson distort the relationship between drama and its related activities in theater and have led to the reactions represented by Antonin Artaud, who castigates the literary theater as a stifling, restrictive art, cut off from the nourishing sources of theater. The alternative, however, is not a nonliterary drama, but perception of the proper connection between theater and drama. As a mode of theatrical art, the medium of drama is *not* language but human presence. Language, vital as it is to the art of the drama, is introduced through the activity of men speaking. But since speaking is such a generalized form of activity, we must modify even that statement by stating that men conversing, men orating, and men reciting are among the activities, and therefore media, of drama. To understand drama, we must return to the source of drama, that is, to theater.

Theater occurs. Therefore, as a subform of theater, drama occurs. It, too, is not a thing but a happening of a distinctive sort. Theater occurs during presentation. So does drama. Drama, too, occurs through the medium of human beings. But so do acrobatic feats, so does the dance. Yet drama differs from these other forms of presentation in one major respect: The presentation of drama is a presentation of an *imagined act*. It is the element of fiction, then, that introduces the crucial distinction between drama and other presentations.

An actor presenting an imagined act is engaged in a double effort: the demonstration of actual skill and the portrayal of virtual existence. He demonstrates actual skill by the way he imitates natural behavior and constructs artificial activity *simultaneously*. In enacting a death scene, for instance, the actor must show how life leaves a body while he clearly articulates his words. What he

imitates, often, is not actuality but a schematic notion of actuality that can be readily perceived by the audience. Breaking his normal rhythm of breathing is one way of indicating the onslaught of death. Originality comes not from absolute fidelity to nature but from a combination of freshly observed features of natural behavior with formal elements of presentation. By using schematic stage activity, he gives the appearance of inner life. This is the imagined act.

The concept of the imagined act is elusive because a dramatic presentation cannot be readily separated into component elements. Although the audience knows that the actor is performing, it also sees him living. If, however, it analyzes *how* the illusion is produced, it finds that not only does stage activity embody a fictional event but that the fictional event also contains an inner life. In performing activity, an actor portrays a character's behavior, which, in turn, reveals the character's inner life. Thus we can speak of the activity (what the actor does), the imagined act (what the character does), and the inner life (what the imagined act reflects). Depending upon the style, or mode, of drama, these planes of recession may be distinct or continuous. At the conclusion of Chekhov's *The Three Sisters*, for instance, the schoolmaster Kulygin comforts his wife, Masha, as her lover departs. Pretending ignorance of her unfaithfulness, he expresses cheer and comfort though he is experiencing deep pain. Here the actor must skillfully perform activity that portrays Kulygin's outward behavior, which, in turn, must suggest his inner life. In *Hamlet,* on the other hand, the actor reciting the soliloquy "To be or not to be" is not portraying Hamlet reciting a soliloquy, but through his verbal activity is giving direct access to the inner life, which, in this instance, is Hamlet's flow of thought. The term "imagined act" will be understood to include both the fictitious behavior and the inner life of that behavior.

In referring to drama, I have used the phrase "imagined act" and avoided the terms "imitation" or "mimesis." Aristotle defined tragedy as an "imitation" of a certain type of serious action. His use of the notion of "imitation" arose from a philosophical view of literature's relation to reality. Included in his use of the word is imitation of imagined events. Unfortunately, the concept of imitation is so closely linked to model and reflection that it seems best to avoid the word. The imagined act includes both imitative and constructed acts, because even in its most documentary state drama subjects historical experience to reconstruction through the operation of the imagination. *Drama occurs when one or more human beings isolated in time and space present themselves in imagined acts to another or others.*

This is truly a broad definition of the term drama. It includes generically all that is meant by tragedy, comedy, skit, serious drama, farce, melodrama, musical play, opera, documentary, and choral recitations. It also includes some forms of dance. To this final inclusion there might be some objection. Can *Giselle* indeed be considered drama? Can *Letter to the World,* Martha Graham's work based on Emily Dickinson's life, be treated as fictional presentation?

In defining any aspect of art, we must realize the ubiquity of artistic materials. The novel employs dialogue; theater employs color and plastic forms; the dance employs fictional situations. In some instances the distinguishing line between two different arts may be blurred, or disappear completely. One art shades into the other, and where one ends and another begins may be exceedingly difficult to determine. This is particularly true when two arts, such as dance and drama, are subforms of a more comprehensive art, the theater. Ballet and modern dance utilize many elements of drama. Usually the framework of a dance piece is imaginative, that is, dramatic. Yet the substance may not be involved with enacting the imagined situation but in constructing spatial forms that use the situation as a springboard. In that case, dance, though theatrical, is not a dramatic form. But when, as in the Bolshoi's *Romeo and Juliet,* the focus remains on the imagined act, ballet becomes a special form of drama.

The considerable emphasis that critics have placed upon genre tends to obscure the common bond that links all forms of drama and, thus, of theater. Eric Bentley has provided a salutary corrective in noting the close connection between "higher" and "lower" types of dramatic expression.[16] The current rejection of traditional forms of drama together with the enlargement of the types of situations drama can contain necessitate a clarification of fundamental premises. Rather than erect unnatural barriers, it is vital to see the natural coherence that exists in any art, to penetrate to the roots of the art, and discover, if possible, organic standards for evaluating contemporary works. As part of this process, it is equally vital to cultivate a way of thinking that will enable one to reach valid conclusions. Thinking about theater and drama demands a dynamic approach, an ability to see experience in flux as well as in comprehensive whole—an ability of prime importance to playgoers, students, critics, readers, and theater practitioners alike.

DRAMATIC ACTIVITY

In examining dramatic activity, we must recognize that a play utilizes modes of activity conventionalized by the historical era in which it is written. The source of its events—whether myth, legend, romance, current events—is shaped to the kinds of activity that the accumulated practice of a theater age approves. Thus, we find the Greek tragic propensity toward propitiation, debate (agon) and revelation (anagnorisis). Episode after episode employs these fundamental activities. The debate is found in *The Oresteia* (between Clytemnestra and the elders after the murder of Agamemnon), in *Oedipus* (between Oedipus and Tiresias, although the entire play is a series of debates as is *Antigone*), and in the patriotic plays of Euripides. Activities of propitiation and revelation occur in almost every Greek tragedy. The uniqueness of such dramatized modes of behavior may be better appreciated if the Greek is compared with a later treatment of the same legend. Although Eugene O'Neill in *Mourning Becomes Electra* makes certain alterations in the Oresteian story, his greatest changes are not in the events but in the activities. The practice of his age as well as his own yearning to discover a psychological equivalent of fate led O'Neill to transform the material into a series of domestic activities. Although there are some activities of intrigue, the most prevalent behavior involves family quarreling and persuasion, owing more to Strindberg than to Aeschylus.

The modes of activity vary from age to age. Stage behavior that was appropriate at one time may be prohibited at another. Dining on stage in serious drama was considered vulgar by seventeenth-century French audiences, though today it has been turned to fine dramatic use in *The Three Sisters, A Streetcar Named Desire,* and many other plays. For us, stage dining creates an impression of daily existence, and is part of the entire tendency of naturalistic drama to emphasize the bodily functions. At present our knowledge of the historical basis of stage activity is limited. We need studies to explore the choice of activity as a projection of socio-aesthetic attitudes. But until these studies are undertaken, we must make tentative efforts to understand the role that activity plays in the entire dramatic experience. To do this, we can address ourselves to three types of questions that emerge from our previous discussion of theater activity.

1. What kind of activity is dramatic activity? Is the activity constructed (artificial) or abstracted from life (natural)?
2. What is the relation of activity to the imagined act? How is dramatic activity evocative?
3. Is dramatic activity actual, virtual, or both?

---

1. What kind of activity is dramatic activity?

By definition dramatic activity is an activity of appearance, or illusion. Onstage we see not an actor but a "character." The activity is not what it seems, but a surrogate for some other activity, either historical, mythical, or fanciful. It is always representing an event, a state of being, an idea that is not or, more likely, cannot be revealed directly. Not imitation, but pretense is its heart—Stanislavski's well-known "as if." Though earth-bound by the very presence of the performer, dramatic activity can liberate the spirit because it juxtaposes a human being in his total physical being with an imagined act to produce an illusion of actuality.

Dramatic activity itself may be natural or artificial. For the most part, twentieth-century theater houses natural activity. We expect the appearance of everyday behavior, if not everyday circumstance. What is done and said onstage is done and said in a manner that is recognized as normative. Even when we witness unusual behavior onstage, such as the ravings of inmates in a mental institution, we accept that behavior as a fair representation of happenings in a historical time and place. Natural activity, however, is not the only kind of dramatic activity that the theater utilizes, and, in fact, the history of drama has seen more artificial than natural activity. Speaking in blank verse, expressing anger through the *mie* (the conventionalized stance of the Kabuki), and wearing masks are all varieties of behavior constructed for dramatic purpose. Products of artistic tradition, these activities refer the spectator not to personal experience but to socio-aesthetic convention. Their impact cannot be judged, therefore, upon their fidelity to actuality but only upon their adequacy or inadequacy in representing the intended imagined act. The dramatist, of course, sees the matter from an opposite point of view. For him, "to imitate an Action is to find objective equivalents of the subjective experience," [17] or "the characteristic and necessary activity." [18] But he as well as the performer and viewer is affected by two operative factors that determine the suitability of any dramatic activity—*selection* and *feedback*.

Selection of the kinds of activities to be included in a presentation operates on two levels: the historical and the personal. Every age seems to find certain recurrent activities peculiarly satisfying. Through the interaction of performers and spectators over a period of time, it amasses a representative collection of activities from which later writers and performers can choose and to which the most original of them contributes. The Greek preference for debate and the modern preference for bodily concern has already been cited. In *Shakespeare at the Globe,* I have shown the frequency with which the finales of Shakespearean and non-Shakespearean plays consisted of trials and quasi-judicial hearings.[19] The commedia dell'arte is filled with the young-wife-deceiving-the-old-husband routine. In recent years the tramp-scratching-his-psyche has taken the stage. In drama each individual creative choice is made within a frame of socio-aesthetic practice so that the theater artist naturally selects his materials from a context of expectations.

Operating in tandem with the factor of selection is the factor of *feedback*. In the cycle of presentation and response, the performer offers activity to the audience. The audience, usually unconsciously, tests this activity against its artistic and personal experience and then signals the performer its reception of his work. Whether or not an activity is plausible, it must bear the stamp of "truth." In the high-wire act, the truth lies in the obvious situation: taut wire, the physical act, danger. In the act of sawing a woman in half, the truth lies in the evidence of the audience's eyes, a truth that conflicts with the audience's logic. In dramatic activity, the truth lies in and arises from a broader context, because the spectator witnesses not merely a superficial activity but an activity with an inner life. A continuous signal reports to his imagination, informing him whether or not what he is seeing is "true." In parallel fashion, the dramatist or performer, in selecting and preparing his activity for presentation, is guided by an inner radar. He includes or eliminates a speech or a bit of business not wholly but largely on the basis of its "truth," that is, its rightness for the intended effect.

What determines rightness, however, is complex. The audience is accustomed to certain conventions, yet it desires variation. The presenter, whether he be dramatist or performer, tries to present activities that can serve as meeting points between himself and the audience. The selective and feedback processes are the means by which contact is made. (See Chapter Four for a further discussion of this point.)

The current habit of mind is to use natural behavior as the referent in the selective and feedback processes. This habit is reflected in the familiar responses to a play or actor: "I did (did not) believe it," "I did (did not) believe him." What determines credibility is often the audience's conviction that such-and-such a sequence of events or such-and-such a person's activity could or could not happen. Because it usually equates credibility and natural activity, a contemporary audience often fails to distinguish between the credibility of activity and that of the imagined act. The imagined act always demands credibility, even though the activity may be fanciful, as we shall see in the discussion of observation scenes below.

To meet the audience's expectation of credible activity as well as satisfy his own artistic sense, the contemporary performer, in turn, uses truth of activity as a sounding board. Again and again current Shakespearean actors endeavor to find "realistic," that is, natural bases for their presentations. In shaping their roles, they constantly use their own personal experience as a point of departure. Their ears are on guard against anything but colloquial rhythm in the verse; heightened speech is considered "false," natural expression, "true." In the drive to project the truth of the inner life, they employ the truth of recognizable behavior.

In reviving plays of the past, however, the current "realistic" tendency clashes with the unabashed artificial activity that prevails in so many early works. Throughout Shakespeare's plays, for example, in tragedy as well as in comedy, we find numerous instances of eavesdropping, or concealed observation. This device also occurs in the plays of Shakespeare's colleagues and so may be considered a typical dramatic activity of the period. It consists essentially of one or more persons engaged in activity while another or others, unknown to them, observe their behavior. Sometimes the observers comment on what they see or hear, sometimes not. Thus one activity occurs within the ambience of another. Probably the most famous observation scenes are the nunnery scene in *Hamlet* (III, i), the handkerchief scene in *Othello* (IV, i), and the letter scene in *Twelfth Night* (II, v). But, of all observation scenes, the most complicated are those in *Love's Labour's Lost* and *Troilus and Cressida*. In each instance we find observers observing observers observing activity.

In *Love's Labour's Lost* four young noblemen abjure love and vow seclusion in order to pursue philosophical studies. In Act IV, scene iii, each in turn steals into a grove so that he can read over a love poem of his own composition. Berowne is on the scene first. At the entrance of the King, Berowne hides himself to watch the King reciting his love poem. The King steps aside to observe Longaville reciting his poem while Berowne watches them both. Then Longaville steps aside to observe the newly entered Dumain. Dumain is thus watched by Longaville, the pair by the King, and the trio by Berowne. They reveal themselves in reverse order: first Longaville scolds Dumain for betraying their vows, the King berates the two of them, and finally Berowne admonishes them all. Less involved but more emotionally complex is the observation scene in *Troilus and Cressida* (V, ii). Troilus and Ulysses observe the amorous exchange between Diomedes and Cressida while they in turn are being observed by Thersites. Throughout, Troilus and Ulysses respond to the scene they are witnessing. Thersites on his part comments both on the lovers and on the observers. In both plays, the genuine passions aroused in the characters depend upon the artificial device of observation.

Observation scenes are not the sole property of the Renaissance but are also found in Roman comedy. In the Renaissance, however, particularly in Shakespeare's work, they underwent their richest formulation. Whether such scenes were originally abstractions from life, that is, attempts to present actual circumstances, we cannot say. Whatever their history, by the time they are utilized by Shakespeare their reference is to theatrical practice not life activity. Since Shakespeare introduced such scenes in more than half the plays he wrote, he must have found them an extremely useful means of enriching the dramatic appeal of his works. Such a device, or convention, enabled him and the playwrights of his period to select dramatic activity from artistic tradition, thereby gaining readily accepted dramatic tools. Whatever feedback occurred related not to life but to imaginative dramatic practice. Invention rather than credibility was the seal of authenticity, and though truth in a general sense was achieved, imaginative use of the dramatic convention was the desired end. Here again I must remind the reader that I have been discussing activity, that is, the external manifestation of presentation. Like the high-wire act, the observation scene is an artificial formulation, obeying its own rules, following its own forms, and judged according to its own context. Obviously, the activity of the high-wire act exists as a form through which daring is displayed in order to thrill the spectator. The observation scene also serves to exploit the tragic or comic possibilities of the juxtaposition of an act and those whom the act provokes or affects. Whether or not it succeeds depends on socio-aesthetic factors.

Activity in drama is the means by which the imagined act reaches the spectator. The processes of selection and feedback play a large part in determining whether or not the spectator shall "believe" the imagined act. When, as in the immediate past, he has been stirred mainly through the agency of natural activity, he finds it difficult to adjust to artificial activity. Audiences and performers alike find the girl-disguised-as-a-boy a contrivance difficult to "believe." Even when they accept the contrivance as a theatrical convention, they do not fully accept it as an adequate analogue of experience. By contrast, the removal and donning of masks to designate inner and outer personality states, as employed by Eugene O'Neill in *The Great God Brown,* is an artifice that is more acceptable as a physical metaphor of reality.

We can see, then, that dramatic activity bridges the entire range of activity from imitation to construction. Yet, rarely does any specific device or activity, as presented to an audience, appear in a pure state. It usually contains both a natural and an artificial aspect. Onstage the "realistic" activity of eating is actually conventionalized, and the performer paces his eating so that it will not interfere with his performing. He "mimes" eating even when he actually chews food. In turn, the "artificial" activity of speaking to oneself is tempered by a naturalness in accordance with audience expectation.

Both in analysis and presentation the task is to find the relevant balance between the natural and artificial aspects of activity. Each aspect makes different demands upon the imagination of the spectator and the skills of the performer, and therefore requires patient attention.

---

2. What is the relation of activity to the imagined act? How is dramatic activity evocative?

Being fictive, dramatic activity always serves as surrogate for an "idealized" activity, no matter what the base of reality or fancy. It refers constantly to another level of life, and therefore has the potential for evoking a wide range of responses in the spectator. The activity witnessed and the life referred to provide magnetic poles between which crackles the excitement of drama. An actor who portrays the dying Romeo does not actually die, but he does refer us to the image of death. Fergusson stresses the inductive process by which observation of external facts leads us to grasp the quality of inner life.[20] We tend to rely on such observation in daily life, but much more so in drama, where the given premise is that all activity is selected by the dramatist to reveal inner life.

Present understanding of the dialectics of activity and the imagined act is influenced considerably by the teachings of Stanislavski. In play analysis one speaks of a text, the lines of the characters, and a subtext, the inner life of the work. Robert Hethmon quotes Lee Strasberg as saying that the actor must "concern himself with the subtext, the inner life of the character; he must avoid an overconcern with words and cues." [21] This approach presupposes a subordination of activity to inner life. An activity is seen to express either a part of the inner life—and that the smallest part—or its antithesis. As a result, the inner life is given undue emphasis at the expense of the texture and shape of the activity, with the effect that the artistic balance between the two is weakened. To avoid this imbalance, we must go beyond Stanislavski's pioneering influence in close analysis toward a more comprehensive approach.

Activity, as I noted, is a way of grouping motion into coherent units of time. Each activity unit embodies some portion of an imagined act. The activity and the imagined act interact with each other in the minds of the audience, doing so in a variety of ways as a result of the artistic relationship between them. We can describe the kinds of interaction according to three factors: *reflection, proportion,* and *depth.*

Positive reflection occurs when the activity corresponds to the inner life. A jealous man venting his jealousy and lovers openly expressing their devotion are examples of positive reflection. The imagined act of the balcony scene in *Romeo and Juliet* is faithfully reflected in the dramatic activity, which takes the form of a lyrical troth-plight. An artistic construction, the verse, allows the inner life to be fully concentrated in one aspect of activity, vocal expression. One of Franco Zeffirelli's extraordinary skills as a director is his ability to discover natural extensions of that expression in gesture. Such harmony of activity and inner life is not often found in modern drama. On the contrary, modern drama is filled with love scenes that suggest the depth of feeling in the characters without fully revealing it. The mismatching of Julie and Liliom in *Liliom* as well as the awkward overtures to adultery of Masha and Vershinin in *The Three Sisters* illustrates how the broken speech, the irrelevant remark, the listening for inner music, can allude to passion. By expressing a casual or trivial notion, a contrary and significant emotion is conveyed. In these instances the reflection is *negative* and the method contrapuntal.

The second factor, *proportion*, involves the comparative size of the activity and the imagined act. In natural activity, the length of a piece of stage business or an activity is roughly equal to the length of the act it reflects. Thus, Volumnia's plea to Coriolanus that he save Rome (*Coriolanus*, V, iii) covers as much time as we might expect were such a plea to be made in life. But, as we watch a man change into a rhinoceros in one of Eugene Ionesco's plays, we are witnessing not only artificial activity but accelerated artificial activity. The imagined act and the stage business that embodies it are out of proportion.

The factor of *proportion* introduces stylistic questions. In theater every activity is, to some extent, a circumscribed and concentrated expression. Natural behavior is least concentrated, the stage activity coming close to a one-to-one relationship with the imagined act. Eating a meal on stage approaches the duration of such activity in life. In addition, certain types of scenes may also reflect one-to-one proportion. Volumnia persuading Coriolanus to spare Rome takes no more time than such a mother's persuasion might occupy in life. But, when a half dozen figures waving flags or battling one another represent the clash of armies, the concentration is extreme and the activity is more sign or symbol than representation.

The effectiveness of sign or symbol depends on its ability to produce the full dimension of the imagined act. This depends upon two factors already considered: selection and feedback. Where the symbol induces strong feedback, it generates a response no whit less pervasive than a more proportionate activity. Only when the feedback is weak does the audience become aware of the disproportion between symbol and intended act.

The third factor concerns the *depth*, or psychological distance, between activity and imagined act. As in artificial activity, the activity and inner life may be so closely connected that no distance exists between the two. This is most characteristic of pure melodrama, in which the visceral thrill of threat and escape, displayed usually in wholly physical terms, is an end in itself. Because the excitement of the moment is sufficient unto itself, one can hardly speak of an inner life distinct from the manifested activity. By contrast—and this appears to be characteristic of the greatest creative artists—the inner life of the activity may be unfathomable; the more one ponders it, the richer seems the interplay.

Negative and positive reflection are also related to the question of depth. Where there is positive reflection, the inner life is an extension of the activity. Where there is negative reflection, a gap seems to exist between the two. Shakespeare's work illustrates the pattern of positive reflection, for what Lear and Hamlet feel they cannot hide. Their explosive reactions express the depth of their passions. Chekhov's characters, on the other hand, illustrate negative reflection, for trivial or inconsequential remarks often cover deep agitation. It is the awareness of the gap between the expressed and unexpressed that contributes so mightily to the poignancy of negative reflection.

Although it is true that the qualities of reflection, proportion, and depth largely determine the evocative power of a play, it is also true that these qualities are vitally affected by the subject and form of the activity selected. Unfamiliar activities or conventions are barriers to the production of spectator response. One of the reasons that *Hedda Gabler* is difficult to produce at present is that a major activity of Hedda's throughout the play, the maintenance of propriety, no longer contains the explosive force it once did. Dramatic activity is the body that bears the power to stir an audience. It must be interesting in itself. But, more than that, the activity must seem an authentic vessel of the experience to be conveyed. Feedback operates here once again. Whether or not the activity is artificial matters little. What matters greatly is the penetrating power of the activity. The effectiveness of man-changing-into-rhinoceros depends upon whether one regards the artifice as a clever idea or a freeing insight. The level of recognition cannot be merely rational. Although a modern audience can understand intellectually the horror that Hedda might feel at being involved in a scandal, fear of scandal no longer strikes to the core of contemporary anxiety. To produce deep penetration of the imagination, an activity must exert strong feedback by being a simplified analogue of complex audience concerns.

3. Is dramatic activity actual, virtual, or both?

Drama, which of all arts comes closest to reproducing life, depends upon weaving illusory forms. Langer identifies three stages in the abstraction of form from actuality: first, the establishment of a realm of illusion by estrangement from actuality; second, the manipulation of the illusion; third, the emergence of "transparency," that is, "insight into the reality to be expressed." [22] This last point is particularly significant for the theory of dramatic activity. To create the illusion of actuality, the activity must be transparent. The spectator must lose his awareness of witnessing a formed activity by seeing through it to the reality intended, that is, the spectator sees not the "presentation" but the "living." This kind of illusion is quite apparent in naturalistic drama, yet it is also a property of more highly theatricalized works.

If the substance of drama were wholly virtual, however, it would be quite distinct from other forms of theater. Fortunately for the protean nature of drama, this is not so. Though a large part of dramatic skill is concealment of skill, another part of dramatic skill is display itself. Some performers hide within a stage character; others exhibit themselves or their skills; the greatest performers do both. We can speak of the activity of the last group as being "actual" as well as "virtual." Stage dueling may serve as an example. The current lack of skill reduces stage dueling to an easily dismissed mock combat. During the Elizabethan age, on the contrary, when the duel was a daily occurrence, stage dueling was a display of skill as well as a narrative event. The boundaries of the duel were fictional, of course. Macduff, not Macbeth, had to win the hand-to-hand combat. But within that frame, when the duel was presented with considerable skill before connoisseurs, the spectator would respond not only to the character's circumstances but also to the performer's abilities. The close link between actual and virtual presentation is illustrated by the fact that many Elizabethan performers were jugglers, tumblers, and dancers besides being actors.

Dueling in the Oriental theater avoided Elizabethan "actuality." It substituted choreographed for "naturalistic" activity and, in so doing, transferred attention from an actual to a virtual skill. Yet, when such a transference occurs, how does it affect the interplay of actual and virtual? To the extent that the spectator sees "through" the activity to the life of the activity, that is, to the extent that the activity is transparent, the activity is a "virtual object." But, to the extent that the spectator appreciates the skill with which the presenter is performing and shaping his activity, the activity is actual. In this latter instance we can speak of the activity as "opaque." Here the spectator is aware of the texture and form of the activity itself and, in sophisticated instances, of the skill involved in realizing that activity. In all likelihood, what we undergo in the theater is a compound of shifting impressions, opacity and transparency being relative imaginative states that combine in slightly different configurations at each presentation.

The idiosyncratic activity of a play is that peculiar window through which we look at some aspect of life. At times we are so engrossed by what we see that we are not aware of the window. Many viewers see *A Long Day's Journey into Night* as a representation of O'Neill's life, not as an artistic performance of that life. At other times, while acknowledging the life beyond, we are conscious of the form, texture, and color of the panes and their supporting fenestration. Throughout theatrical history, dramatic activity varies in the degree to which it tends toward the first state, that is, the transparent, or the second, the opaque. At all times drama contains both tendencies in different proportions, and each age seeks to achieve its own balance between the actual and the virtual.

In this discussion, dramatic activity has been treated as a single entity. But it is quite apparent that there are not one but many dramatic activities. They embrace the entire range of presentation: mimetic, acrobatic, gymnastic, musical, gestural. They can be combined in different ways and made to serve different purposes. As a consequence of this variety, therefore, the recognition of the features of a dramatic activity must be a preliminary step in the analysis of the dramatic life of a presentation. The activity must first be identified. Normally, it is embedded in the dialogue of a script, though it may be described in a scenario or devised in rehearsal. Second, the nature of the activity must be recognized. What is its connection with actuality? What skills are needed to perform it? What is its evocativ_ potential? Why was it selected? Finally, the context of the activity must be understood. Against what historical or imaginative background will it be viewed? In dealing with revivals of plays, this question is critical, for the original context of the activity may be different from the context within which it is now viewed. An appreciation of the difference between these two contexts is preliminary to mediating these differences. This threefold analysis of activity will thus lead us to consider in greater detail the dynamics of dramatic action.

2 Foundations

⊚ To the Puritan, the theater was the house of the devil. For devil read flesh, and indeed the theater was, and is, a house of flesh, of sensuous surfaces that beguile the fancies of the audience. The body is displayed in all its various physical manifestations, insisting on appreciation. Skin, hair, coloring, tone, tongue exudes, sweeps, highlights, resounds, ullulates. Attention, as the Puritans rightly feared, was truly upon the flesh.

Yet, to the nineteenth- and twentieth-century pioneers of the Art theater movement, the theater was a temple of the spirit. It housed the tragic awareness of destiny, the comedic joy of existence, the aspiring yearnings of man. In its essence, as men such as Yeats, Stanislavski, and Gordon Craig saw it, theater was holy, a form of secular religion and, therefore, heir to the spiritual institutions of the past. Flesh might be displayed, yet theater was not concerned with flesh, but only with the eternal, humanizing quest.

In a parallel manner, Nietzsche polarized these contradictory views as the Dionysian and the Apollonian, the subrational, physical exaltation and the super-rational, intellectual vision. And, of course, the theater encompasses both. It is flesh. It is spirit. The art of the drama is, to a large extent, the art of relating one to the other. I have called the flesh "activity," the spirit "inner life." The present chapter will investigate the dialectical interplay between the two.

TYPES OF
DRAMATIC ANALYSIS

Such investigation is hampered, however, if one adopts the horizontal approach of conventional dramatic criticism. This procedure, laid down in part by Aristotle and followed in whole by many a successor, studies a play by striation. Plot is analyzed as a vein running through a play; character and spectacle are other veins; theme, above all, is disentangled from the rest and examined separately. The astute critic recognizes, of course, that this method is merely a means of dealing with the material, that he must see the dramatic work as a whole. Despite this recognition, however, the habit of mind that chooses to treat a play as a collection of strands inhibits an appreciation of it as a sequence of total experiences. The horizontal method is essentially literary. Working from a script, one can more easily distinguish elements of plot and character. But drama in its theatrical expression does not permit such distinction. As a scene unfolds, it is impossible to know what is "plot" and what "character." One responds to a totality of living.

I propose to use a vertical method of analysis. Although it will be necessary to consider matters of plot and character, they will be related to segmented wholes, that is, coherent sections of a play. In large measure such analysis owes a good deal to the working methods of the theatrical director. He sees the overarching development of a play as composed of "units of action," or, in the jargon of the Stanislavski-oriented performer, of "beats." Our aims, however, require that we go beyond the director to a more comprehensive view of dramatic function. To employ the vertical method effectively, a proper habit of mind is needed. It requires the ability to differentiate the coherent sections of a play. It requires the capacity to see the whole and the parts simultaneously. It requires the knack of remembering a flow of changing images, and, ultimately, the insight to see form in an art that does everything it can to mask that form.

The vertical method, which is essentially concerned with the analysis of the interplay between activity and imagined act, is bound by temporal progression. Rather than treat a play as movement along separate paths of plot, character, and so forth, it envisions the progression of the play in its entirety. The elements of analysis, therefore, are not plot and character but units of time: what occurs within these units and how they relate to one another. Units of time are, in fact, the contextual frames within which the drama evolves, and the first step in our dramaturgical analysis is to discern them in a dramatic work. The temporal characteristics of a particular type must not, however, be imposed upon all drama. This, unfortunately, was persistently the case throughout the Renaissance, especially in France, when the Horatian-derived five-act division was often imposed upon unsuitable material.

TIME AND
SEGMENTATION

To avoid preconceptions about how units of time are used in the drama and what their contents may be, I shall start with the fundamental assumptions so far put forward. That theater occurs makes it a temporal art. Add presence to duration and we have activity. But "activity," as a word, does not have any inherent temporal value. Activity can encompass a lengthy or a brief span of time; it can apply to crossing the sea or crossing the street. In order to utilize the concept of activity in the analysis of drama, it must be related to the broader subject of time, or rather to the aspect of time particularly relevant to the theater.

Time is not accessible to direct observation. We perceive time only through some kind of manifestation. Historically, perception of time first depended upon observation of natural phenomena. Changes from light to dark, heat to cold, budding to decaying, all afforded means of recognizing—and marking—the workings of time. These phenomena, emanating from seen and unseen powers, from the sun and moon, from the rotation of the earth, provided the first clock. The Chaldeans charted the phases of the moon. The Plains Indians harnessed their ceremonies to the sun. Seasonal levels of the Nile as well as passage of the sun gave the ancient Egyptians an annual rhythm. Satisfied at first with gross measurements of years, seasons, months, and days, man increasingly segmented time, dividing the month into three or four units, the day into twelve or twenty-four units. In order to control time man had to be able to discriminate phases of it with finer precision. In other words, man had to objectify his perception of the passage of time.

Perception of time gradually shifted from the observation of phenomena to the noting of signs. For a long period neat division of time into equal segments faltered on the lack of coincidence between different natural phenomena, namely between lunar and solar cycles. However, successive refinements of observation and arrangement, first in Julius Caesar's calendar and later in Pope Gregory's revision of it, reconciled the discrepancies in a satisfactory way. Subsequently, more subtle refinements of the hour, minute, and second became feasible with the development of the mechanical and then the electric clock. With greater refinement has come greater uniformity. In 1964 the chemical element cesium, by international agreement, became the standard for determining the length of the second. Because so many of our activities are now determined by the clock—work, celebrations, amusements, dining, and so forth—we need no longer rely upon observations of natural phenomena for an awareness of time. Think of how many people now labor in windowless rooms where awareness of time's passing can come only from the clock or the completion of regular tasks.

Unfortunately, in the course of becoming chained to clock-time, our perception of other temporal manifestations has become blunted. At one time the rhythm of the heavens and earth was reflected in the rhythm of life. Traditionally, life was composed not of years but of sequences of activity that fell into coherent segments. These activity-defined segments were only loosely correlated to clock-time. More often they were marked by the harmony of events. There were the natural events of birth and death, the natural processes of maturation and decay. There were the social sequences of learning and wooing, which led to the ritual events of confirmation (in the secular world, graduation) and marriage. The rhythm of life neatly divided into seven ages by an earlier day seems remote at present, though it still beats within us. Each age of man, as Jaques scornfully remarks, has its own idiosyncratic behavior, and, although in a rough sense each age is but a segment of our three score years and ten, the length of each is still characterized by the activity carried on not by the span of years. In ignoring this rhythm of life, we do not still it. We merely sublimate the beat, which continues within us. One of the intriguing struggles of modern life occurs between our aspirations to be timeless and the persistent rhythm of existence.

The manifestation of time in nature is by means of celestial, terrestrial, or chemical activity. The manifestation of time in life is by means of human activity. Developing one's perception of time-as-activity requires concentration. In daily life the act of segmenting existence into units of activity is complicated by three factors: the intricacy and multiplicity of strands of behavior, the inconclusiveness of many of our acts, and the difficulty of separating ourselves from the experiences that we are undergoing and observing. Not until an experience is complete do we recognize that it has a coherence that differentiates it from all other experiences. Only when we go through an unusual or catastrophic event are we aware of it as a distinct segment. Yet, we need but look about us and attend to the patterns of activity that we and others follow in order to perceive the fact that our lives consist of differentiated units of time marked by characteristic behavior.

Grouping these units may or may not be difficult. Units of time devoted to work periods or class meetings are marked off from each other in highly defined ways by clock-time and assigned space. Academic scheduling in our society illustrates perfectly how an organic activity like learning is subordinated to nonorganic segmentation. But units of time filled by exchanges between parent and child, husband and wife, colleague and colleague are often so undefined, so extended in time, so dissipated in effect that it is normally difficult to discern the temporal phases into which these relations fall. Sociologists and psychiatrists, such as Erving Goffman and Eric Berne, in differentiating recurrent "dramatic" or game patterns in everyday life, make us aware of such phases of daily existence.[1]

The patterns that are blurred in life are defined in the theater. The very form of theater insures this. The gathering together of an audience and its knowledge of a reasonably specific playing time provide the frame of clock-time. Periodic intermissions emphasize this frame, cutting it off from sensed-time and yet promising a return. Within the frame, whether it be the two-hour frame of modern commercial theater or the five-day frame of the City Dionysia, the audience experiences a sensed-time induced by the units of activity that are presented. The framing itself heightens the duration. The spatial arrangement further concentrates the block of time reserved for the presentation. Within the temporal-spatial frame, the audience perceives time as activity and through the perception enjoys a heightened sense of life.

When an acrobat walks the high wire, time is transformed into a series of feats. The feats, usually arranged in a sequence of mounting difficulty, occur in the same frame of time as the one in which the spectators exist. In the drama, however, this heightened sense of time is exceedingly complex. The duration of the performer's activity is congruent with the audience's attendance, and he can therefore produce the same kinds of skill sensations as an acrobat. At the very same time, the imagined act observes its own time scheme, communicated through but often distinct from the dramatic activity. That time scheme, which is illusory, is related to the ways man conceives time to pass. The "classical" tendency is to shape the imagined act so that its duration coincides with the duration of the presentation. That tendency found its fullest expression in the doctrine of the unity of time, particularly in France. A counter-tendency of the Elizabethan theater was to compress a narrative sequence of considerable duration into two hours running time. A third tendency, most evident in recent years, is to expand a few moments of life time—as experienced in a dream or an instance of memory, for example—into an evening's presentation. From this variety of relationships between played and imagined time stems innumerable possibilities.

Temporal awareness, as we have seen, is linked to segmentation through signs or activity. Temporal sensation, particularly in the theater, depends equally upon segmentation. We can start with a simple axiom: A human being's attention to any presentation is not constant; it either increases or decreases. If it decreases too much, the individual will not attend to the presentation. Conversely, it cannot increase indefinitely. For example, if a play arouses a sensation of terror, it cannot intensify that sensation indefinitely without forcing the individual either to shut off his response in self-protection or vent his tenseness in contradictory behavior such as laughter. A rhythm of involvement and disengagement becomes mandatory, particularly where strong attention is concerned, and it is this rhythm that provides the basis for theatrical segmentation.

In drama the division of time into segments is never mechanical. The performer imposes "meaning" upon his presentation by the way he designates the major and minor units. This segmentation may be *formal* or *organic*. Formal segmentation can be defined as the performer's marking of the presentational units by convention. The intermission is such a convention. So is the bow of a magician after he has performed a trick. Organic segmentation reflects the rhythm of the presentation without any conventional recognition by the performers. Within the division of an act exists a sequence of segments. Although the individual segment is not formally defined, it has a cohesiveness arising from its inner structure. In performance each segment is differentiated organically by the pacing of the performer, and, though variations of phrasing may occur among performers, each performer produces a series of activity-defined segments.

Vertical analysis depends upon the recognition of both formal and organic segments. But what the performer achieves effortlessly as part of his art, the reader has difficulty accomplishing through the mere perusal of a script. Usually the script suggests but does not specify the segmentation of activity. In order to undertake vertical analysis of a script, a reader must first understand dramatic structure.

There are two aspects of the activity-defined segment that should be scrutinized. One is the aspect of *linkage:* how segment A is tied to segment B, these to C, and so forth. The other is the aspect of *substance:* what happens within each segment. The linkage of segments involves the entire matter of dramatic structure and is, in fact, the subject of initial consideration in most critiques of dramatic form. In this study, I have reversed the order in the belief that it is first vital to secure an image of the internal operation of a dramatic segment, and only then study how such segments are joined together. I shall therefore devote the present chapter to a definition of the variables that compose a dramatic segment and treat the subject of linkage in Chapter Five. There is, however, one aspect of linkage that demands immediate attention; I shall call it *nesting* for the moment.

Nesting, as used here, refers to "a set or series of similar things, each fitting within the one next larger." In this instance the "set or series" is composed of segments. An entire presentation is a segment of time differentiated from the preceding and succeeding surrounding time by the assemblage of an audience. This major segment is further segmented into subordinate formal units such as acts and scenes. All this is obvious. But we must pursue the segmentation further, for each scene can be subdivided, and then further subdivided, until we arrive at the individual activity, which, in truth, can be subdivided into its constituent motions.

Consider an extremely simple activity: A woman sews a button on a shirt. Such a task may be considered as a whole and described as such: sewing a button on a shirt. This same task also consists of a series of sub-tasks: threading the needle, arranging the shirt, selecting the button, sewing it to the material, cutting the thread. These sub-tasks are activity-defined segments nesting within the major activity. Just as the second is subordinate to the minute, and the minute to the hour, so too is one activity segment subsumed within another.

The concept of nesting is useful as long as the task we are examining is static. In conceiving work to be done or in remembering work already done, we can envision a totality—sewing, subdivided into time segments. Clearly this is not how we experience segmentation in the theater, where, as we encounter activity, we gain a sense of the rhythmic units through a process of accretion. *Accretion* is "the growing together of separate parts into a single whole." As we receive successive impressions of a presentation, we link them into coherent units and then add unit to unit by internalizing each as part of the unit before. Moreover, we absorb the segmental pattern of presentation kinesthetically rather than perceive it focally, that is, we absorb it with our muscles as well as our minds. (See additional discussion in Chapter Four.) For the purpose of understanding the theater experience we need to attend to the process of accretion. For the purpose of analyzing the play script, we need to comprehend the concept of nesting. The two ideas are complementary.

One impediment in analyzing *nesting* and *accretion* in drama is the absence of an adequate vocabulary for designating the superiority and inferiority of segments. We have the term "act." We have the term "scene." Each tends to overlap the other, although, when both terms are employed, scene is always a subordinate part of an act. But we have no other terms except "beat," which merely means a segment and has a particular connotation with regard to Stanislavski. We have only to compare our inarticulateness to the relatively precise vocabulary of music, at least traditional music. The nesting system of beats, bars, measures, and movements enables the musician to discriminate among the parts of a composition. The absence of a proper vocabulary in dramaturgy has inhibited the growth of a reliable system of analysis. At this stage of knowledge, however, it is first necessary to define the concepts for which language is required and then gradually develop the appropriate vocabulary.

Initially I shall utilize the term *segment* to denote any coherent unit of theatrical time that nests within a formal dramatic unit, such as act or scene. At once the question will arise: How can one determine what portion of an act or scene composes a coherent unit? Unfortunately, there are no formulae. The French method of designating each section between entrances as a *scène* is sometimes applicable, but not invariably so. We are thus left with analytic means and must determine segmental coherence through a study of structure. As we become more adept at discerning the forms of theatrical activity, we shall be able to differentiate organic segments more readily. To commence this process we shall first examine a formal segment of activity from the nondramatic theater: an acrobatic act.

THE THEATRICAL SEGMENT

My purposes in investigating a nondramatic segment are (1) to identify succinctly the variables that compose all theatrical segments and (2) to explore the ways in which these variables function. Such a theoretical examination will give a basic model of *how* theater works and thus enable us to better appreciate the clues embedded in a play script. It will help us see what is omitted by the text and supplied by the performers. Rope dancing, or high-wire walking, offers an intriguing subject for investigation. One of the most ancient of performing arts, rope dancing has entertained kings at their coronations and princes at their weddings. It is so precise, so measured a performance that it clearly reveals all its features to the spectator. The thrills it evokes arise from the motions displayed deliberately and distinctly before us.

The elements of the act are simple enough. There is the acrobat and a steel wire of about 7mm. in diameter. The wire is stretched either horizontally or diagonally, at great or moderate height, taut or slack. Each variation of the wire has its own place in the hierarchy of danger. The high wire is more dangerous than the low one, the slack more than the taut, the diagonal, at times, more than the horizontal. The acrobatic artist performs a variety of tricks upon the wire from simple walking to riding upon a bicycle to turning somersaults.[2] Usually he performs the trick that lies at the forefront of his capacity, always attempting the more difficult feat: If he has worked with a net, he removes it; if he has walked the wire with ease, he adds a blindfold or attempts a somersault. Whatever the specific task, he operates at the juncture where he might fail. His act is the result not only of his training and skill but also of contemporary fashion. As soon as Blondin astonished the world by crossing a wire stretched over Niagara Falls, a bevy of Blondins sought to imitate him. Both the personal and social factors influencing the act comprise what I shall call the *precipitating context*.

The *precipitating context* embraces all the relevant factors that govern the theatrical segment. It includes events antecedent to the commencement of the segment as well as the geographical environment established for it. For example, it includes the personal history of the artist performing a particular trick: Is he doing so for the first time? Has he always done it successfully? Did he almost fall the last time he tried it? What is the atmosphere of the hall or tent? All these factors contribute to the context. In general, however, we can speak of the precipitating context in two ways: by noting the *contrast* and the *vector* inherent in the context.

Within the precipitating circumstances there can be varying degrees of *contrast* between the effort and the expected result. Obviously the higher the wire the greater the contrast and, consequently, the greater the task and anxiety. There is greater contrast in an acrobat attempting a new feat for the first time than an experienced acrobat performing the identical trick for the hundredth time. That is why the ring master will announce a first effort, for only when the audience knows about this greater contrast does it experience that thrill. Actually, the contrasting elements create the context. In the nature of the acrobatic profession, the tasks must always be sufficient to produce a thrill. Out of the context, there then emerges a *vector*, that is, a sense of where the contrasting elements are pointing. When the new feat is announced, all energies and all attention are directed toward the moment the act is realized. In other words, the context sets a framework for the future, within which the task will be performed. The preciseness of the vector will vary from circumstance to circumstance. In life it may be unclear, even seem not to exist. But in the theater the vector of a precipitating context tends to be defined by the performer and the performing situation.

Arising from the context then is a direction. In the case of wire walking, it is a direction set for the performance of one or a series of feats. The acrobat concentrates his energy to accomplish them. As we can readily see, in this type of segment at least, the performer sets a goal and determines a path to that goal. He infuses that path with his energy. But where is the focus of his attention? Henry Thétard reports a conversation with the acrobat Maïss: "It is necessary [for the rope walker] not to have any distraction, to work as if one were alone in the hall, eyes continually fixed at a point aimed at, an imaginary point that one creates oneself in the center of the apparatus."[3] It is to such a point that all one's energy must be directed. The importance of this type of concentration to a performer is explained by Michael Polanyi in distinguishing between subsidiary awareness and focal awareness: "If a pianist shifts his attention from the piece he is playing to the observation of what he is doing with his fingers while playing it, he gets confused and may have to stop. This happens generally if we shift our focal attention to particulars of which we have been aware only in their subsidiary role."[4] In *The Tacit Dimension*, Polanyi elaborates his analysis of the relation between ability to perform an act and the performer's focus of attention: "In the exercise of a skill, we are aware of its several muscular moves in terms of the performance to which our attention is directed."[5] This projection of awareness is central to our understanding not only of how a performer works but also how human energy can be directed. At this point we are concerned only with the performer, but we shall later extend our discussion to include fictional characters as well.

In focusing his attention at "an imaginary point," the wire walker harmonizes all his energies in the pursuit of the path marked by the vector. That point, as Maïss indicates, is not an image of the feat but a virtual point of concentration. He seems to suggest that it takes on intangible, but nonetheless imaginative reality. We can speak of this imaginative process as projection, and the imaginary point as the acrobat's project. By an effort of concentration, the performer projects, throws himself forward at a target, and then gathers his full forces to relate to that target. Such a concept of focus underlies Sartre's term, *projet*. In *Question de Méthode*, the prelude to his *Critique de la Raison dialectique*, Sartre rejects the suitability of the term "will" for the understanding of man's acts. For him, "projet" is both more inclusive and more accurate. "The most rudimentary behavior must be determined both in relation to the real and present factors which condition [the behavior] and in relation to a certain object, still to come, which it is trying to bring into being. That is what we call *the project*." [6] The project, then, is the translation of the conditions of the precipitating context through activity toward a future object. Implicit in Sartre's thought and central to my use of the term is the concreteness of the object projected. It is not an idea, but an image of the future that the performer attempts to attain. For the wire walker, whose circumstance is potentially unsteady, the imaginary point offers a fixed and stable target to which he is related both visually and kinesthetically. The project is not merely a creation of the mind but the focus of body and mind together. Applied to the wire walker, the project is the means for channeling his energies in the accomplishment of the task. The task is, of course, a consequence of a clearly defined *intent*. In the case of wire walking, the intent is implicit in the context, for the acrobat sets up particular conditions in order to perform a particular trick. He determines height and tautness of the wire and defines the effect he wishes to produce. Within the performance itself, however, the intent is given physical reality as a project. (See pp. 70 ff. for application to drama.)

What inhibits the acrobat from achieving his goal is the actual or potential *resistance* in the situation. By resistance I mean any impedance in the pursuit of the project. For an experienced performer, walking across the wire is easy indeed. Yet even so, there is some resistance, minimal though it may be. The more difficult the task he has set himself, the greater the resistance. For example, "the forward somersault is in all circumstances more difficult than the back, because it is turned 'blind' so to speak, without the aid of the eyes." [7] The inability to see the wire as one comes round is an aspect of resistance inherent in the trick itself. In this instance as in most performances, the resistance is built into the act, is fully anticipated, and thus, if the performer has calculated accurately, is overcome through the full display of his art and skill. There can be variations in the act, however, due to environmental factors. At certain temperatures a wire will become "wavy," a condition that must be overcome before a trick can be undertaken. Consequently, the performer faces two types of resistance: that which is foreseen and so allowed for in the project; that which is unforeseen, that may develop within the segment, and faced spontaneously in the course of the segment.

Both in the preliminary context and in every phase of the performance, there is evident contrast between the project and resistance. In the precipitating context of the high-wire act the contrast is potential and basic: a fine strand and a human being in motion. Add a bicycle and the contrast appears even greater. This contrast is both actual and imaginative. It is actual in that we can see the disproportion between man and wire. It is imaginative because we the audience sense with our own bodies just how difficult wire walking must be. Within the segment itself, as the acrobat moves to the center of the wire to perform his act, the contrast sharpens even more. It lies between his intent, manifested through the project, and the conditions he seeks to overcome. What fills the gap between the points of contrast is *tension*.

Derived from the Latin *tensus*, meaning stretched, tension suggests the invisible lines of force between two contrasting poles. These lines are determined by the nature of contact between project and resistance within the segment and between segment and audience within the theatrical experience. In the latter case tension is induced sympathetically as the audience witnesses the tension of the performance. If the controlled danger of the acrobat should turn to real danger, through a misstep, for instance, tension would turn to tenseness. Tension, as I have stated, is induced by our perception of contrast. Between prize fighters physical contact does not produce the effect of tension as much as their wary sparring because in actual contact, the two poles of contrast have become one. The spectator can no longer perceive the separate energies. On the other hand, in watching two figures circle each other, the gap between them, and so the potential conflict, is apparent. Tension is allied to expectation. It is a result not only of what is seen but of what is about to happen.

Is it possible for theatrical presentation to exist without the factor of tension? I doubt it, for unless there is some contrast between the performer's project and the accomplishment of that project, there is nothing to arouse attention. The very act of presentation supposes the closing of the gap between the present and the future. But how great the tension must be to retain an audience's attention is a matter of cultural habit.

Two principal variables govern tension: *intensity* and *velocity*. Changes of intensity are themselves consequences of changes in forms of resistance. Thus, the tension varies as resistance increases or decreases, becomes more open or covert, more direct or oblique. Usually, the most intense moments occur when the forces of the project, confronting resistance most critically, create an unresolved state of tension. This unresolved state in turn induces an urge for resolution in the audience.

Velocity, the second variable, relates to spatial tension. If a spectator could stop time as a rope walker is about to turn a somersault, he would witness a potential state of tension. He would have the sensation that time is held back, that the moment is retarded before it changes into the next moment. The pause before the acrobat turns the somersault would be a moment of low velocity succeeded by the somersault itself, a moment of high velocity. Throughout theatrical segments, moments of high and low velocity succeed each other in infinite combinations.

Tension, then, is intangible but real. It seems analogous to electricity. It has force but no mass, and like electricity exists only when an optimum relationship is established between "magnetic poles." It is thus a factor of structure rather than a property of any physical body, occurring only when the project and resistance of an activity are brought into critical proximity. In the course of a performance there are successive cross-sections of increasing and decreasing tension. As a result, the successive states of tension create an intangible shape. If we can envisage a three-dimensional flow of time bound by the electrostatic force of tension, we would see the shape of the energy produced by the activity. To this shape I apply the word "action."

Action is one of those words widely used in dramatic practice and criticism. It is an elusive word, because performers and writers have failed to make a careful distinction between either activity and action or between the action of an entire segment and the activity of an individual performer. In acting and directing, action has come to be used as a substitute for motivation. Actors speak of "playing an action" which is meant to stand for "pursuing an intent." As I utilize the term, action is a result, not a tool. The actors fulfilling their projects generate the activity that, in turn, produces the theatrical tension. The sequence, or path, of theatrical tension is the action, the flow of which creates the illusion of inner life. The configuration of the activity thus contains the action so that activity and action can never be truly separated except for analytic purposes. But just as an audience cannot receive the sensation of the action except through the activity, so the performers cannot create the action except through the activity.

Theoretically, action can assume an infinite variety of shapes. In practice, it does not, because the very nature of presentation predetermines a definite shape. When an audience gathers together, it fixes its attention upon the presenters and the presentational space. As psychologists have long known, people do not maintain steady concentration. To elicit the same level of attention, a presentation must increase in interest. To raise the level of attention and so give the sensation of a satisfying experience, there must be considerable intensification of action. As an audience watches the rope walker, it is affected by two intimately related aspects of the presentation. It is absorbed by a heightening of tension and by the sensuous surfaces of physical movement. When a sequence of feats is performed, it is presented in an ascending order of difficulty and artistry just as almost every theatrical event presents material of maximum interest at the end or near the end of a performance. Linear intensification is simply the inherent requirement of any theatrical situation.

How such linear intensification is organized is another matter. Here variation enters. Though a segment proceeds largely

through intensification, there must also be reduction of intensity since human beings respond in phases. An unremitting increase in intensity would only force an audience to react self-protectively by dropping its attention. Consequently, a theatrical segment must have a rhythmic character. Its pulsation must be organic, involving not so much a beginning, middle, and an end, but intensification and decrescence, that is, a falling of tension. In the act of turning a somersault, the portion leading to the somersault is the period of intensification, the portion where the performer walks off the wire and bows is the *decrescent*. The somersault is the *crux* of the act. In essence, this is the modular unit of all theatrical action.

I have used the word "crux" to specify the time when the rhythm of the action reaches maximum intensification. It is a point where either a sudden shift from tension to decrescence takes place or a period of intensification is sustained. In one sense, the idea of crux is similar to the notion of crisis, which John Howard Lawson defines as a "dramatic explosion . . . created by *the gap between the aim and the result*—that is, by a shift of equilibrium between the force of will and the force of social necessity." [8] But, as a term, "crux" has broader application. In dramatic criticism crisis has normally suggested a moment of decision, and, although many a crux is such a moment, there are many others in which the extremity of intensification is not expressed in a shift of direction so much as in a subsidence of tension. It is particularly essential in the analysis of non-Aristotelian drama to distinguish between the intensification-relaxation pattern implied by the word "crux" and the issue-decision pattern implied by the word "crisis." I shall therefore utilize the former term, allowing for the fact that a crux might also be a crisis in the traditional sense.

In envisioning a theatrical segment, we can regard it in one of two ways. We can recall the entire performance from beginning to end as a continuum (a temporal image), or we can remember particular moments of the performance (spatial images). It is exceptionally difficult, if not impossible, to do both simultaneously. When we recall the act of an acrobat sliding down a diagonal wire, we can visualize the temporal sequence: his mounting the wire, his pivot on the raised platform, and his descent. Alternately, we can concentrate on the particular moment when the performer is poised on the raised platform, ready to slide down. We can imagine his quiet stance in contrast to the long run of cable—so slender and seemingly insubstantial; in short, we can remember the spatial design of the moment. But if we imagine that design vividly, we cannot, at the same time, vividly imagine the temporal sequence of climb, poise, and descent.

The spatial examination of a segment consists of isolating a series of cross-sections cut through time. In the wire-walking act, the image of the performer poised on high is just such a cross-section. We see splayed out the dichotomy of potential act and potential resistance. The moment is not one of rest but one of nervous and muscular preparation, *"of tendency . . . incipient change of direction,"* in Henri Bergson's words.[9] The performer is anticipating the next instant, is leaning into the future, we might say. He is *becoming*.

In its turn, temporal examination reveals an alternate picture. Where the former was static, the temporal picture is dynamic. It can be imagined as rhythmic progression. There is movement forward against intangible but nevertheless actual resistance. The progression passes through discernible stages: ascent, pause, and swift descent. In the example of wire flying, there is unmistakable climactic release. Decrescence is accompanied by applause. We are thus aware of change or accomplishment.

Obviously, the temporal and spatial views of an activity are mutually exclusive. But though they are exclusive, they are also complementary. Each kind of perception is partial, but both are necessary for a total comprehension of a segment. What I have described has, in fact, an analogue in quantum physics. In studying the structure of the atom, physicists discovered that they could account for certain behavior of an electron through a particle theory and for other behavior through a wave theory. To reconcile these two theories of physical behavior, Niels Bohr proposed a theory of complementarity. To illustrate this theory, Louis De Broglie draws an analogy to

> two faces of an object that can never be seen at the same time but which must be visualized in turn, however, in order to describe the object completely.

Then he goes on to explore the application of Bohr's principle to general experience. He avers that

> this notion of complementarity seems to have taken on the importance of a true philosophical doctrine . . . [for] it is in no way evident that we [can] describe a physical entity by means of a single picture or a single concept of our intellect.[10]

An activity segment is an entity similar to an electron in that it requires just such a complementary view; as in the case of the electron, we need to alternate a spatial image (the position of the performers) and a temporal image (the progression of the performance).

In defining the variables of a theatrical segment, I have given definitions that may seem to suggest they are entities in themselves. This is certainly not intended. A term such as *resistance* does not refer to an object or a fixed state, but is, rather, a generic expression covering all forms of impedance to a project. As such it is one of the variables. Within every theatrical segment, as in every moment of life, there is resistance. The very act of breathing involves the resistance of tissue to air. All resistance varies in *source* and *strength*. It can arise from inanimate material conditions or proceed from the individual himself or from other individuals. Whatever its source, resistance in a theatrical segment must manifest itself in activity, if human, or in spatial mass or direction, if inanimate. On stage inanimate resistance may be manifested through an object such as a locked door, for instance. Manifestation of resistance will also vary according to strength. A taut wire will exert less resistance than a slack wire. Space itself offers resistance. The distinguishing mark of the dancer, for instance, is seen in his walk; he displaces space, makes its resistance evident, and then overcomes that resistance. In other theatrical forms, the resistance is far more active. But regardless of the circumstances we are dealing with, resistance is always present as a variable. And what is true of resistance is also true of the other variables I have defined. *Project, decrescence, crux, becoming,* and the rest are all terms defining dynamic processes. They should be regarded not as having a fixed character but as embracing specific possibilities. *Project* embraces different ways in which the individual orients himself to the future. *Crux* embraces different stages of intensification between project and resistance. *Becoming* embraces differing potentialities for expending energies. *Decrescence* embraces a wide range of adjustments to the accumulated pressures of the segment. As we explore the implications and applications of these terms, it is essential to remember that they are valid only as guides to the actual interplay that produces dramatic action.

To sum up, I have examined a theatrical segment in which the activity is artificial and therefore self-contained. This activity arises from *precipitating contexts*, which, in the instances studied, are almost wholly the creation of the acrobat or performer. Inherent in these circumstances are elements of resistance, against which the performer exerts skill and force as expressions of his project. In passing through the segment, he adjusts the project as he meets resistance, thus marking successive states of becoming. At some point it becomes clear whether the project or the resistance will dominate. This is the crux, which in turn determines the nature of the change or readjustment that the segment has gone through. This is the decrescent.

The pattern described above is the basic model of all theatrical segments, whether dramatic or not. As we have seen in Chapter One, gymnastic or acrobatic activities primarily display skill and the daring that is required by the skill. Their segments tend to be highly defined. The forms can be readily perceived. There is, however, one other type of activity segment that needs to be examined before turning to the dramatic. This type falls somewhere between the gymnastic and the dramatic, and is generally classified under the heading of Happenings. In this category are grouped such examples as: a nude woman playing a cello on stage; an audience visiting a cave where various "performers" cook food; players enacting the Civil War as a game; an audience viewing a tennis game played without tennis balls and then, in darkness, hearing the sound of a tennis ball struck by rackets.

Happenings, as these examples illustrate, are activity-centered. In large part they consist of undirected or, in Michael Kirby's phrase, "non-matrixed" sequences of activity.[11] They lack any causal connection to each other and thus any sense of progression.

Progression, as we have seen, is related to purposeful activity. But contemporary theater has questioned the viability of such a concept, and in certain Happenings one encounters activities that exhibit no progression whatsoever. Movements, gestures, and sounds are merely random attempts to spark subliminal responses by breaking down logical reaction and substituting disconnected reaction. To accomplish these ends, such presentations rely principally on contrast, the main element that Happenings share with other theatrical segments. By juxtaposing hitherto unconnected activities, the Happening often creates a type of theatrical metaphor based on unexpected contrasts. Instead of progression, the Happening substitutes varieties of contrast. In doing so, it gives us an object lesson in activity counterpoint and reminds us of the importance of this factor in theatrical presentation.

In addition, many Happenings are out of phase with the expected rhythms of segmented time. Often through repetition of simple activity, repetition that goes beyond the usual endurance of onlookers, the agents of a Happening deliberately avoid decrescence. Of course, their ability to do so is relative. Sooner or later a segment, whether musical or visual, must end. The activity may be merely repeating chords or stirring up endless lathers of soap. Its endlessness has meaning only in terms of the time clock of the onlooker. Such prolonged activity is calculated to break down barriers in the spectators, to transport them to another plane of response (if they do not first depart in disgust). What we find in such cases is a reduction of emphasis upon the interaction between agent and resistance and a transformation of the audience into the resistance against which the performers project their energies.

Lastly, the Happening eschews logically apprehended contrasts. It thrives on the accidental juxtaposition of activities, purporting to find in such accidents richer possibilities of presentation. To the extent that the Happening is a product of accident, it also loses any impress of segmentation. Where accidents dominate, ability to control an ending is lost. In fact, this tendency coupled with the inclination to confront the audience directly makes the Happening a game more than a theatrical presentation. Games offer a wide variety of experience, but should not be confused with the theater experience. Insofar as the Happening remains a theatrical event, we can analyze its form in the same way as we analyze the acrobatic act. When it becomes a game, its social character changes radically and must be analyzed according to a different set of principles.

The groundwork has now been prepared for a consideration of the dramatic segment.

THE DRAMATIC SEGMENT

Because dramatic activity is a theatrical act of presentation, it is governed by many of the conditions we discovered in our analysis of wire walking. There is interplay between audience attention and presentation. The performer must project his energies and establish fields of tension between himself and other actors or objects. No matter what character he may play, the pattern of intensification and decrescence still goes on. All the features of a spatial-temporal field that are evident in nondramatic presentations are also present in dramatic presentation. Whatever shape an action may assume, it is governed by the essential structure of the presentational situation.

In abstracting from idea or observation, the performer translates his material into presentational form. This does not mean that he must follow a formula. There are no formulas. But there are variables (project, resistance, etc.) which compose recurrent shapes. The same variables can be arranged in quite new combinations, but they cannot be ignored. Whatever the impulse for theatrical creation, the source material must be transformed into shapes of action. At the moment I am not concerned with the creative process. Studies of this subject, such as those undertaken by Harold Rugg in *Imagination* and Arthur Koestler in *The Act of Creation,* make it quite clear that the creative act is not a mechanical manipulation of matter into form. Here I would merely like to emphasize that dramatic activity obeys presentational requirements independent of its subject matter. Its first content—as Marshall McLuhan might use the term—is the human being in defined space and time. The imagined act is contained within and subservient to that first content. Consequently, whatever the particular subject matter of a play, its shape is already partially defined by the medium through which it acts.

How would our analysis differ if we were to examine a dramatic presentation of the high-wire act? Instead of an actual wire stretched thirty feet off the floor, there might be an imaginary line on the stage. Instead of a superb *fil-de-fériste* like Blondin or Con Colleano, we might find a master mime such as Marcel Marceau. Using the same outline of activity, Marceau would pantomime the rope dance. The differences between his presentation and that of Blondin or Colleano would be twofold: in the act itself, and in its sympathetic reflection in the audience.

In the act itself the principal motions achieved by the acrobat would be reflected in the body of the mime. By concentrating on the salient features of tempo, stride, posture, and so forth, Marceau would create the essential visual structure of wire walking, thus producing a virtual image, or illusion. Naturally, his attention would shift from the acrobatic skill to the mimetic skill, in short, from the actual need to maintain balance to the imitation of the acrobat maintaining balance. In the audience there would be a similar shift, from imminent danger to the illusion of imminent danger. The spectator would experience a double image. First, through the process of feedback, he would mentally "check" the mimed wire walking against the actual feat, marveling or not, as the case may be, at the acted version. Second, he would see the mimed presentation as an act in itself, obedient to its own nature and enjoyed for itself alone. This would not be an either/or situation, in which we would see first one then the other image, but it may be characterized as a both/and situation, in which the illusion and its referent are contained simultaneously in the spectator's imagination. In fact, the presence of both images creates the kind of contrasting gap that sparks mental tension.

Dramatic activity, it is apparent, lacks the unity of the acrobatic activity. Instead it has a contradictory nature. It is a presentation "in itself," arousing intrinsic interest for what is perceptible; it is also a representation, a window into imagined life. The environment of the activity has the same double character. It has actual physical existence as a stage, what the psychologists call a "geographical environment." It also has virtual existence as a sign or symbol of the imaginative. In that dimension it serves as "behavioral environment" for the performer. The agents are both performers and characters. Thus, the dual nature of dramatic activity allows artists to produce an infinite variety of effects. In an art that is wholly constructed, such as music, the elusive yet provocative *trompe l'oeil* of drama is not readily available. That pleasant deception is possible only where two planes of reality are simultaneously evoked by the interplay between stage activity and the imagined act.

In the preceding chapter, a preliminary examination of the relationships between the two revealed that true imitation is rarely possible. Instead, we find abstraction. Just as the mime abstracts a form from the acrobatic act, so the performer abstracts from a total experience to produce his work. When Bernard Shaw creates St. Joan and John Osborne creates Luther, neither is rendering historical portraits. One could justifiably say that these figures are more Shaw and Osborne than Joan and Luther. Yet the fact that each author turned to these figures indicates that each one saw in the historical personage a sympathetic element. That is, in abstracting from history, they selected those aspects of Joan and Luther that could illuminate the contemporary imagination. Can we say that the results are pure illusions, unconnected to their sources? By no means. What each author has done is to select certain features of the original model. These features, fused with the attitude of the writer, have effected an "idealized" form, by which I mean an image corresponding to what the author regards as the essence of the historical figure. He thus structures a role in which the incidents and even the language belong to history. To that extent Joan is the historical Joan, Luther the historical Luther. But the form and attitude of the roles are Shaw's and Osborne's.

We have, then, two planes of immediate experience: the activity actually presented to us containing the form and attitude of the author and the historical act from which it was drawn. In the case of a masterpiece, the stage activity comes to stand for history in the popular mind, *Richard III* being the most notable example.

But even for the sophisticated mind, dramatic artifice and historical fact shade into one another, for through the stage activity the performers attempt to evoke the idealized sign of Joan's celestial voices and Luther's burning conscience. As a result, the actor oscillates continuously between mirroring the historical act and creating its theatrical analogue according to the demands of presentational form. We can better appreciate the process by considering a specific activity: Joan persuading the Dauphin to join her in redeeming France.

The episode is a typical persuasion segment, the main lines of action being a force (agent) exerted to bring about a change of mind in an opponent. Shaw's originality resides principally in the *quality* of the resistance and thus the quality of the energy needed to overcome the resistance. A unique realism of the intellect, unabashed self-knowledge and self-interest, guides the Dauphin. Against this Joan brings the force of her naïve conviction and sharp common sense. In order to accomplish this persuasive action, the performer playing Joan must infuse her activity with the fervor appropriate to Joan. As she pleads with the Dauphin, she must act as though she is ignorant of the outcome of the segment, though as an actress she knows quite well that the actor playing the Dauphin will show how the Dauphin yields to her. The actor playing the Dauphin carefully calculates his resistance. As a performer he projects a path for himself similar in most essentials to that of the acrobat. He exerts the kind of energy that the acrobat uses in walking the wire and passes through successive states of becoming. Both actor and acrobat aim at an imaginary point in order to maintain physical direction. But there are also differences.

The dramatic performers' energies are directed not toward the accomplishment of the historical act but toward the creation of a shape of action. As stated earlier, theatrical tension is produced by the spatial and temporal structures created by the performers. The same is true of drama. The dramatic contrast between "Joan's will" and the "Dauphin's reluctance" is achieved through the careful modulation of project and resistance. The resultant tension between the actors is then perceived as tension between characters as well as interaction of performers.

The relation of activity to the imagined act may occur at different levels of abstraction. In many instances the illusion of life on stage seems to be the concretization of a similar life that has gone on or is going on. Albert Finney as Luther is a mirror of an actual Luther undergoing similar activities. The actors playing Edmund and James Tyrone in *Long Day's Journey into Night* seem to be reflections of a real Eugene and James O'Neill. In turn, the imagined act of the characters is a reflection of the dramatist's conception of actuality. To appreciate that concept, the audience imaginatively passes through a series of receding planes. It perceives the activity through which it sees the imagined act, and finally, by experiencing and absorbing the imagined act and its inner life, the audience grasps the concept underlying the entire work.

There need not be, however, a mediating plane of a fully articulated fiction. In the presentation of artificial activity the connection between stage, imagined act, and concept is often short-circuited. This can be illustrated by Peter Weiss' *Marat/Sade*.

At one point in the play a choral figure enters with a bucket and funnel, places the funnel in a hole cut into the floor of the stage, pours the contents of the bucket—blue paint—into the funnel. This activity in itself does not reflect any specific life activity, but is, instead, a visual pun. It represents the pouring out of the blue blood of the French aristocracy, and thus alludes to an actual historical activity. In this way the dramatic activity refers to the *idea* of an activity, and its execution, therefore, is not and cannot be measured by faithful reflection of life activity. As the business is used in the play's context, it has comic force as a sarcastic comment on the equality with which common and aristocratic blood was shed. Generally, we can say that the more schematized the dramatic activity, the more likely it will short-circuit reference to life activity and be a direct reflection of an intellectual concept.

From this discussion of dramatic activity, it is apparent that the crucial difference between the nondramatic and the dramatic theatrical segments lies in the area of *resonance*. By resonance I mean the continued reverberation of the segment's action in the imagination of the audience. In terms of gross structure, the two types of segments are similar. The dramatic segment, however, is an instrument of incomparably greater richness, more subtly elaborated and varied, with the result that its resonance is more extensive and powerful. Because dramatic activity, even in its most direct depiction of life (for instance, in a documentary play), is reduced to a severely restricted time-space, it can be potentially a source of immense impact upon the audience *if* the selection of elements and the shape imparted to them create a sympathic resonance. These two factors are critical. Selection of elements respond, as previously shown, to feedback, to the audience's sense of what is essential truth. In that respect the audience's response may be associational. The audience responds because it recognizes in a stage act a reflection of personal experience. But of equal importance, if not more so, is the shape of the action, or structure. In a persuasion scene, such as I have cited, the audience is involved in pressures and counter-pressures on a purely structural level. Not that all persuasion scenes produce the same response, but all persuasion scenes are structured toward bringing a character to a point of decision. The process by which he is brought to that point and the nature of the decision jointly provoke the resonance. In effect, the segment is an atom of imaginative energy. The right conjunction of activity, imagined act, and audience can release this energy. (See Chapter Four for further discussion of this subject.)

The reader may wonder how my theoretical model of wire walking applies to specific plays. This model, which has enabled me to illustrate a vocabulary and its application, has, I hope, also established another point, the primacy of the activity segment. Although it is usual for a person to first become acquainted with a play through reading, the first contact, in terms of artistic intention, is meant to be made through activity. That is why I have stressed and started with the concept of the activity and its substance. In turning now to plays, which in fact means turning to scripts of plays, we must first consider exactly what is the relation between the text and the activity it is supposed to represent.

I have already alluded to the common notion of the play, and therefore the script, as the soul and the theatrical performance as the body of drama.[12] Such a simplified statement of the connection between script and production is no longer fashionable. In the humanities, students are encouraged to take into account the mounting of plays in their study of drama. Unfortunately, the worthy aim leads to the rather difficult task of trying to imagine an entire production of the script that one is reading. But such an accomplishment is difficult enough for people actively involved in theatrical production. It is beyond most lay readers. In fact, the impression that one is seeing the script on stage often consists of fragmentary glimpses of living experience. It would be much easier to gain a sense of dramatic rhythm without having to conjure up bodily forms and three-dimensional locales. Of all forms of verbal expression, the dramatic is most loosely woven. Between sentences and words room is left for human impulse to move toward and away from individuals or incipient events. A rhythm of intensification and decrescence is written into any competent script, and it is awareness of this rhythm that makes play reading enjoyable. By becoming sensitive to the open spaces in the dialogue, we begin to feel the gestures, the reactions, the pauses that they imply, and thus begin to sense the pattern of action.

Naturally, the words of a production are most easily preserved. Therefore, in those plays where the spoken word is the principal conveyor of the activity, a greater portion of the presentation is recorded. This is particularly true of poetic drama, in which a higher portion of the dramatic activity is oral, than of gestural drama. Two examples, both showing the sadistic pleasures of mockery, will serve to illustrate the varying degree to which scripts contain the presented activity. Toward the end of *Twelfth Night* (IV, ii), Feste, urged on by Sir Toby, visits the imprisoned Malvolio, pretending to be Sir Topas the Curate. After abusing Malvolio in his disguise as the priest, Feste returns in his own person, leads Malvolio to think that he will assist him in gaining freedom, and then, pretending the return of Sir Topas, addles Malvolio by switching from one character to another. Yet in this entire segment, Malvolio remains concealed. Only his hand, flourishing a letter for Olivia, is revealed. Feste does actually don a disguise as Sir Topas, but his doing so is gratuitous, because Malvolio cannot see him. Feste's abuse of the steward, and the comedy derived from it, is almost completely verbal, and gesture, though it could be elaborated, has little to do with the progress of the activity.

Gestural expression is far more important in Molière's *Les Fourberies de Scapin* ("The Deceits of Scapin"), in which we find another scene of deception and abuse. Scapin has determined to revenge himself upon his master, Géronte. He invents a story that a town bully, furious at Géronte for thwarting his sister's marriage to Géronte's son, is roaming the town, determined to beat the old man. Scapin induces his master to crawl into a large sack so that Scapin can drag him safely through the town to his home. When the old man is in the sack, Scapin pretends to speak to the bully in the course of which conversation he finds occasion to beat the bag though crying out all the time that he is being struck. Twice Géronte pops out of the bag when Scapin leads him to think that the bully is gone. Three times he is thrust into the bag. The third time, however, Scapin is so carried away by his device that he does not notice the old man emerging from the bag, whereupon the trick is discovered. It is apparent that this scene depends not upon *more* activity but more *gestural* activity. Feste's pretended sympathy is more closely reflected in the words of the text than Scapin's double take when the old man appears. Because *Scapin* relies so heavily upon facial reaction and visual movement, it is inevitable that a smaller portion of the total activity can be recorded in the text of that play.

Unfortunately, all plays tend to be read at a common level of completeness, or, what is even worse, the scripts that seem to record a high proportion of the presented activity—Shakespeare's in particular—are read as though they contained *all* there is of the play. This is misleading, for although it is true that some scripts record a higher proportion of the finished work than others, no script can ever record the complete play.

What applies to the dramatic activity also applies to the dramatic action. Just as the script is a partial record of the activity, so is it a partial preserver of the action. Again there will be differences among scripts and also among dramatic modes. In Chapter One I argued that several different kinds of relationships can exist between activity and imagined act. Where the activity and the inner life of the imagined act are antithetical, the action is less readily evident in the text. It is suggested indirectly as is the case in Chekhov's works. Chekhov hints so often at a disparity between what is actually done, that is, what we see happening on stage, and the flow of tensions among and within the characters.

The action must be deduced from the context not only of a segment but from linkage between segments. Just as in the theater we perceive the action through the stage activity, so in reading we must perceive the action through the limited fragments of activity contained in the script. We must remember, however, that the performers who communicate the action through their activity have already read the play. They shape their activity to accord with what is to come. In reading we have an incomparably more difficult task, to sense the action without knowing the future. That is why plays should not be read, but *reread*.

I shall now ask the reader to read carefully the following brief segment from John Millington Synge's *Riders to the Sea*, the piece I have chosen to illustrate the application of the analytic method that I have hitherto constructed. Obviously, one scene from one play cannot adequately demonstrate the analysis I recommend. This instant is merely a preliminary example. In the following chapter I shall examine a variety of scenes to show how different ways of arranging the variables in a dramatic segment produce distinct dramatic modes.

Riders to the Sea, based on material gathered by Synge from the lives of the Aran islanders, proceeds quite directly from the specific to the ideal. In his book *The Aran Islands* Synge describes in detail the hard struggle of these people for subsistence upon three small isles situated off the west coast of Ireland. The bleakness and precariousness of their existence matched only by their fortitude and resignation impressed themselves upon his imagination and led to the composition of *Riders to the Sea*. Compressing many divergent observations and events into one incident, Synge introduces an old woman, Maurya, waiting for word of whether or not one of her sons, Michael, has drowned at sea. Her last children, two daughters and the youngest boy, Bartley, go on with their tasks of daily living. Maurya's premonitions of disaster fail to keep Bartley from embarking for Connemara on the mainland where he hopes to sell their two horses. In going down to the sea, he drowns. The report of his death is mingled with the report of Michael's drowning. In a final paean, Maurya mourns for the men of her family, who have all been lost to the sea, and accepts the workings of God.

Even this summary cannot help distorting somewhat the substance of the play. I have merely sketched the general subject. Now let us turn to a very brief segment: the departure of the youngest son. It consists of eighteen brief speeches and occurs shortly after the beginning of the play. Nora has brought the clothes of a drowned man to be examined so that the family might learn whether or not they belong to Michael. But before she and her older sister, Cathleen, can examine the garments, they hear their mother getting up from her bed. The girls hasten to hide the clothes. As they do so, Nora tells Cathleen that the priest will not prevent Bartley from traveling to the mainland. Maurya enters. Almost immediately there is an exchange between her and Cathleen over the likelihood of Bartley's departure. The mother maintains that the priest will not let him go. Immediately someone is heard outside. Looking out the window, Nora reports that Bartley is hurrying toward them.

NORA (*looking out*): He's coming now, and he in a hurry.

BARTLEY (*comes in and looks round the room. Speaking sadly and quietly*): Where is the bit of new rope, Cathleen, was bought in Connemara?

CATHLEEN (*coming down [from the loft where the turf or fuel is stored]*): Give it to him, Nora; it's on a nail by the white boards. I hung it up this morning, for the pig with the black feet was eating it.

NORA (*giving him a rope*): Is that it, Bartley?

MAURYA: You'd do right to leave that rope, Bartley, hanging by the boards. (BARTLEY *takes the rope.*) It will be wanting in this place, I'm telling you, if Michael is washed up to-morrow morning, or the next morning, or any morning in the week, for it's a deep grave we'll make him by the grace of God.

BARTLEY (*beginning to work with the rope*): I've no halter the way I can ride down on the mare, and I must go now quickly. This is the one boat going for two weeks or beyond it, and the fair will be a good fair for horses I heard them saying below.

MAURYA: It's a hard thing they'll be saying below if the body is washed up and there's no man in it to make the coffin, and I after giving a big price for the finest white boards you'd find in Connemara.

She looks round at the boards.

BARTLEY: How would it be washed up, and we after looking each day for nine days, and a strong wind blowing a while back from the west and south?

MAURYA: If it wasn't found itself, that wind is raising the sea, and there was a star up against the moon, and it rising in the night. If it was a hundred horses, or a thousand horses you had itself, what is the price of a thousand horses against a son where there is one son only?

BARTLEY (*working at the halter, to* CATHLEEN): Let you go down each day, and see the sheep aren't jumping in on the rye, and if the jobber comes you can sell the pig with the black feet if there is a good price going.

MAURYA: How would the like of her get a good price for a pig?

BARTLEY (*to* CATHLEEN): If the west wind holds with the last bit of the moon let you and Nora get up weed enough for another cock for the kelp. It's hard set we'll be from this day with no one in it but one man to work.

MAURYA: It's hard set we'll be surely the day you're drownd'd with the rest. What way will I live and the girls with me, and I an old woman looking for the grave?

> BARTLEY *lays down the halter, takes off his old coat, and puts on a newer one of the same flannel.*

BARTLEY (*to* NORA): Is she coming to the pier?

NORA (*looking out*): She's passing the green head and letting fall her sails.

BARTLEY (*getting his purse and tobacco*): I'll have half an hour to go down, and you'll see me coming again in two days, or in three days, or maybe in four days if the wind is bad.

MAURYA (*turning round to the fire, and putting her shawl over her head*): Isn't it a hard and cruel man won't hear a word from an old woman, and she holding him from the sea?

CATHLEEN: It's the life of a young man to be going on the sea, and who would listen to an old woman with one thing and she saying it over?

BARTLEY (*taking the halter*): I must go now quickly. I'll ride down on the red mare, and the gray pony'll run behind me. . . . The blessing of God on you.

> *He goes out.*

MAURYA (*crying out as he is in the door*): He's gone now, God spare us, and we'll not see him again. He's gone now, and when the black night is falling I'll have no son left me in the world.

CATHLEEN: Why wouldn't you give him your blessing and he looking round in the door? Isn't it sorrow enough is on every one in this house without your sending him out with an unlucky word behind him, and a hard word in his ear?

> MAURYA *takes up the tongs and begins raking the fire aimlessly without looking round.*

For the most part the activity of the segment is clear though there are several vital points that are not explicitly stated or described. We can secure a better sense of what has and what has not been recorded by examining the following chart: On the left are listed those constituent motions that are conveyed through dialogue or stage direction. On the right are posed questions concerning other motions that are not stated, but that must be considered to fill out the activity of the segment.

Explicit Activity	Implicit Activity
Bartley hurries to door of hut. He enters and looks about. Cathleen descends from the loft, gives orders to Nora. Nora offers rope to Bartley.	*Is there a shift from hurry to hesitancy? Does he exchange a glance with his mother? Is he startled to see everyone assembled? Does he hesitate when he says his first lines? Is there a pause before he speaks? Where is Maurya looking?*
As he is about to take it, Maurya warns him not to touch the rope. Bartley answers by taking it. He starts to make a halter. Bartley tries to explain the obvious need for his trip.	*What is Maurya's reaction when he ignores her advice?*
Maurya and Bartley argue, but, when reason fails, Maurya pleads desperately that her last son is more important than anything else in the world.	*Does Bartley approach Maurya, or Maurya, Bartley? Do they look at each other?*
Bartley continues his work with the rope, gives orders to Cathleen.	*How does Bartley make the transition from Maurya to Cathleen? Is there a pause?*

Explicit Activity	Implicit Activity
Maurya mocks everything he says, asks a bitter question but is ignored.	*Does her voice become louder, softer, sharper?*
Bartley changes into a newer coat, asks for information about the ship. Nora reports its imminent arrival. Bartley takes his tobacco and purse.	*Do the girls ignore the mother? Both in the same way? Where does Bartley secure his tobacco and purse? Are they special items? Where are they placed in relation to Maurya?*
At Bartley's prediction of his return, Maurya turns to the fire and covers her head with her shawl.	*Is this activity a sign of mourning? Had she been gazing at Bartley until then?*
Cathleen scolds her for her words about Bartley. Bartley takes up halter and announces he is about to go. He stops for a moment in the doorway facing his family, then, giving his blessing, he leaves.	*Does Maurya make any sound during the last two speeches of Cathleen and Bartley? How long is the pause that Bartley holds? Is his last sentence directed toward the family or to the mother? Does he gaze at Maurya? If so, is she aware of him?*
Maurya cries out, lamenting the death she feels is imminent.	*Which stage direction is correct? Does Maurya cry out before Bartley leaves or after?*
Cathleen asks Maurya how she could have denied Bartley her farewell.	*Is Cathleen's voice scolding or despairing? Is her question rhetorical?*

Immediately, we can see that the implicit activity involves the reactions of the four people to one another, the ocular exchange or lack of it between mother and son, and the timing, including pausing, of the rhythm in the segment. Especially crucial is the pause near the conclusion of the segment when Bartley hesitates in the doorway. We shall consider the significance of this activity shortly.

It is useful in examining activity to first define, without being rigid, the nature of what is happening within a segment. One can do this by summarizing the detailed sequence of activity, but it is sometimes simpler, and theatrically more pointed, to sum up in a single phrase the kind of activity contained in a segment. Just as there are character types which recur in play after play, so there are segmental types which run throughout dramatic history. Our example dramatizes a farewell. There are also persuasion, confessional, messenger, and many other segmental types. In fact, we can better understand the artistry of a playwright by identifying these segmental types. In that way, the particular skill he brings to the type can be appreciated.

The segment we are analyzing contains a farewell situation. In form it adheres to natural activity, Synge's inspiration having come from the lives of the Aran islanders. The first thing to note about this farewell segment is its relative inarticulateness. There is no true expression of farewell, no demonstration of affection, no physical contact between brother and sister or between son and mother. Thus, we modify the type by describing the segment as an abortive farewell.

The particular treatment of the farewell segment in this play leads us directly to an analysis of the action. In order to visualize the shape of the action, we shall search for the ways Synge utilizes the variables described earlier in this chapter. What is the precipitating context? What is the project of each character? What path does the tension follow? Where is the crux of the segment? By answering these questions, we shall arrive at a total image of the segment as experience and art.

Precipitating context

The information supplied before the segment begins establishes the precipitating circumstances. Maurya, fearful that her youngest son wants to make the trip to the Connemara fair, has either asked the priest to prevent him from doing so or believes that the priest will do this. Bartley, on the other hand, intends to go, and the description of his hurrying to the door verifies that decision. The circumstances are thus very simple. Maurya, waiting to hear whether or not one son has drowned, does not want the younger one to leave the island. Bartley intends to go. Initially the daughters seem not to take sides but to accept events. The *vector* of the incipient segment points toward a confrontation between mother and son. The *contrast* lies in their attitudes and in the juxtaposition of youth and age.

Projects

Earlier in this chapter (see pp. 46–47) I introduced the concept of project without exploring it fully. When applied to acrobatic performance that concept is much simpler than when applied to the dramatic act. In an acrobatic performance, the project is the concrete focal point of the energies of the performer. In drama it is the focal point both of the performer and the character. The performer attempts to achieve the form of the character's project, in Jan Kott's phrase, he "mimes" the character's project.[13] For instance, Bartley is attempting to fulfill his role as man of the house, one task of which is selling the horses at the fair. His project is the "living out" of the masculine role as it has been defined in the past by his brothers and his father before them. For the character the outcome of this conflict is uncertain. He lives from moment to moment. For the performer the outcome follows a shape of action set in rehearsal. He acts "as if" he were living from moment to moment although he actually paces himself to fulfill a general structure, allowing for minor variations in accord with audience response.

In introducing the term "project," I am departing from common usage. It seems necessary to do so in order to distinguish accurately how human energy is expended through activity. Every segment, as we know, has an impelling force of some sort. Customarily this force is termed "drive" or "motivation." Actors speak of what characters "want" or of "their action," that is, the purpose of their activity. Their usage, however, is but one part of the larger concept of project. Bartley, we have seen, "wants" to sell the horse, but the image of the future is not the act of selling the horse, nor is it even the abstract idea of fulfilling the male role. His energies are gathered to fulfill a mode of male behavior. The act of picking up the pipe is part of that effort at fulfillment. In his entire being is the total image of how he should behave. To illustrate the point on a simple level, I can speak of a man wanting to make money. That is his intent. However, to know that man I would have to know his project. One cannot live out the abstract purpose of wanting to make money, only the concrete project. The urge to make money may manifest itself in one's imagination and behavior negatively, that is, as escaping a poverty one has known, or positively, as owning a yacht or walking into an exclusive hotel. It is in such a way that *the project is the concrete focal point of a character's energy, and it is the project that the performer enacts.*

In calling the impelling force of a scene "motivation" or "intention," actors usually think of "conscious will" though they may also include the idea of "impulse" and "subconscious drive." The project, by contrast, encompasses all kinds of energies that human beings exert. Some people dream into the future. Others concentrate their energies consciously. At one extreme we have determined efforts to achieve a specific goal. At the other, generalized impulses. For the purposes of analysis, we should discriminate between the project, the concrete image of a character's energy, and the energy itself. That energy, or impelling force, can be conscious or unconscious, rational or irrational, defined or vague. For the energy as a totality, of whatever type, I shall use the term "motivation." When the energy is conscious and specific, I shall call it "intention." Thus, I would speak of Bartley's *intention* to go to Connemara as part of his larger *motivation* of fulfilling his new role as man of the house. The *project* is the mode of behavior he is trying to achieve.

Two of the variables affecting motivation are *strength* and *directionality*. Motivation can be vigorous or weak. In most presentations, the leading figures tend to possess strong drives. This is not necessarily always the case, as seen in the plays of Chekhov and Beckett. Related to strength is directionality. Motivations may or may not be fixed upon specific goals. Vague purposes may be pursued passionately and specific ends may lack vigorous pursuit. There is much force in Lear, but to what end? His aims are diffuse. And though Chekhov's three sisters want to go to Moscow, they lack the energy to sustain their aspirations. Just how much energy a dramatic character must apply to hold our interest is hard to say. We expect drama to be composed of strong situations, yet contemporary drama is filled with the impression of weakness. This is often accomplished by retaining strength, but diffusing purpose, thus giving the effect of feebleness. In *Who's Afraid of Virginia Woolf?*, George's apparent spinelessness at the outset arises from the want of clear purpose rather than lack of vigor. Throughout our work we will encounter the equation: *dramatic progression is a product of the proportion between strength of motivation and the directionality of motivation.*

A third variant of motivation is *source*. As mentioned earlier, motivation in drama is often thought to arise from an exertion of will. To a substantial extent this is so, though the nature of will may be analyzed in quite different ways, depending upon whether one is a behaviorist, a Freudian, or a Marxist. At this point it is not necessary to choose between various views of human will but to recognize that the will as a source of motivation is merely one source among many. Motivation may arise from impulse, instinct, reason, and so forth. It may stem from a common source in human nature, as in Renaissance thinking, or from the unique context of individual existence. It may reside primarily in spiritual yearning or sexual longing. As manifested in a dramatic work, motivation will arise from that source which a particular society and a particular author accepts as valid.

We now return to our analysis of the segment from *Riders to the Sea*. In this play the source of motivation resides in endurance of a cruel environment, an endurance embedded in a traditional way of life. What moves the characters is their sense of community and their place in the communal scheme. "For these people the outrage to the hearth is the supreme catastrophe," Synge observes. They live "in a world of grey, where there are wild rains and mists every week in the year, and their warm chimney corners, filled with children and young girls, grow into the consciousness of each family in a way it is not easy to understand in more civilized places." [14]

BARTLEY: His intention is specific: he plans to take the hooker, or ship, to Connemara and comes to the house ostensibly to secure the few things he requires for the trip. From his behavior, it is evident that his intention is strong enough to withstand the mother's objections. His motivation, which encompasses this intention, arises from the circumstances that he is the last and the only man of the house. Thus, he is trying to fulfill the role of the responsible male. Moreover, intentionally and motivationally, he seems to wish for his mother's approval of what he is doing although this is not explicitly stated. All these factors are subsumed within the project. Bartley enacts the traditional masculine role of his society by projecting an image of himself into this role. The projection includes giving orders to the women, taking up his tobacco, and receiving the traditional support of the household. Being young, however, and rushed too soon into responsibility by the disappearance of his older brother Michael, Bartley finds a gap between his project and his circumstances on one hand and between his project and his mother's recognition of it on the other.

MAURYA: Her project is negative. It is to resist the coming of the inevitable, that is, the loss of her youngest son. She envisions this event so vividly that she cannot acquiesce in his departure. She does not look beyond the immediate matter of Connemara. She wishes Bartley to remain, and though the intention and the general motivation that support it are strong, the objective is diffuse, for though the intention is focused upon the immediate issue, her motivation, given the circumstances, does not have a specific goal. How can she permanently keep Bartley from assuming his role as man, that is, how can she permanently keep him from the sea? The diffuseness of her motivation helps to explain the indirect way she applies her energies to keeping Bartley from his trip.

THE DAUGHTERS: Cathleen's and Nora's intentions, with differences in quality, are similar. They both wish to assist Bartley. The strength of Cathleen's intention causes her to assist Bartley actively and even to defend him against Maurya. By nature Nora is more passive. Cathleen's project appears to parallel Bartley's. She fulfills the role of woman in the household. She does not question, but she participates in carrying through the routine of life. Nora's project is somewhat different. Her youth is a contributory factor. So is her status in the household. There is no explicit clue to her project and yet we can sense it. She does as she is told, but she does not initiate activity. Rather, she witnesses, empathizes, and seems to project a capacity for sympathy, which is absorbed into her mother's final paean. In Nora's case then, passivity and diffuseness are characteristics of her project.

Action (path of the tension)

Bartley's arrival activates the precipitating context. Within the duration of the segment, we can see that he is the *impelling agent*. It is his determination that propels the segment forward. Tension is produced by the discrepancy between his project and Maurya's resistance. Its path is as follows: Bartley rushes in, looks about, then asks for the new rope; Maurya remonstrates, linking the new rope to Michael's disappearance. In the first half of the segment, Bartley and Maurya speak directly to each other. He argues that he needs the rope to take the horses to the fair. "The fair will be a good fair for horses." She insinuates that his first duty is to remain to bury Michael when he is found. He answers her either by ridiculing or disputing her faith in finding Michael, depending upon individual interpretation. Her next answer changes the nature of her appeal. Bartley must remain, she suggests, because there is a cruel sea and he is her last son. Thus, to this moment he has countered every appeal with arguments, and she has revealed step by step her true concern until the deep fear that really haunts her is revealed. To this fear Bartley has no answer.

From this point onward, Bartley does not speak directly to Maurya except to include her in his last sentence. He assumes the role of man of the house, thus living out his project, which she attacks. Cathleen alone replies directly to her. The tension, which threatens to become higher pitched, leading to direct conflict, becomes diffused throughout the room. We are aware of the tension, but it is a tension by negation. We sense the tension by Bartley's failure to reply. For instance, Maurya's prediction of his death demands response and the failure to arouse it makes us more aware of the gap that exists between mother and son. It is that gap which produces tension in the characters and induces in the audience a parallel though vicarious tension.

The most intense moment also occurs where the gap is broadest. At the very end of the scene, the dramatist has inserted ellipses to mark an activity before Bartley speaks the last words, "The blessing of God on you." Two speeches later Cathleen tells us what he did. She asks her mother angrily, "Why wouldn't you give him your blessing and he looking round in the door?" At his exit, there is the following picture: Bartley poised in the doorway, turned toward his family, waiting; Maurya, turned toward or away from him, ignoring him, ignoring his silent request as he had ignored her previously. A yawning abyss lies between his need for her blessing and her refusal to give it. No word defines that gap, yet it is the *crux* of the segment.

Can we say that a change has taken place in the segment? Not a great change. But then a great change does not occur in this play. The only change is that what is expected to happen does happen. The action lies in how the people live through this fulfillment of the inevitable. Although Bartley impels the action, attention is principally upon Maurya. Her stubbornness is all she has with which to fight the inevitable. Bartley intends to leave. He leaves. One more door closes on Maurya. Yet she resists to the point of withholding her blessing, a refusal of the utmost significance.

The path and the quality of intensity are determining elements of what I have previously called the shape of the action. In this instance the tension offers the potential for a confrontation that never occurs. This type of tension can be termed *oblique*. Oblique tension is characterized by implied conflict between characters. The parties themselves do not overtly admit to its existence. They insinuate, they do not argue. Forms of ironic tension may also be considered oblique. Where the audience knows of a danger that the character does not, tension proceeds by indirection. The opposite of the oblique conflict is the *direct*. Characters confront each other, aware of the tensions that exist between them. The most direct conflict, of course, is physical battle, although it is not necessarily the most intense. The distinction between oblique and direct tension is not one of quantity but of quality. In the Bartley-Maurya segment, the most intense moment is also the most oblique, so oblique that it finds active expression in performance only.

The shape of the action thus moves from fairly direct to oblique opposition. Throughout, the activity counterpoints the underlying action. Not that the activity implies one meaning and the action another but, rather, the domesticity of the activity does not fully express the powerful undertow of yearning that flows through the action. Only three times does the potential force that inhabits the individual projects come to the surface: once when Maurya cries out "What is the price of a thousand horses against a son where there is one son only?"; a second time when Maurya draws the shawl about her head; a last time when Cathleen berates her mother for being "an old woman with one thing and she saying it over." These outbursts or revelations of deeper emotions only accentuate the unspoken feelings of the characters. If we turn back to our list of activities, we will see that it is the implicit activity that is instrumental in communicating these unspoken feelings and thus conveying the shape of the action.

As we know, the shape of action is not only temporal but spatial. Consider again the moment when Bartley stands in the doorway waiting for his mother's response and Maurya sits unresponsive, with her shawl about her head. Both are in states of becoming, states that are not completed. He is enacting a waiting, she a refusal to fulfill the purpose of his waiting. The physical gap between them, expressing as it does a spiritual gap, arouses a sense of poignancy in the audience.

The oblique quality of the segment coming to a crux at Bartley's departure is apparent enough from the play script itself. Happily, however, there is external evidence that the dramatist consciously shaped the segment toward this end. In a definitive edition of Synge's plays, Ann Saddlemyer has not only produced a careful version of the text but also reproduced many extracts from the notebooks that Synge kept in 1902 and 1903.[15] The departure of Bartley, who is named Patch in the preliminary drafts, appears in two earlier versions. The first draft is fragmentary. The line, "Isn't it a hard and cruel man won't hear a word from an old woman, and she holding him from the sea?" is prefigured as "Isn't it a cruel thing he wont hear what I'm saying and I holding him back from death and destruction and the danger of the sea?" This version is corrected in pencil, "he" and "I" being crossed out and a more indirect phrasing substituted so that the revised line reads, "Isn't it a hard and cruel thing when a man wont hear the thing his mother is saying and she holding him from being destroyed upon the sea?" [16]

In the second draft of the segment, the corrections reveal more explicitly that Synge sought to shape the action obliquely. Twice Maurya (in this version called Bride) openly begs Patch (Bartley) to remain. "Dont go Patch for the weather's broke now and there'll be danger on the sea. Dont go Patch if it was a hundred horses you had itself. (Patch gets down a halter and begins settling the rope.) What is a hundred horses against a son in a house where there is one son only?" Later she pleads, "Dont go heir of my heart, dont go Patcheen and leave an old woman alone." The first three of these overt pleas are crossed out by Synge. [17] The last one remains, but only temporarily, because in the final text, he eliminated all direct confrontation between mother and son.

The notebooks also illustrate how deliberately Synge defined the crux. In both early drafts, stage directions indicate that Patch (Bartley) leaves without hesitation. At first, he goes out after the line, "I'll ride down on the mare and the other horses will follow me." [18] In the second draft, he goes out after the revised line, "I'll ride down on the mare and the grey pony will run after." [19] For the final draft, Synge added an ellipsis and the line, "The blessing of God on you." That the three dots were significant and intentional is further demonstrated by a corrected state of the play as published in *Samhain,* a review edited by William Butler Yeats. *Riders to the Sea* appeared in the September 1903 number, and after publication Synge revised the copy, apparently for the Vigo edition. In the Bartley segment, as it appears in *Samhain,* there are two other points where pauses are indicated. An ellipsis follows the word "kelp" and the word "bad" (in the phrase "if the wind is bad") as well as before "The blessing of God on you." Synge himself struck out the dots after "kelp" and "bad" and left the only ellipsis for the end, thus stressing its crucial importance.[20]

Taken together, the tightrope act and the sequence from *Riders to the Sea* provide a composite model of a segment of action. In drama the segment is the building block. So far we have concentrated upon its internal structure. This structure will vary considerably in form and type, but the variables I have identified will be found in all instances. From these building blocks plays are constructed.

3 Variations

● No single model of action can represent the multifarious depictions of life contained in the thousands of scenes of dramatic history. At best, a model can define the components of drama so that a more systematic examination of plays can be undertaken. And yet, the theater is a conservative art. With all the variety of scenes it has known, patterns of action recur with amazing frequency. Perhaps no one can reduce all drama to thirty-six situations as Georges Polti has tried to do. But on comprehensive consideration of dramatic form, one finds more repetition than might be expected.

In examining variations and recurrence in dramatic patterns, the reader must have a clear idea of the factors he is comparing. Usually, drama critics, to the extent that they compare different types of drama, compare subject matter, themes, and style, principally linguistic style. But they give scant consideration to the various ways in which the elements of action are treated by different playwrights and performers. In effect, to draw an analogy from art history, they study the recurrent use of the Madonna as a theme and the attitudes different artists bring to that subject, but comment little upon an artist's handling of the elemental components of art: line, mass, color, space, and so forth. To appreciate the similarities and dissimilarities in historical dramatic form, one cannot ignore the elemental components of drama, including precipitating context, project, resistance, crux, and decrescence. How they are arranged by a theatrical artist determines the kind of segment which he produces.

ACTIVE AND REACTIVE TENDENCIES IN DRAMA

A dramatic segment shows one of two tendencies in its linear development. It inclines toward being either *active* or *reactive*. The precipitating context of each segment points a direction (vector) for the action. One type of vector promises confrontation which usually arises from tension between project and resistance. Bartley intends to leave; his mother tries, indirect though her method may be, to hinder his departure. The action moves toward a crux when neither will yield to the other. In contrast, another type of vector points not toward a confrontation but toward some sort of sustained emotional release. The reactive pattern occurs, in fact, because the precipitating context is sufficiently explosive to excite such an extended release. It can be clearly distinguished from the active pattern through the absence of constantly applied pressure by one character on another. Hitherto dramatic theory has taken sufficient account of active segments. It is time that we recognize the reactive element, for any single play is a composite of both.

Most enactments of suffering, which Aristotle names as one of the three structural elements of tragedy, are reactive. The brief subsegment in Sophocles' *Electra* in which the disguised Orestes gives Electra the urn supposedly containing his ashes is just such a reactive segment. Accepting the reported death of Orestes without suspicion, Electra bewails her loss. During this segment, the vector of action is pointed not toward a moment when she will discover that the urn-bearer is her own brother but toward the full expression of her grief. Throughout, Orestes stands by without speaking directly to Electra though he may indeed react to her words:

ELECTRA: Sir, give it to me, by the Gods. If he
　is hidden in this urn—give it into my hands,
　that I may keen and cry lament together
　for myself and all my race with these ashes here.
ORESTES (*speaking to his men*): Bring it and give it to her, whoever
　　she is.
　It is not in enmity she asks for it.
　One of his friends perhaps, or of his blood.
ELECTRA (*speaking to the urn*): Oh, all there is for memory of my
　　love,
　my most loved in the world, all that is left
　of live Orestes, oh, how differently
　from how I sent you forth, how differently
　from what I hoped, do I receive you home.
　Now all I hold is nothingness,
　but you were brilliant when I sent you forth.
　Would that you had left life before I sent you
　abroad to a foreign country, when I stole you
　with these two hands, saved you from being murdered.
　Then on that very day you would have died,
　have lain there and have found your share,
　your common portion, of your father's grave.
　Now far from home, an exile, on alien soil
　without your sister near, you died unhappily.
　I did not, to my sorrow, wash you with
　the hands that loved you, did not lift you up,
　as was my right, a weight of misery,
　to the fierce blaze of the pyre. The hands of strangers
　gave you due rites, and so you come again,
　a tiny weight inclosed in tiny vessel.
　Alas for all my nursing of old days,
　so constant—all for nothing—which I gave you;

my joy was in the trouble of it. For never
were you your mother's love as much as mine.
None was your nurse but I within that household.
You called me always "sister." Now in one day
all that is gone—for you are dead. All, all
you have snatched with you in your going, like
a hurricane. Our father is dead and gone.
I am dead in you; and you are dead yourself.
Our enemies laugh. Frantic with joy, she grows,
mother, no mother, whom you promised me,
in secret messages so often, you
would come to punish. This, all this, the Genius,
the unlucky Genius of yourself and me,
has stolen away and sent you back to me,
instead of the form I loved, only your dust
and idle shade. Alas! Alas!
O body pitiable! Alas!
O saddest journey that you went, my love,
and so have ended me! Alas!
O brother, loved one, you have ended me.
Therefore, receive me to your habitation,
nothing to nothing, that with you below
I may dwell from now on. When you were on earth,
I shared all with you equally. Now I claim
in death no less to share a grave with you.
The dead, I see, no longer suffer pain.

CHORUS: Think, Electra, your father was mortal,
and mortal was Orestes. Do not sorrow too much.
This is a debt that all of us must pay.[1]

Throughout this segment, Electra's grief becomes increasingly
intense and desperate. The precipitating context includes her previous debate with Clytemnestra, the report of Orestes' death, and
most immediately, the presence of the funeral urn. This context
propels the action, which does not move, however, toward a
"closed" crux, that is, a crux in which a project and resistance
confront each other. Rather, it moves toward an "open" situation
in which Electra must adjust to the dreaded facts. The action is a
working out of the pressures aroused by the precipitating events.
It may be divided into the following stages: reception of the
"body," evocation of the past, testing the present, reiteration of
the past, testing the present again with awareness of the broken

promise for the future, unrestrained lament (the *crux*), and the longing for death, for the future (the *decrescence*).

The reactive tendency is not confined to the expression of passion. It is also manifested in segments of revelation as illustrated in a brief choral scene from *Macbeth* (II, iv). The scene occurs immediately after the discovery of Duncan's murder. First, Ross, one of the courtiers, meets an Old Man, and, second, Macduff joins them to reveal the latest political events. The entire scene makes one action-unit, but each of the two halves composes an autonomous segment. The first half is not at all related to plot sequence, for the Old Man who appears here initially is never seen again.

The precipitating circumstance is Duncan's murder. As I have shown elsewhere,[2] Shakespearean drama is structured on a reactive basis. This example dramatizes one reaction to Duncan's murder not merely, or even principally, in terms of human reactions but in terms of natural and cosmic reactions. The activity that Ross and the Old Man engage in is conversational report. They exchange news of natural and supernatural responses to the king's murder. The action, we discover, moves toward mounting astonishment of universal horror. The tension is modulated somewhat because these figures are not centrally involved in the events of the play (though the Old Man issues a warning to Ross at the very end of the scene). Note how Shakespeare structures the action.

OLD MAN: Threescore and ten I can remember well;
   Within the volume of which time I have seen
   Hours dreadful, and things strange, but this sore night
   Hath trifled former knowings.
ROSS: Ha, good Father,
   Thou seest the heavens, as troubled with man's act,
   Threatens his bloody stage: by th' clock 'tis day,
   And yet dark night strangles the travelling lamp.
   Is't night's predominance, or the day's shame,
   That darkness does the face of earth entomb,
   When living light should kiss it?
OLD MAN: 'Tis unnatural,
   Even like the deed that's done. On Tuesday last,
   A falcon, towering in her pride of place,

Was by a mousing owl hawk'd at, and kill'd.

ROSS: And Duncan's horses (a thing most strange and certain)
Beauteous and swift, the minions of their race,
Turn'd wild in nature, broke their stalls, flung out,
Contending 'gainst obedience, as they would make
War with mankind.

OLD MAN: 'Tis said, they eat each other.

ROSS: They did so; to th' amazement of mine eyes,
That look'd upon 't. (II, iv, 1–20)

First, a general reaction, on a less emotionally tense, more philosophical level, is initiated. The Old Man puts his reaction into the
perspective of age. Ross then personalizes the response by pointing out the strangeness of nature, asking the Old Man why
the darkness: night's=evil's predominance or day's=goodness'
shame? The Old Man can only answer that what is happening is
unnatural, and he illustrates with the case of the falcon. Ross
betters him with the story of Duncan's horses. The Old Man
chimes in with a horrifying description of their end: " 'Tis said,
they eat each other." Ross suddenly intensifies the recital by testi-
fying that he witnessed this act. Thus, the tension mounts as a consequence both of the contents of the stories and the characters'
proximity to them, the action passing from impersonal rumor to
personal involvement. The change is revealed: nature has been
overthrown. But what of the crux in the action-block? Where
does it occur? It occurs at the very end of the unit when Ross
admits his amazement at seeing the horses eat each other.
Whether or not even more gruesome news would have followed,
we do not know. We have here what may be described as a
crisis in suspension. Into the midst of their horrified reaction
comes Macduff.

Who is the Old Man? Although he may not quite personify Father Time, he is a measure of human experience. "Threescore and
ten," the proverbial extent of a man's life, he can remember well.
He goes beyond man's life, encompassing a length of witnessing
against which the particular events of the murder can be viewed.
These events surpass all "former knowings." To Ross, he is "good
Father." But, as we see, his knowledge is abstract and lacks the
particularity that Ross himself has. In these two characters then,
we have the reaction of time itself as well as that of the individual

within time. As the segment progresses, the Old Man maintains a narrative or journalistic tone in reporting the strange news of the time. It is Ross who progresses from question to report to witnessing. The leap from report to witnessing is sudden, unexpected, decisive. Regard once again the construction of the last two lines and imagine the characters' emotive responses that should accompany them.

OLD MAN: 'Tis said, they eat each other.
ROSS: They did so; to th' amazement of mine eyes,
    That look'd upon 't.

The rhythmic sequence is an oral equivalent of a camera lens zooming into a close-up of strained features. General astonishment becomes immediate.

The projects of both figures are dissimilar, but only in degree. Absorption into experience seems to be the key to the Old Man. Imaginatively, he must adjust to the unnatural deed, draw it within himself in the fullness of time. Ross, too, absorbs the implications of the deed but lacks the experience to measure it. The disruption in nature disquiets him. His project is to fulfill his role as courtier, yet the murder threatens to destroy this role. His goals are exceedingly nebulous. A vague impulse to assimilate the horror of the time propels him, and, as the lines illustrate, he does not even seem to have the intention of sharing his personal knowledge. "And Duncan's horses" merely continues the enumeration of the unnatural acts besetting the time. In confirming the cannibalism of the peerless horses, Ross reveals unresolved amazement. Natural order has indeed been violated. He stood by and watched. His project has not been achieved. He has not and cannot, at this point at least, assimilate the horror of the catastrophe. In this we see an analogue of future action, for it takes Ross a long time to come to terms with the bewildering events of which he is witness.

What we find in this reactive segment can be seen in reactive segments generally. Projects tend to be directed toward adjusting to the precipitating context or venting the repressed thoughts, feelings, or experiences released by the precipitating circumstances. In most instances the motivation is not likely to be specific, and, in effect, the segment, unlike an active one, tends to be experience-oriented rather than goal-oriented. Concentration upon amazement occupies Ross far more than achieving a specific goal. Such is the case of Electra, too, in the segment previously cited. Her grief-sharing with the supposedly-dead Orestes is an end in itself. She craves the sensation of death. Her reaction advances from her awareness of separation from him to an outburst of grief leading to the penultimate line: "Now I claim/in death no less to share a grave with you."

In both *Macbeth* and *Electra*, each reactive segment has a crux near the end of the action. As we have seen, the crux in the selection from *Macbeth* occurs when Ross reveals his personal observation of the cannibal horses. The crux in the selection from *Electra* occurs when Electra bursts into wild lamentation. Though Ross' response is more implicit than Electra's, each crux involves a leap into intense emotionality. Thus, the crux in these two units is not a moment of decision or realization, but cumulative release.

What is the nature of the resistance that the project meets in the reactive segment? We cannot speak of resistance in the same forceful sense as in the active segment. What hinders Electra from immediately expressing her lament? What prevents Ross from revealing his own involvement? We must consider here how human experience is transmuted into dramatic form. Natural emotional reactions encompass a wide variety of expression. At their most intense level they may be inarticulate, physically as well as orally. True grief, for instance, cannot be presented because it is not communicable. Instead it must be ordered so that it can be perceived. As we shall see, even then it cannot be too fully realized because room must be allowed for audience response. Therefore, the crux of a reactive segment represents the level that is most nearly inarticulate, yet most completely expressive of the individual's extreme state of mind. Between the initial precipitation and the crux lies the path of reaction. In essence, this path is "artificial," that is, it is shaped to bring the audience to the proper level of response. Frequently, time is stretched so that the minute stages of response can be expressed. Electra, addressing the urn, bewailing her inability to prepare her brother's body for cremation, imagining the triumph of their enemies, gradually comes to the crux. By retarding her outburst, Sophocles enables us to share her emotions. In *Macbeth*, by retarding Ross' personal involvement in the unnatural reactions, Shakespeare accentuates the suddenness of Ross' astonishment, and thus of our own.

In the reactive segment, the resistance is internalized. The character must bring his total being into accord with the precipitating context. This is particularly true of verbal as differentiated from gestural drama. The verbal drama seems to permit the character to bring separate aspects of self into touch with circumstances. In sequence, memory, funereal rites, and defeat occupy Electra's thoughts. The present fact of darkness, former events, and personal presence prepare for Ross' unresolved amazement. The imagination of the character must traverse the path of response before reaching its most intense revelation. Each stage suggests the ultimate intensity but does not realize it until all the causes for grief are brought into the total configuration. Electra's grief for Orestes must traverse the path of both personal devotion to the dead and ritual responsibility to the corpse. The shape of the ritual is the resistance which provides a vehicle for her personal expression.

The tendencies of the *active* segment are most easily discerned in the line of drama that came down from the Greeks through the Romans and the French to Ibsen. Ibsen did not discard the intrigue of the well-made play; he merely internalized it. *Hedda Gabler* exhibits both the manipulation of events and the psychological basis for the manipulation. The last half of Act IV provides an excellent example both of Ibsen's skill in dramatic construction and of the active segment.[3]

Type of activity

At its most fundamental level, the play's activity is both conversational and domestic. As in so many middle-class and lower-middle-class dramas, the activity, which consists of a kind of domestic socializing, allows for informality and intimacy. It may occasionally embrace formal receptions, but by and large relies upon a marked degree of casualness. Conversation rarely begins in the midst of a situation but evolves from occasional and trivial chatter to momentous revelations. Yet, however undirected the conversation appears to be, it is always aimed toward an ultimate confrontation. In the present segment the conversation is organized into coercive activity.

Precipitating context

Lövborg is dead. Unknown to anyone but Tesman, Hedda has destroyed Lövborg's manuscript. Moreover, she has urged Lövborg to kill himself "beautifully" and given him a pistol for the purpose. By chance Thea has preserved all the notes for the manuscript so that Tesman, to relieve his conscience, agrees to collaborate with Thea in reconstructing Lövborg's work. The moment before the segment begins is low-keyed. Thea and Tesman are working together in an inner room, and it is not apparent that they threaten Hedda in any way. No one seems to know of her responsibility for the destruction of Lövborg's manuscript or, for that matter, her encouragement of his death. Strong contrasts exist, however, between the working couple, Thea and Tesman, and the conversing couple, Hedda and Brack. As the segment proceeds, the proximity of the working couple exerts a restraint upon the conversing couple.

Projects

HEDDA: For the first time in the play, Hedda is not chafing at the boredom of her existence. She experiences an inner exaltation under the impression that she has secretly directed Lövborg to his godlike twilight. At this point then, her project is to taste fully the sensation of the moment, to remain perched upon its ecstatic height.

TESMAN: His aim is far more specific than Hedda's. His intention is to restore Lövborg's manuscript and thus make amends for his responsibility in leaving it with Hedda. This intention is, however, only the particular manifestation of a broader project. Pouring over scraps of information produces physical and psychological delight. Therefore, in specifically making amends he is also fulfilling the image of himself that he prefers.

THEA: Beyond the intention of rescuing Lövborg's work (her "child"), she seeks to relive that physical and spiritual relationship she had with Lövborg when he was writing his book. Her abject service to the man (first Lövborg and later Tesman) results in the man achieving himself more completely.

BRACK: His project is hidden at the beginning of the segment, but gradually asserts itself. From the previous action of the play, it is clear that he envisions a special role for himself in the Tesman house. That it could go beyond the intimacy of confidant is hinted at but not established. Within the project of becoming "the one cock of the roost," his intention is one, to discover Hedda's responsibility for Lövborg's death, and two, to use the information when he gets it to exercise control over Hedda.

The shape of the action in the segment

The segment primarily involves Hedda and Brack; Tesman and Thea merely counterpoint the dominant action. Brack is the impelling agent. His gentle pressure is directed at Hedda. The nature of the resistance is, first, Hedda's euphoria, and then, throughout the segment until the crux, her inability to perceive her involvement. Step by step Brack destroys her illusion about Lövborg's death and then reveals the trap into which she has fallen. Thus, the overall shape of the action will emerge from *how* Hedda makes her discoveries.

To what degree is my division of the action accurate? If the dramatist has not formally marked segments in the text, may not my analysis be purely interpretive and as arbitrary as any other reader's? Certainly, interpretation does enter into the segmental process, but it is essential to distinguish between imaginative and descriptive interpretation. Segmenting the action for purposes of analysis is a descriptive process which depends on careful examination of the dramatic components. A segment embraces a phase of action which contains a development, crux, and decrescence. The balancing of projects and resistance as extensions of the precipitating circumstances reveals the vector of a segment. By tracing the vector to its resolution, the reader can determine the conclusion of one segment and the commencement of another. To master this method requires practice, preferably in the study of the finest drama, because, as it turns out, the finer the drama, the simpler and more precise is the segmental pattern. There may indeed be true differences of interpretation, but they will be richer if they emerge from detailed reexamination of the text (my division of the segment is specified in square brackets).

[*Subsegment A contains three subordinate units, each with a crux.*]

> HEDDA *crosses to the stove and sits in the armchair. Presently* BRACK *goes up to her.*

HEDDA (*in a low voice*): Oh, what a sense of freedom it gives one, this act of Eilert Lövborg's.

BRACK: Freedom, Miss Hedda? Well, of course, it's a release for him—

HEDDA: I mean for me. It gives me a sense of freedom to know that a deed of deliberate courage is still possible in this world,—a deed of immutable beauty.

BRACK (*smiling*): Hm—my dear Miss Hedda—

HEDDA: Oh, I know what you're going to say. For you are a kind of specialist too, like—hm!

BRACK (*looking hard at her*): Eilert Lövborg was more to you than perhaps you are willing to admit to yourself. Am I wrong?

HEDDA: I don't answer such questions. I only know that Eilert Lövborg has had the courage to live his life after his own fashion. And then —the last great act, with its beauty! [*crux*] Ah! that he should have the will and the courage to turn away from the banquet of life—so early. [*end of unit A1*]

BRACK: I am sorry, Miss Hedda,—but I fear I must dispel a pleasant illusion.

HEDDA: Illusion?

BRACK: Which couldn't have lasted long in any case.

HEDDA: What do you mean?

BRACK: Eilert Lövborg did not shoot himself—voluntarily.

HEDDA: Not voluntarily!

BRACK: No. The thing did not happen exactly as I told it.

HEDDA (*eagerly*): Have you concealed something? What is it?

BRACK: For poor Mrs. Elvsted's sake I idealised the facts a little.

HEDDA: What *are* the facts?

BRACK: First, that he is already dead. [*crux*]

HEDDA: At the hospital?

BRACK: Yes—without regaining consciousness. [*end of A2*]

HEDDA: What more have you concealed?

BRACK: This—the event did not happen at his lodgings.

HEDDA: Oh, that can make no difference.

BRACK: Perhaps it may. For you must know that Eilert Lövborg was found shot in—in Mademoiselle Diana's boudoir.

HEDDA (*makes a motion as if to rise, but sinks back again*): That is impossible, Judge Brack! He cannot have been there again to-day.

BRACK: He was there this afternoon. He came to claim something, he said, which they had taken from him. Talked wildly about a lost child—

HEDDA: Ah—so that was why—

BRACK: I thought probably he meant his manuscript; but I hear he destroyed that himself. So I suppose it must have been his pocket-book.

HEDDA: Yes, no doubt. And there—there he was found?

BRACK: Yes, there. With a pistol in his breastpocket, discharged. The ball had lodged in a vital part.

HEDDA: In the breast—yes.

BRACK: No—in the bowels. [*crux of subsegment A*]

HEDDA (*looks up at him with an expression of loathing*): That too! Oh, what curse is it that makes everything I touch turn ludicrous and mean? [*end of A3*]

[*Subsegment B contains four units.*]

BRACK: There is one point more, Miss Hedda—another element of vulgarity in the affair.

HEDDA: And what is that?

BRACK: The pistol he carried—

HEDDA (*breathless*): Well? What of it?

BRACK: He must have stolen it.

HEDDA (*leaps up*): Stolen it! That is not true! He did not steal it! [*crux*]

BRACK: No other explanation is possible. He *must* have stolen it,— [*end of B1*] Hush!

> TESMAN *and* MRS. ELVSTED *have risen from the table in the back room, and come into the drawing room.*

TESMAN (*with the papers in both his hands*): Hedda dear, it's almost impossible to see under that lamp. Think of that!

HEDDA: Yes, I am thinking.

TESMAN: Would you mind our sitting at your writing table—eh?

HEDDA: If you like. (*Rapidly.*) No, wait! Let me clear it first!

TESMAN: Oh, you needn't trouble, Hedda. There is plenty of room.

HEDDA: No no, let me clear it, I say! I'll take these things in and put them on the piano. There! [*crux*]

> She has drawn out an object, covered with sheet music, from under the bookcase, places several other pieces of music upon it, and carries the whole into the inner room, to the left. TESMAN *lays the scraps of paper on the writing-table, and moves the lamp there from the corner table. He and* MRS. ELVSTED *sit down and proceed with their work.* HEDDA *returns.*

HEDDA (*behind* MRS. ELVSTED'S *chair, gently ruffling her hair*): Well, my sweet Thea,—how goes it with Eilert Lövborg's monument?

MRS. ELVSTED (*looks dispiritedly up at her*): Oh, it will be terribly hard to put in order.

TESMAN: We must manage it. I'm determined. And arranging other people's papers is just the work for me. [*end of B2*]

> HEDDA *goes over to the stove, and seats herself on one of the footstools.* BRACK *stands over her, leaning on the arm-chair.*

HEDDA (*whispers*): What did you say about the pistol?

BRACK (*softly*): That he must have stolen it.

HEDDA: Why stolen it?

BRACK: Because every other explanation *ought* to be impossible, Miss Hedda.

HEDDA: Indeed?

BRACK (*glances at her*): Eilert Lövborg was here this morning, wasn't he?

HEDDA: Yes.

BRACK: Were you alone with him?

HEDDA: Part of the time.

BRACK: Did you not leave the room whilst he was here?

HEDDA: No.

BRACK: Try to recollect. Were you not out of the room a moment?

HEDDA: Yes, perhaps just a moment—out in the hall.

BRACK: And where was your pistol-case during that time?

HEDDA: I had it locked up in—

BRACK: Well, Miss Hedda?

HEDDA: The case stood there, on the writing-table.

BRACK: Have you looked since, to see whether both the pistols are there?

HEDDA: No.

BRACK: Well, you needn't. I saw the pistol found in Lövborg's pocket, and I knew it at once as the one I had seen yesterday—and before, too.

HEDDA: Have you it with you?

BRACK: No; the police have it.

HEDDA: What will the police do with it?

BRACK: Search till they find the owner.

HEDDA: Do you think they will succeed?

BRACK (*bends over her and whispers*): No, Hedda Gabler,—not so long as I say nothing.

HEDDA (*looks frightened at him*): And if you do *not* say nothing,— what then? [*crux*]

BRACK (*shrugs his shoulders*): There is always the possibility that the pistol was stolen.

HEDDA (*firmly*): Death rather than that.

BRACK (*smiling*): That's what people *say*—but they don't do it. [*end of B3*]

HEDDA (*without replying*): And supposing the pistol was not stolen, and the owner is discovered, what then?

BRACK: Well, Hedda—then comes the scandal.

HEDDA: The scandal!

BRACK: Yes, the scandal—of which you have such a mortal dread. You will, of course, be brought before the court—both you and Mademoiselle Diana. She will have to explain how the thing happened—whether it was an accidental shot or murder. Did the pistol go off as he was trying to take it out of his pocket to threaten her with? Or did she tear the pistol out of his hand, shoot him, and push it back into his pocket? That would be quite like her; for she's an able-bodied young person, this same Mademoiselle Diana.

HEDDA: But *I* have nothing to do with all this repulsive business.

BRACK: No. But you will have to answer the question: Why did you give Eilert Lövborg the pistol? And what conclusions will people draw from the fact that you did give it to him?

HEDDA (*lets her head sink*): That's true. I did not think of that.

BRACK: Well, fortunately, there's no danger, so long as I say nothing.

HEDDA (*looks up at him*): So I am in your power, Judge Brack. You have me at your beck and call, from this time forward. [*Crux of subsegment B begins.*]

BRACK (*whispers softly*): Dearest Hedda—believe me—I shall not abuse my advantage.

HEDDA: I am in your power none the less. Subject to your will and your demands. A slave, a slave then! (*Rises impetuously.*) No, I can't endure the thought of that! Never! [*Crux of Subsegment B ends.*]

BRACK (*looks halfmockingly at her*): People somehow get used to the inevitable.

HEDDA (*returns his look*): Yes, perhaps. [*end of B4*]

[*Subsegment C contains three units.*]

(*She crosses to the writing-table. Suppressing an involuntary smile, she imitates* TESMAN's *intonations.*) Well? Are you getting on, George? Eh?

TESMAN: Heaven knows, dear. In any case it will be the work of months.

HEDDA (*as before*): Think of that! (*Passes her hands softly through* MRS. ELVSTED's *hair.*) Doesn't it seem strange to you, Thea? Here are you sitting with Tesman—just as you used to sit with Eilert Lövborg?

MRS. ELVSTED: Ah, if I could only inspire your husband in the same way.

HEDDA: Oh, that will come too—in time.

TESMAN: Yes, do you know, Hedda—I really think I begin to feel something of the sort. But won't you go and sit with Brack again?

HEDDA: Is there nothing I can do to help you two?

TESMAN: No, nothing in the world. (*Turning his head*) I trust to you to keep Hedda company, my dear Brack!

BRACK (*with a glance at* HEDDA): With the very greatest of pleasure. [*crux*]

HEDDA: Thanks. [*end of C1*] But I am tired this evening. I will go in and lie down a little on the sofa.

TESMAN: Yes, do dear—eh?

> HEDDA *goes into the back room and draws the curtains. A short pause. Suddenly she is heard playing a wild dance on the piano.* [*crux*]

MRS. ELVSTED (*starts from her chair*): Oh—what is that?

TESMAN (*runs to the doorway*): Why, my dearest Hedda—don't play dance-music to-night! Just think of Aunt Rina! And of Eilert too!

HEDDA (*puts her head out between the curtains*): And of Aunt Julia. And of all the rest of them.—After this, I will be quiet. (*Closes the curtains again.*) [end of C2]

TESMAN (*at the writing-table*): It's not good for her to see us at this distressing work. I'll tell you what, Mrs. Elvsted,—you shall take the empty room at Aunt Julia's, and then I shall come over in the evenings, and we can sit and work *there*—eh?

HEDDA (*in the inner room*): I hear what you are saying, Tesman. But how am *I* to get through the evenings out here?

TESMAN (*turning over the papers*): Oh, I daresay Judge Brack will be so kind as to look in now and then, even though I'm not here.

BRACK (*in the arm-chair, calls out cheerfully*): Every blessed evening, with all the pleasure in life, Mrs. Tesman! We'll get on capitally together, we two!

HEDDA (*speaking loud and clear*): Yes, don't you hope so, Judge Brack? You as the one cock of the roost—

> *A shot is heard within.* TESMAN, MRS. ELVSTED, *and* BRACK *leap to their feet.* [crux of subsegment C]

TESMAN: Oh, now she is playing with those pistols again.

> *He throws back the curtains and runs in, followed by* MRS. ELVSTED. HEDDA *lies stretched on the sofa, lifeless. Confusion and cries.* BERTA *enters in alarm from the right.*

TESMAN (*shrieks to* BRACK): Shot herself! Shot herself in the temple! Think of that!

BRACK (*half-fainting in the arm-chair*): Heaven help us—people don't *do* such things! [end of C3]

The segment divides into three major units: Brack disillusioning Hedda, Brack trapping Hedda, Hedda reacting to the trap. In the first two subsegments Brack steadily but gently presses Hedda to two moments of realization. Each time Hedda's response is the crux, for the goal of Brack in each instance is to effect a change in Hedda's state of mind. During these two subsegments Brack drives her from a euphoric to a trapped state. Out of her sense of entrapment comes the final defiant act of self-destruction that follows. It is evident that the segment proceeds along a path of succeedingly significant discoveries for Hedda.

Brack is the impelling agent. But our attention focuses only secondarily upon the information he plays out and primarily upon its impact on Hedda. Here we have an instance of the separation of impelling force and the focus of audience interest. The action holds our attention as long as Hedda continues to interest us. Moreover, the responses intimated in the text are only a small part of the deep and critical response she undergoes, which must be conveyed by the actress. Yet, one might ask, with so much emphasis upon Hedda's response, why is this segment not reactive? Primarily because the structure is not reactive. The structure of the reactive segment is far more open-ended. In it a force precipitates a response but does not press it to a crux. Orestes, for instance, presents Electra with the urn, but she herself undergoes a sustained reaction to the crux. In *Hedda Gabler*, however, Brack is driving toward the moment of confrontation. He is playing a game in order to bring Hedda to a particular point of realization, which, he believes, will in turn lead to the behavior he desires. The crux of the entire passage is typical of all active segments. It occurs when Hedda realizes she is in Brack's power. In this particular instance, the crux comes in two closely connected waves. It begins when she grasps the fact of her vulnerability, manifested in the text by the words "So I am in your power." The realization sinks in, more and more deeply.

HEDDA (*looks up at him*): So I am in your power, **Judge Brack. You have me at your beck and call, from this time forward.**

BRACK (*whispers softly*): **Dearest Hedda—believe me**—I shall not abuse my advantage.

HEDDA: I am in your power none the less. **Subject to your will and your demands.** A slave, a slave then!

The full extent of her entrapment strikes her at this point. The words in bold type mark additions in the final draft of the play, demonstrating that Ibsen added nothing to the facts but amplified the inner realization. A secondary crux, anticipating the next segment, follows when Hedda rises impetuously and says, "No, I can't endure the thought of that! Never!" But she rapidly subsides when Brack comments that "People generally get used to the inevitable." Her answer, "Yes, perhaps," reduces the pitch of the crux and brings this segment to a close (the decrescence). In an earlier draft both Brack's remark and her reply did not appear.

The last subsegment is completely reactive. Brack reacts to his sense of triumph acting out his project of being the one cock of the roost. Tesman and Thea respond to the early stages of their task. Focus, however, is upon Hedda and her response to her new status. On stage, whether speaking to Thea and Tesman or to Brack, she maintains composure. To the very end she hides her native ferocity from others. But it is when she is offstage that Ibsen reveals her inner torment through the tempestuousness of her piano playing. The crux of the subsegment naturally occurs at the sound of the shot. There is the subsidiary discovery by the three people in the parlor, but at the sound itself we in the audience receive the full impact of Hedda's death.

The pattern of active segments building to a crux and followed by a reactive segment as in this section of *Hedda Gabler* mirrors the normal pattern in many plays. No drama consists wholly of active or of reactive tendencies. Even within brief units of action qualities of both activeness and reaction always exist. How, then, can we distinguish one tendency from another? Distinctions are based on emphasis, the active segment depending upon continuing pressure, the reactive segment upon an initial charge that sets off a chain response. It is a matter of the *kind* of energy exerted to reach the crux.

A simple analogy might clarify this point. The black keys on a piano can be either sharp or flat, depending upon whether one is ascending or descending the scale. Of themselves the notes do not change, but, in context, a note reveals itself in relation to other notes. So may we think of the energies and counter-energies of the characters. If the impelling figure is exerting force to bring about a change, he is producing an active segment; if he is adjusting emotionally and psychologically to a precipitant, then he is creating a reactive segment. Because Brack exerted sustained energy to produce a confrontation with Hedda, the segment is active. Because Electra internalizes her shock upon receiving her brother's ashes, the segment is reactive.

Within each of the two tendencies, the active and reactive, there are recurrent patterns. Every audience is familiar with melodramatic scenes, not unlike the one in *Hedda Gabler*, in which a villain forces a heroine to a fateful decision. As yet, because systematic and thoroughgoing study of such recurrent scenes has not been undertaken, it is too early to produce a comprehensive chart of activity types. But that these types do exist, there is no question. For example, Electra's lament over the supposed ashes of her brother follows a recurrent sequence. She reviews the past twice, tests the present twice, cries out in grief, and yearns for a future, death. An almost identical sequence can be found in Clov's reactive speech toward the conclusion of *Endgame*. Prompted by Hamm, Clov recalls memories of the past that he has kept hidden, realizes the facts of the present, and envisions his future, also death. Amazingly, this reactive sequence of a person remembering the past, facing the present, and projecting the future recurs in a number of plays that are otherwise dissimilar. Lopahin exulting at the purchase of the cherry orchard in Act III, Maurya lamenting her dead menfolk, and Blanche recounting her life at Belle Reve exhibit analogous patterns of remembrance of the past, awareness of the present, and yearning for the future. However varied their subjects and styles may be, these segments all reveal the durability of a specific sequence of action.

INTENSITY
AS A VARIABLE

In the previous chapter, I demonstrated that action is the term applied to an intangible nexus of energies, or tension. Variations in tension, whether between characters or between presentation and audience, are measured in relative degrees of intensity. As a segment evolves, intensity constantly shifts, either lessening or increasing. In the selection from *Hedda Gabler* previously cited, it is apparent that Judge Brack steadily increases pressure upon Hedda. The gradual intensification produces a distinctive dramatic rhythm, quite unlike a sequence characterized by irregular pressures and sudden eruptions. A comparison of the *Hedda Gabler* segments and Scene 8 of *A Streetcar Named Desire* readily reveals the differences.

Scene 8 is divided into six segments. The masked intensity of the action is high. Both Stanley and Stella know that Mitch is not coming to the birthday party, which is now already half over. Blanche senses disaster but tries to fend it off by pretense. The audience knows that Stanley intends to give Blanche a bus ticket to Laurel, the town she was forced to leave, and is waiting for the blow to fall. Although the precipitating context points toward a confrontation between Blanche and Stanley, the substance of much of the scene is not concerned with bringing this confrontation about. In the first segment, Blanche impels the action by trying to create a party-like atmosphere. Stanley is unyielding and arouses Stella's scorn. Her remarks cause Stanley to erupt. He stalks out to the porch at the end of the segment, and the intensity subsides. Now Blanche pressures Stella for information, receives no reply, and insists on calling Mitch. Stella undertakes a parallel action of attempting to shame Stanley, which he counters with a less intense yet nevertheless strong appeal to their own satisfactions. Again the intensity subsides, if not completely to its level in the beginning then at least to a level not much greater. The third segment begins with the lighting of candles on the cake. Stanley stands aside, offering sarcastic comments but making no move toward the confrontation. Blanche responds to his sarcasm sufficiently to spark another eruption. Again there is a brief subsiding until the telephone rings. Stanley asserts himself by picking up the receiver before Blanche. The subject of the call (whether it will be Stanley or Mac who decides where the team will bowl) does not have immediate relevance to the action of the scene, but the dramatic intensification does. In the argument, Stanley asserts himself vigorously. His energy, though directed at someone other than Blanche, is in strong spatial contrast to Blanche's sense of impending doom. The fourth segment ends. Now Stanley concentrates on the promised confrontation. A false amiability seems to lessen but in fact serves to increase intensity, not in comparison to the end of the fourth segment but in relation to the beginning of the scene. Because Stanley displays less energy here than at any other time in the scene, the intensity is implied rather than fully expressed. Blanche's reaction on receiving the ticket raises the action to a more intense though not extreme pitch because her full response is reserved for Scene 9. Thus the fifth segment ends.

There is a brief reduction in intensity, but Stella presses Stanley for an explanation of his action. This segment is a reprise of the second segment, but at a higher level of intensity. This time Stanley reveals his full credo: he is common, he pulled Stella off her plantation columns, and he revels in having done so. At the end of this revelation, a sudden shift occurs. Stella goes into prenatal labor.

It is apparent that the pattern of intensification in this scene differs considerably from that in *Hedda Gabler*. Within any individual segment of *Streetcar*, the shifts of intensity are greater. There are sudden leaps from unspoken foreboding to wild explosion. For the scene as a whole, the action undergoes irregular and violent swings of intensity, quite unlike the steady intensification in *Hedda Gabler*. We can speak of the degree of change in intensity, whether extreme or slight, as the *amplitude* of intensity, and the rhythm of the change, whether violent or steady, as the pattern of amplitude.

In physics and mathematics, amplitude indicates the extreme of a fluctuating quantity such as the swing of a pendulum. So, too, is there a swing of intensity in a segment. In the theater an audience is not aware of dramatic intensity in absolute terms. Only by comparison with what precedes and follows is it cognizant of changes in force, a type of relativity found in visual perception too. In *Art and Illusion*, E. H. Gombrich, citing an experiment in which chicks perceived relationships between different degrees of grayness rather than absolute values of lights, points out that "we respond to light intervals . . . rather than to the measurable quantity of light reflected from any given object." [4] Performers, by the variation of amplitude within a segment and the speed with which the amplitude changes, not only create distinctive forms but also produce variant impacts upon an audience.

Drama has long been associated with great amplitude. Melodrama principally relies upon strong swings of intensity. When critics and audience experience works of lesser amplitude than they are accustomed to, they tend to call such works "undramatic." Both Chekhov and Shaw have been criticized for "talkiness," lack of plot, and lack of drama. Though these charges are no longer seriously advanced, there is insufficient recognition of how the works of these writers differ from those of more conventional dramatists. One of the first things to note about Chekhov's drama-turgy is its spatial character. Instead of adopting the narrative method of the Elizabethans, in which various strands of actions are treated in sequence, he chose to give an illusion of simultaneity. That is, he brings several strands of action on stage at one time and, by juggling them, manages to convey the sense of spatial relationship between one action and another. This technique is directly connected to his manipulation of amplitude. Although Chekhov does not totally avoid action of great intensification, he generally employs slight modulations of intensity, so that an audience geared to high amplitude intensity cannot perceive initially that anything is happening in a Chekhov play. Only with time and exposure do audiences gradually perceive the amplitude of Chekhov's action. At the same time the rhythm of his segments tends to be undulating so that one action flows into another. Since each character has an individual rhythm out of which his activity emerges and into which it descends, the overall rhythm tends to embrace the segments in a gently shifting, sometimes pulsating, bubbling rhythm.

The particular quality of Chekhov's dramatic style can be seen in the two major segments from Act II that I quote below (my commentary is supplied in square brackets). In overall shape these segments are reactive, but reactive in a special way, that is, not in response to a specific event so much as to a general state of being. The first segment begins with Lyuboff's entry to the grounds adjoining the cherry orchard. She is followed by Gayeff and Lopahin. They have returned from town where they have had lunch.

[*Subsegment A: Active.* LOPAHIN *is the impelling agent. He meets no overt opposition, however. The resistance arises from the inability of* LYUBOFF *and* GAYEFF *to focus their attention on the impending auction of the cherry orchard. The subsegment has neither a strong nor clearly defined vector, principally because the resistance to* LOPAHIN *is so oblique.*]

LOPAHIN: We must decide definitely, time doesn't wait. Why, the matter's quite simple. Are you willing to lease your land for summer cottages or are you not? Answer in one word, yes or no? Just one word!

LYUBOFF ANDREEVNA: Who is it smokes those disgusting cigars out here—? (*Sitting down*)

GAYEFF: The railroad running so near is a great convenience. (*Sitting down*) We made a trip to town and lunched there—Yellow in the side pocket! Perhaps I should go in the house first and play one game—

LYUBOFF ANDREEVNA: You'll have time.

LOPAHIN: Just one word! (*Imploringly*) Do give me your answer!

GAYEFF (*yawning*): What?

[*She reacts to the senseless trip to town.*]

LYUBOFF ANDREEVNA (*looking in her purse*): Yesterday there was lots of money in it. Today there's very little. My poor Varya! For the sake of economy she feeds everybody milk soup, and in the kitchen the old people get nothing but beans, and here I spend money—senselessly—(*Dropping her purse and scattering gold coins*) There they go scattering! (*She is vexed.*)

YASHA: Allow me, I'll pick them up in a second. (*Picking up the coins*)

LYUBOFF ANDREEVNA: If you will, Yasha. And why did I go in town for lunch—? Your restaurant with its music is trashy, the tablecloths smell of soap—Why drink so much, Lyonya? Why eat so much? Why talk so much? Today in the restaurant you were talking a lot again, and all of it beside the point. About the seventies, about the decadents. And to whom? Talking to waiters about the decadents!

LOPAHIN: Yes.

GAYEFF (*waving his hand*): I am incorrigible, that's evident—(*to YASHA irritably*) What is it?—You are forever swirling around in front of us?

YASHA (*laughing*): I cannot hear your voice without laughing.

GAYEFF (*to his sister*): Either I or he—

[*Reaction reaches peak in GAYEFF's irritation at YASHA.*]

LYUBOFF ANDREEVNA: Go away, Yasha. Go on—

YASHA (*giving LYUBOFF ANDREEVNA her purse*): I am going right away. (*Barely suppressing his laughter*) This minute. (*Goes out.*)

[**Subsegment B:** Active. Persuasion activity. LOPAHIN *presses the issue of the auction.*]

LOPAHIN: The rich Deriganoff intends to buy your estate. They say he is coming personally to the auction.

LYUBOFF ANDREEVNA: And where did you hear that?

LOPAHIN: In town they are saying it.

GAYEFF: Our Yaroslavl aunt promised to send us something, but when and how much she will send, nobody knows—

LOPAHIN: How much will she send? A hundred thousand? Two hundred?

LYUBOFF ANDREEVNA: Well—maybe ten, fifteen thousand—we'd be thankful for that.

LOPAHIN: Excuse me, but such light-minded people as you are, such odd unbusinesslike people, I never saw. You are told in plain Russian that your estate is being sold up and you just don't seem to take it in.

[*He demolishes defenses, appears to bring* LYUBOFF *to a point of decision.*]

LYUBOFF ANDREEVNA: But what are we to do? Tell us what?

LOPAHIN: I tell you every day. Every day I tell you the same thing. Both the cherry orchard and the land have got to be leased for summer cottages, it has to be done right now, quick—The auction is right under your noses. Do understand! Once you finally decide that there are to be summer cottages, you will get all the money you want, and then you'll be saved.

LYUBOFF ANDREEVNA: Summer cottages and summer residents—

[*This is the crux. She fails to face the unpleasantness of the problem.*]

it is so trivial, excuse me.

GAYEFF: I absolutely agree with you.

LOPAHIN: I'll either burst out crying, or scream, or faint. I can't bear it! You are torturing me! (*To* GAYEFF) You're a perfect old woman!

GAYEFF: What?

[*Decrescence comes in form of* LOPAHIN'S *outburst against* GAYEFF *and in his effort to depart.*]

LOPAHIN: A perfect old woman! (*About to go*)

[*The next few lines serve as a transition.*]

LYUBOFF ANDREEVNA (*alarmed*): No, don't go, stay, my lamb, I beg you. Perhaps we will think of something!

LOPAHIN: What is there to think about?

LYUBOFF ANDREEVNA: Don't go, I beg you. With you here it is more cheerful anyhow—(*A pause*)

[**Subsegment C:** *Reactive. The confessional.*]

I keep waiting for something, as if the house were about to tumble down on our heads.

GAYEFF (*deep in thought*): Double into the corner pocket—Bank into the wide pocket—

LYUBOFF ANDREEVNA: We have sinned so much—

LOPAHIN: What sins have you—?

GAYEFF (*puts a hard candy into his mouth*): They say I've eaten my fortune up in hard candies—(*Laughing*)

> [*Note the juxtaposition of* GAYEFF's *ludicrous sins with* LYUBOFF's *real sins.* LYUBOFF *reveals her deep-seated anguish.*]

LYUBOFF ANDREEVNA: Oh, my sins—I've always thrown money around like mad, recklessly, and I married a man who accumulated nothing but debts. My husband died from champagne—he drank fearfully—and to my misfortune I fell in love with another man. I lived with him, and just at that time—it was my first punishment—a blow over the head: right here in the river my boy was drowned and I went abroad—went away for good, never to return, never to see this river again—I shut my eyes, ran away, beside myself, and he after me—mercilessly, brutally. I bought a villa near Mentone, because he fell ill there, and for three years I knew no rest day or night, the sick man exhausted me; my soul dried up. And last year when the villa was sold for debts, I went to Paris and there he robbed me of everything, threw me over, took up with another woman; I tried to poison myself—so stupid, so shameful—And suddenly I was seized with longing for Russia, for my own country, for my little girl—(*Wiping away her tears*) Lord, Lord have mercy, forgive me my sins! Don't punish me any more! (*Getting a telegram out of her pocket*) I got this today from Paris, he asks forgiveness, begging me to return—(*Tears up the telegram*)

> [*Only at this crux does she reveal the pressure that has compelled the revelation: the telegram from her lover.*]

That sounds like music somewhere.

> *Listening.*

> [*Response to the orchestra is the decrescent. Here and elsewhere Chekhov uses the decrescent to counterpoint the previous action. He contrasts* LYUBOFF's *suffering with her thought of a party.*]

GAYEFF: It is our famous Jewish orchestra. You remember, four violins, a flute and double bass.

LYUBOFF ANDREEVNA: Does it still exist? We ought to get hold of it sometime and give a party.

LOPAHIN (*listening*): Can't hear it—(*Singing softly*) "And for money the Germans will frenchify a Russian."

[*Subsegment D: Reactive, then active. It concentrates on* LOPAHIN. *At first reactive, the action becomes mildly active when* LYUBOFF *urges* LOPAHIN *to marry. Once again there is no direct resistance. Yet* LO-PAHIN's *assent lacks will.*]

(*Laughing*) What a play I saw yesterday at the theatre, very funny!

LYUBOFF ANDREEVNA: And most likely there was nothing funny about it. You shouldn't look at plays, but look oftener at yourselves. How gray all your lives are, what a lot of idle things you say!

LOPAHIN: That's true. It must be said frankly this life of ours is idiotic—(*A pause*) My father was a peasant, an idiot, he understood nothing, he taught me nothing, he just beat me in his drunken fits and always with a stick. At bottom I am just as big a dolt and idiot as he was. I wasn't taught anything, my handwriting is vile, I write like a pig—I am ashamed for people to see it.

LYUBOFF ANDREEVNA: You ought to get married, my friend.

LOPAHIN: Yes—That's true.

LYUBOFF ANDREEVNA: To our Varya, perhaps. She is a good girl.

LOPAHIN: Yes.

LYUBOFF ANDREEVNA: She comes from simple people, and she works all day long, but the main thing is she loves you. And you, too, have liked her a long time.

[*The crux here indicates decision, but the quality of the decision is flaccid. The pause marks the end of the subsegment.*]

LOPAHIN: Why not? I am not against it—She's a good girl. (*A pause*)

[*Subsegment E: The action now shifts to* GAYEFF *and* FIERS. *The segment hovers between active and reactive.*]

GAYEFF: They are offering me a position in a bank. Six thousand a year—Have you heard that?

LYUBOFF ANDREEVNA: Not you! You stay where you are—

FIERS (FIERS *enters, bringing an overcoat. To* GAYEFF): Pray, Sir, put this on, it's damp.

GAYEFF (*putting on the overcoat*): You're a pest, old man.

FIERS: That's all right—This morning you went off without letting me know. (*Looking him over*)

> [GAYEFF's *rumination about doing something* (*active*) *is contrasted with* FIERS *doing something for him. The main action is reactive as* FIERS *remembers the past.*]

LYUBOFF ANDREEVNA: How old you've grown, Fiers!

FIERS: At your service.

LOPAHIN: She says you've grown very old!

FIERS: I've lived a long time. They were planning to marry me off before your papa was born. (*Laughing*) And at the time the serfs were freed I was already the head footman. I didn't want to be freed then, I stayed with the masters—(*A pause*) And I remember, everybody was happy, but what they were happy about they didn't know themselves.

LOPAHIN: In the old days it was fine. At least they flogged.

FIERS (*not hearing*): But, of course. The peasants stuck to the masters, the masters stuck to the peasants, and now everything is all smashed up. You can't tell about anything.

GAYEFF: Keep still, Fiers. Tomorrow I must go to town. They have promised to introduce me to a certain general who might make us a loan.

> [GAYEFF *reechoes the motif of active thought.*]

LOPAHIN: Nothing will come of it. And you can rest assured you won't pay the interest.

LYUBOFF ANDREEVNA: He's just raving on. There aren't any such generals.

[*Major Segment I ends here. Major Segment II begins. Youth enters.*]

[*Subsegment A is a brief introduction. It expresses the warm love that* LYUBOFF *extends to the young.*]

> TROFIMOFF, ANYA *and* VARYA *enter.*

GAYEFF: Here they come.

ANYA: There is Mama sitting there.

LYUBOFF ANDREEVNA (*tenderly*): Come, come—My darlings—(*Embracing* ANYA *and* VARYA) If you only knew how I love you both! Come sit by me—there—like that.

> *Everybody sits down.*

[*Subsegment B:* LOPAHIN, *the impelling agent, tries to provoke* TRO-FIMOFF, *but then disarms himself by inviting* TROFIMOFF'S *attack. See p. 180 for further discussion of this subsegment.*]

LOPAHIN: Our perennial student is always strolling with the young ladies.

TROFIMOFF: It's none of your business.

LOPAHIN: He will soon be fifty and he's still a student.

TROFIMOFF: Stop your stupid jokes.

LOPAHIN: But why are you so peevish, you queer duck?

TROFIMOFF: Don't you pester me.

LOPAHIN (*laughing*): Permit me to ask you, what do you make of me?

TROFIMOFF: Yermolay Alexeevich, I make this of you: you are a rich man, you'll soon be a millionaire. Just as it is in the metabolism of nature, a wild beast is needed to eat up everything that comes his way; so you, too, are needed.

Everyone laughs.

[*Subsegment C: This subsegment contains the peculiarly Chekhovian activity of "speechifying."* TROFIMOFF (*proudly?*) *rejects the notion of pride, predicts perfection through work, and denigrates the present behavior of the intellectuals.*]

VARYA: Petya, you'd better tell us about the planets.

LYUBOFF ANDREEVNA: No, let's go on with yesterday's conversation.

TROFIMOFF: What was it about?

GAYEFF: About the proud man.

TROFIMOFF: We talked a long time yesterday, but didn't get any-where. In a proud man, in your sense of the word, there is something mystical. Maybe you are right, from your standpoint, but if we are to discuss it in simple terms, without whimsy, then what pride can there be, is there any sense in it, if man physiologically is poorly con-structed, if in the great majority he is crude, unintelligent, profoundly miserable. One must stop admiring oneself. One must only work.

GAYEFF: All the same, you will die.

TROFIMOFF: Who knows? And what does it mean—you will die? Man may have a hundred senses, and when he dies only the five that are known to us may perish, and the remaining ninety-five go on living.

LYUBOFF ANDREEVNA: How clever you are, Petya!

LOPAHIN (*ironically*): Terribly!

[*Obviously* TROFIMOFF *speaks seriously, but for the others his talk is entertainment.*]

TROFIMOFF: Humanity goes forward, perfecting its powers. Everything that's unattainable now will some day become familiar, understandable; it is only that one must work and must help with all one's might those who seek the truth. With us in Russia so far only a very few work. The great majority of the intelligentsia that I know are looking for nothing, doing nothing, and as yet have no capacity for work. They call themselves intelligentsia, are free and easy with the servants, treat the peasants like animals, educate themselves poorly, read nothing seriously, do absolutely nothing; about science they just talk and about art they understand very little. Every one of them is serious, all have stern faces; they all talk of nothing but important things, philosophize, and all the time everybody can see that the workmen eat abominably, sleep without any pillows, thirty or forty to a room, and everywhere there are bedbugs, stench, dampness, moral uncleanness—And apparently with us, all the fine talk is only to divert the attention of ourselves and of others. Show me where we have the day nurseries they are always talking so much about, where are the reading rooms? They only write of these in novels, for the truth is there are not any at all. There is only filth, vulgarity, orientalism—I am afraid of very serious faces and dislike them. I'm afraid of serious conversations. Rather than that let's just keep still.

> [*His serious speech comes to an end with his denunciation of serious conversation. He does bring to the surface the more universal impulse toward silence that appears shortly. The segment moves toward a purgation of talk, but it does so in contrast to talk, gradually slipping from* TROFIMOFF's *somewhat active stance to* GAYEFF's *purely reactive speech.* LOPAHIN, *"the beast," takes up* TROFIMOFF's *theme. He, it turns out, is the only one to really work. (Is he a comic prefiguration of* TROFIMOFF's *future?) He is a worker, but his thought is fustian. His speech commences soberly, but at "Lord" shifts to bombast. A lull follows.*]

LOPAHIN: You know I get up before five o'clock in the morning and work from morning till night. Well, I always have money, my own and other people's, on hand, and I see what the people around me are. One has only to start doing something to find out how few honest and decent people there are. At times when I can't go to sleep, I think: Lord, thou gavest us immense forests, unbounded fields and the widest horizons, and living in the midst of them we should indeed be giants—

LYUBOFF ANDREEVNA: You feel the need for giants—They are good only in fairy tales, anywhere else they only frighten us. (*At the back of the stage* EPIHODOFF *passes by, playing the guitar.*)

> [*It is evident that* EPIHODOFF'*s passing by at this moment signifies more than a chance stroll but an intrusion among them of the general ineptness in life.*]

LYUBOFF ANDREEVNA (*lost in thought*): Epihodoff is coming—

ANYA (*lost in thought*): Epihodoff is coming.

GAYEFF: The sun has set, ladies and gentlemen.

TROFIMOFF: Yes.

> [*The third speech comes from* GAYEFF. *It is the* reductio ad absurdum *of speechifying. The others react heatedly and mockingly, bringing on the silence toward which the vector of the action is aimed.*]

GAYEFF (*not loud and as if he were declaiming*): Oh, Nature, wonderful, you gleam with eternal radiance, beautiful and indifferent, you, whom we call Mother, combine in yourself both life and death, you give life and you take it away.

VARYA (*beseechingly*): Uncle!

ANYA: Uncle, you're doing it again!

TROFIMOFF: You'd better bank the yellow into the side pocket.

GAYEFF: I'll be quiet, quiet.

[*Subsegment D: "The taste of silence." Reactive. All imbibe the silence. The "sound of a snapped string," whether imaginary or not, is an echo of a life passing away. It will be followed by the entrance of the* STRANGER. *After the reverberation of the string, a premonition of death falls upon the group.* FIERS' *response links dread and freedom.* LYUBOFF's *remark, awakening all to time, "Twilight is falling," is the decrescent.*]

> *All sit absorbed in their thoughts. There is only the silence.* FIERS *is heard muttering to himself softly. Suddenly a distant sound is heard, as if from the sky, like the sound of a snapped string, dying away, mournful.*

LYUBOFF ANDREEVNA: What's that?

LOPAHIN: I don't know. Somewhere far off in a mine shaft a bucket fell. But somewhere very far off.

GAYEFF: And it may be some bird—like a heron.

TROFIMOFF: Or an owl—

LYUBOFF ANDREEVNA (*shivering*): It's unpleasant, somehow. (*A pause*)

FIERS: Before the disaster it was like that. The owl hooted and the samovar hummed without stopping, both.

GAYEFF: Before what disaster?

FIERS: Before the emancipation. (*A pause*)

LYUBOFF ANDREEVNA: You know, my friends, let's go. Twilight is falling. (*To* ANYA) You have tears in your eyes—What is it, my dear little girl? (*Embracing her*)

ANYA: It's just that, Mama. It's nothing.

[*Subsegment E: The* STRANGER *is the impelling agent. His physical appearance is extremely important. He is a creature from another world. How he is dressed will feed back to the audience whether he represents a worker, an outcast, a bandit, etc. What does the "shabby white cap" and overcoat convey? He poses a threat though he starts politely enough.*]

TROFIMOFF: Somebody is coming.

> A STRANGER *appears in a shabby white cap, and an overcoat; he is a little drunk.*

THE STRANGER: Allow me to ask you, can I go straight through here to the station?

GAYEFF: You can. Go by that road.

THE STRANGER: I am heartily grateful to you. (*Coughing*) The weather is splendid—(*Declaiming*) Brother of mine, suffering brother—Go out to the Volga, whose moans—(*To* VARYA) Mademoiselle, grant a hungry Russian man some thirty kopecks—

> VARYA *is frightened and gives a shriek.*

> [*Through the* STRANGER'S *declamation Chekhov satirizes the earlier speechifying and shows to what it is reduced. The activity with the money reechoes the earlier motif of* LYUBOFF'S *improvidence as well as poses a larger issue of the* STRANGER'S *intrusion upon the decaying gentry. The women's reactions serve as the crux.*]

LOPAHIN (*angrily*): There's a limit to everything.

LYUBOFF ANDREEVNA (*flustered*): Take this—Here's this for you— (*Searching in her purse*) No silver. It's all the same, here's a gold piece for you—

> [*The final politeness of the* STRANGER *is undercut by his offstage laughter.*]

THE STRANGER: I am heartily grateful to you. (*Goes out. Laughter*)

[*Subsegment F: This subsegment is the decrescent to the second major segment. It is a reprise of previous reactions. Only* LYUBOFF's *announcement to* VARYA *is fresh. Toward the end of the subsegment, the action assumes a ludicrous tone. To the one serious issue,* LOPAHIN's *marriage to* VARYA, LOPAHIN *responds as a buffoon, ridiculing further the activity of speechifying, but distorting it in his incorrect remembrance of* OPHELIA's *name. The mention of sins in the quotation echoes* LYUBOFF's *confession.*]

VARYA (*frightened*): I'm going—I'm going—Oh Mama, you poor little Mama! There's nothing in the house for people to eat, and you gave him a gold piece.

LYUBOFF ANDREEVNA: What is to be done with me, so silly? I shall give you all I have in the house. Yermolay Alexeevich, you will lend me some this once more!—

LOPAHIN: Agreed.

LYUBOFF ANDREEVNA: Let's go, ladies and gentlemen, it's time. And here, Varya, we have definitely made a match for you, I congratulate you.

VARYA (*through her tears*): Mama, that's not something to joke about.

LOPAHIN: Achmelia, get thee to a nunnery.

GAYEFF: And my hands are trembling; it is a long time since I have played billiards.

LOPAHIN: Achmelia, Oh nymph, in thine orisons be all my sins remember'd—

LYUBOFF ANDREEVNA: Let's go, my dear friends, it will soon be suppertime.

VARYA: He frightened me. My heart is thumping so.

LOPAHIN: I remind you, ladies and gentlemen, August 22nd the cherry orchard will be auctioned off. Think about that!—Think!—(*All go out except* TROFIMOFF *and* ANYA.)[5]

> [*Chekhov emphasizes the futility of the action by the circular method of having* LOPAHIN *return to his initial warning. The first major segment began with the reminder that the orchard will be auctioned.*]

In the large frame of the action, the active portions are propelled by Lopahin (on the issue of the orchard), by Lyuboff (on the issue of the marriage), and by Trofimoff (on the issue of the future). These parallel active efforts flounder and are reduced to absurdity. Most of the action is reactive: to the past, with all its pain, and to the nostalgia of nature. One may say that this is a farewell scene to the orchard. The crux (and one of the climactic moments of the play) is the common response to the "snapped string," filled as it is with foreboding. It is succeeded by two decrescent waves: irruption of the "stranger," ludicrousness of the group.

For the most part, the action is oblique. Without movement toward confrontation, the amplitude of intensity is bound to be relatively low. Yet there is change of intensity. It comes mainly from the mounting concentration of a figure's attention upon the facts of his own life. Perhaps the greatest change of amplitude occurs during Lyuboff's recital of her past. But even that is lessened because the anxiety and guilt she feels are undercut by Gayeff's muttering about billiards. Often the action promises confrontation, only to be dissipated in the inability of one or another character to face the project of another or tackle the resistance he or she encounters. Lopahin asks for a decision on the matter of leasing the land for cottages. "Answer in one word, yes or no? Just one word!" Lyuboff queries, "Who is it smokes those disgusting cigars out here—?" Even when Lopahin presses his point, "Just one word!" neither Lyuboff nor Gayeff can grasp the challenge or understand his insistence. There is no lack of projective energy in Chekhov. What is lacking is the directness which would make such projective energy explosive.

Hedda Gabler, as we have seen, exhibits a conventional pattern of action moving from oblique to direct confrontation. *The Cherry Orchard* shows the avoidance of confrontation. Scene 8 of *A Streetcar Named Desire* reveals a variation of oblique and direct patterns in rich counterpoint. Within some subsegments there is the usual pattern of movement from oblique to direct conflict. For instance, the scene opens with Blanche endeavoring to keep a semblance of party cheer though she recognizes the unspoken disaster that hangs over the evening. The tension causes Stella to speak sharply to Stanley, the consequence being an explosive confrontation between him and the women. Thus, we see a sudden shift from oblique to direct attack with a leap in amplitude. This pattern recurs in subsegments three and four. In subsegments two and six the action tends to be direct and develops by intensification. Yet taken as a whole, the scene utilizes an interesting variation of the oblique-direct pattern. The conclusion of Scene 7 leads the audience to expect that Stanley will confront Blanche with his knowledge of her past and give her the bus ticket back to Laurel. The vector thus points to a crux between Stanley and Blanche. But at the beginning of Scene 8, the audience soon learns, Stanley's project is not directed at Blanche, but at Stella. In subsegments one and two Stanley confronts Stella first by shouting at her and then by mollifying her. In the third subsegment, he confronts Blanche, but not on the expected issue. He attacks her for calling him a "Polack." In the fourth subsegment, he confronts Mac on the telephone, asserting his authority as captain of the bowling team. Each of these confrontations has succeeded in building the tension of the scene, but obliquely by being concerned with issues other than the central one. In the fifth subsegment, Stanley, deliberately feigning amiability, precipitates the expected confrontation by handing Blanche his gift of the bus ticket. In comparison to the energy he has expended in the previous subsegments, he uses very little to bring the scene to its crux. The last confrontation, that between Stanley and Stella, develops the issues dramatized in subsegments one and two. At this point Stanley completes his credo of masculine superiority and delight in the common pleasures of the flesh. Throughout the scene, Williams has delayed Stanley's direct attack upon Blanche at the same time as he stressed Stanley's assertion of manhood to Stella. By doing so, he increases the gap between Stanley's power and Blanche's vulnerability, with the effect that the attack on Blanche seems to be incidental cruelty rather than hotly contested revenge. He also postpones Blanche's major confrontations to the two scenes that follow.

In general, contemporary taste prefers the methods of Chekhov and Williams to those of Ibsen. Leaps in amplitude and sudden shifts from oblique to direct or from direct to oblique confrontation characterize the work of modern dramatists such as Brecht, Pinter, Osborne, and Albee. The techniques of obliquity have been considerably extended so that unconnected juxtaposition (extreme obliquity), such as Stanley's telephone conversation with Mac, is frequently employed to evoke deeply ingrained emotions.

CRUX AS
A VARIABLE

The shape assumed by changes in intensity, that is, the shape of
the action, is ultimately determined by the way theater artists
handle crux. It is already clear that dramatic tension cannot increase or decrease indefinitely. Within each segment there occurs
some moment when the projects of the characters either shift direction, cease, or evolve into something new. That moment may
be a highly concentrated point of time. For example, a moment of
reversal, what is often called a turning point, tends to be instanta-
neous. Arnolphe's soliloquy opening Act IV of *The School for
Wives* illustrates this. Until that time in the play Arnolphe has
endeavored to thwart Horace's attentions toward Agnes, the ward
whom Arnolphe has raised painstakingly to become his innocent
and thereby faithful wife. At the end of Act III, expecting to gloat
at Horace's defeat, he learns that instead he has been outwitted.
He ordered Agnes to throw a brick at Horace when he came to
woo, but the innocent girl tied a love letter to it. Being unknown
as Agnes' guardian, Arnolphe is forced to hear Horace read the
love letter to him. After Horace's departure, Arnolphe expresses
his frenzy at the thought of losing Agnes. The soliloquy opening
Act IV continues the reactive pattern of the final speech of Act
III. Arnolphe bemoans Agnes' indifference. He mortifies himself
with remembrance of her loveliness. He is appalled to imagine
that she might slip away from him just as he is ready to marry her.
Then in an instant he vows, "No, no! Good God, no, no!" In decid-
ing to fight for her, he shifts from a reactive to an active stance.
This pattern of sudden shifts at crucial moments characterizes
The School for Wives throughout. Structurally the play portrays
the alternating phases of self-satisfaction and frustration through
which Arnolphe passes.

The crux here is a moment of decision. But the crux may be
more extensive or, on the other hand, more abortive. When Elec-

tra bursts into sustained wailing as she longs for union with the supposedly dead Orestes the crucial moment is thus extended. In Scene 8 of *Streetcar*, Blanche's response at the crux is also extended. Action seems momentarily suspended as she stares at the bus ticket. The crux is also somewhat abortive because she rushes out before expressing her full hysteria, but that very incompleteness contributes to the impression of a sustained crux.

This shift of direction is also related to amplitude. The first segment in Scene 8 (*Streetcar*) contains extreme changes in intensity. The ominous tone of the party persists. Stella berates Stanley, but instead of a gradual intensification, there is a sudden outburst, the outburst itself being the crux. Both *The Cherry Orchard* and *Hedda Gabler* display less extreme shifts. The sound of the snapped string and Hedda's discovery of Lövborg's sordid death are not less powerful but certainly less violent. Naturally, the greater the amplitude of the crux the more devastating the impact upon the audience.

Identification of crux within a segment is only the first step toward understanding the contents of the crux. Often the crux embodies internal changes of realization or acceptance, frequently unspoken. In *Hedda Gabler* the crux of each of the segments usually occurs at moments of realization. Gradually, Brack forces Hedda to face the implications of her situation, the crux in each instance being the moment she loses an illusion. The active segment thus leads to a reactive crux. By comparison, Electra's reactive segment leads her, at the crucial moments of painful wailing, to strive for unity with the "dead" Orestes. In that case the reactive force leads to an active crux. Though these shifts from active to reactive or the reverse are not invariable, they do constitute one pattern of crucial action.

What happens within a crux may be further distinguished by reversal or augmentation. When Hedda learns how Lövborg died, she is forced to retreat. She can no longer maintain her illusion about Lövborg. In the major crux, she is forced to accept the full implications of Brack's power and begin adjusting to them. In both instances Hedda changes direction, and, though the changes are not so absolute as Arnolphe's, they can be characterized as reversals. Yet not every crux involves reversal. Hedda's act of burning Lövborg's manuscript (end of Act III) is a major crux of augmentation. It is a continuation of Hedda's drive to control Lövborg's life and, until that point in the play, her most destructive act. Stanley's rape of Blanche in Scene 10 of *Streetcar* is another example of augmentation in a crux.

In segments where confrontation is sharp, it is relatively simple to identify the crux and perceive the kind of reversal or augmentation that occupies it. This is particularly so in Aristotelian drama with its highly concentrated action and linear structure. In non-Aristotelian drama, on the other hand, the quality and elaboration of the crucial moments are quite different. They are often sustained for longer periods and are sometimes oblique and suggestive rather than direct and decisive. These patterns are especially apparent in Shakespeare's works. The banquet scene in *Macbeth* (III, iv) illustrates a sustained and elaborated crux, and the first heath scene in *King Lear* (III, ii) illustrates an oblique and suggestive one.

In *Macbeth*, Shakespeare foreshortens the ceremonial welcome of the banquet scene and comes immediately to the first crux, the disclosure that Fleance lives. This is a partial reversal for Macbeth. It takes 20 lines. Another 10 are taken up with the murderer's reassurance that Banquo is dead: "Safe in a ditch he bides." Another 20 lines lead to Macbeth's discovery of the Ghost's presence. The next 75 lines are devoted to two waves of response to his two discoveries of the Ghost. A new subsegment begins when Macbeth queries, "What is the night?" and begins to ponder the meaning of Macduff's absence. Another crux, arising as a consequence of the earlier reaction, occurs when he determines to abandon all scruples: "For mine own good,/ All causes shall give way."

In the overarching pattern of the scene, we thus find two cruxes early in the action and a final crux near the end. The main portion of the action is devoted to the sustained responses of Macbeth. A crux commences each time that Macbeth sees the Ghost. If we examine his first response in detail, we observe the following structure. The segment commences when Macbeth invokes the presence of Banquo:

> Here had we now our country's honour roof'd,
> Were the grac'd person of our Banquo present.

The Ghost enters. During the next 6 lines, tension mounts as we wait for Macbeth to see the "blood-bolter'd" Banquo. Lennox beckons Macbeth to a supposedly empty seat:

LENNOX: Here is a place reserv'd, Sir.
MACBETH: Where?
LENNOX: Here, my good Lord.

Seeing the Ghost, Macbeth is startled. "What is't that moves your Highness?" Lennox asks. Macbeth responds in fear and wonder, at first paralyzed by the apparition as Lady Macbeth tries to explain away his unaccustomed behavior, and then, after the Ghost departs, horrified by the memory of the visitation. In this reactive segment, then, the shape of the action proceeds from (1) a brief invocation, (2) a sudden heightening of the amplitude of tension, and then (3) radiating from the explosion of the crux, a paralytic reaction followed by a penetrating memory of the reaction. It is typical of the plenitude of Shakespearean structure to repeat this pattern in a nearly identical manner immediately afterward. The one change is that the paralysis of the first segment is replaced by frenzy in the second, thus heightening the amplitude of Macbeth's response.

The heath scene in *King Lear* (III, ii) is also reactive, although in this instance the spark for the reaction has been struck in Act II, scene iv. Lear enters in a highly emotional state. He has already been raging at the elements, and at this moment is reaching the peak of his response. The Fool is with him. By the end of the segment he has or is trying to control himself. "I will be the pattern of all patience," he says, "I will say nothing." What is the path that the segment takes? We must first consider Lear's reaction, since he impels the scene, and then consider the shape of the segment by considering his relation to the Fool.

Storm still. Enter LEAR *and* FOOL.

LEAR: Blow, winds, and crack your cheeks! rage! blow!
   You cataracts and hurricanoes, spout
   Till you have drench'd our steeples, drown'd the cocks!
   You sulph'rous and thought-executing fires,
   Vaunt-couriers of oak-cleaving thunderbolts,

Singe my white head! And thou, all-shaking thunder,
Strike flat th' thick rotundity o' th' world!
Crack Nature's moulds, all germens spill at once
That makes ingrateful man!

FOOL: O Nuncle, court holy-water in a dry house is better than this
rain-water out o' door. Good Nuncle, in, ask thy daughters blessing;
here's a night pities neither wise men nor Fools.

LEAR: Rumble thy bellyful! Spit, fire! spout, rain!
Nor rain, wind, thunder, fire, are my daughters:
I tax you not, you elements, with unkindness;
I never gave you kingdom, call'd you children,
You owe me no subscription: then let fall
Your horrible pleasure; here I stand, your slave,
A poor, infirm, weak, and despis'd old man.
But yet I call you servile ministers,
That will with two pernicious daughters join
Your high-engender'd battles 'gainst a head
So old and white as this. O, ho! 'tis foul.

FOOL: He that has a house to put's head in has a good head-piece.

The cod-piece that will house
Before the head has any,
The head and he shall louse;
So beggars marry many.
The man that makes his toe
What he his heart should make,
Shall of a corn cry woe,
And turn his sleep to wake.

For there was never yet fair woman but she made mouths in a glass.

Enter KENT.

LEAR: No, I will be the pattern of all patience;
I will say nothing.

Lear's response comes in four waves. First, he challenges the
stormy elements to destroy him and the world. Second, he frees
these elements from allegiance and abases himself before them.
He deliberately exposes himself to their fury with a claim of in-
firmity. Whether or not he expresses an apocalyptic vision or his
own self-pity, he cries for absolute destruction. But immediately
following, in the third wave, he accuses the elements of complicity
with his daughters, thus renewing his anger. Finally, he again

vows silent endurance. Of these four waves, two are vigorous and angry, two are cries of resignation. Each of the two waves of resignation is preceded by a speech of the Fool in which he advises compromise. In the first, the Fool pleads with Lear to return and "ask thy daughters blessing." Lear does not respond to him. In the second, the Fool reiterates the motif of housing (shelter), this time with an obscene turn. During this second speech or song, the crux of the segment occurs, for this is when Lear shifts from "O, ho! 'tis foul" to "No, I will be the pattern of all patience." This shift from accusation to endurance is accompanied by an inward turning and disillusionment. His shift is both comment and reaction. Thus the segment, reactive in structure, moves from a pitch of anger to a stoic endurance by way of an inner concentration on sexual and emotional corruption.

This segment illustrates Shakespeare's subtle forms of juxtaposition whereby he creates a metaphor of action. Lear at first relates not to the Fool but to the stormy elements and then to himself. For Lear the duration of the Fool's speeches are silences in which at first he waits for an ultimate destruction that does not come and then struggles with his rage, vowing a stoicism that he cannot possibly fulfill. If we read Lear's speeches without the Fool's, we suddenly become aware of the loss not of a supporting character but of an entire dimension of action. Initially the Fool attempts to persuade Lear to submit, in part counseling expediency, in part expressing pity for himself. The second speech reveals that he has turned away from Lear, that he has turned inward, and thus in his song parallels Lear's state. In turning inward, the Fool turns to a lechery of the flesh and of the emotions. The crux, Lear's interior shift and the Fool's song of frustration, together compose a metaphorical action, which exists as a theatrical possibility, not as a textual fact. How two actors physicalize that moment will determine its true nature.

ACTIVITY AND
ACTION

The internal dynamics of a segment, it must be obvious, do not function independently of the outward form of activity. In analyzing variations in dramatic progression, I have so far been describing those factors that most critically govern the temporal structure of a sequence. Equally significant in determining the shape of a dramatic segment is the nature of the activity and its relation to the action.

Each age fosters archetypal dramatic activities. They recur in play after play of the age, utilized in different ways by different writers but nevertheless present in a discernible form. It is beyond the scope of this book to investigate the socio-aesthetic basis for each typical activity. I can merely call attention to the presence of such types. As we come to recognize that the drama of each age stresses distinctive metaphors of action, we can proceed to study the historical reasons for their existence. At this juncture I can only give a structural analysis of one of these types.

A prime example of a recurrent activity type is the debate segment in Greek drama. The activity of debate combines both form and content, for not only do the Greek dramatists introduce the substance of debate but they also maintain its form. Albin Lesky ascribes the popularity of this form to "the Athenian passion for legal strife," [6] and in commenting on the debate sequences in *Ajax*, J. C. Kamerbeek notes that they follow "the taste of the Athenian public for lawsuit speeches" and that the exchange of personal taunts between Agamemnon and Teucer was "a practice well-known in the Attic law-courts." [7] The debate form can thus be understood for what it was, a transferal of a mode of action from the courts to the theater.

A perusal of the ancient drama will immediately reveal how frequently this kind of activity occurs. In the seven surviving tragedies of Sophocles there are full debate segments in five (*Electra,*

Ajax, Antigone, Oedipus at Colonus, Philoctetes), and a less formal but nonetheless structured debate in one (*Oedipus*). Aeschylus does not rely so completely upon formal debate except in the *Eumenides* though his work is filled with elements of debate. Euripides, especially in his patriotic plays, employs the debate mode, and in Aristophanes' work, debate features prominently in *The Frogs*.

The two debates in *Ajax,* one between Teucer and Menelaus and the other between Teucer and Agamemnon, illustrate this type of activity. The precipitating context is sharply defined. Teucer feels compelled to bury his dead brother, Ajax. The Atreidae, Menelaus and Agamemnon, are determined to assert their authority and punish Ajax's treachery, if only symbolically, by prohibiting the burial of his corpse. The two debates dramatize clashes of will. Teucer is relatively powerless, the Atreidae all powerful. Nevertheless, Teucer's project, his image of himself fulfilling the ritual burial due the corpse, gives him strength to resist. Menelaus and later Agamemnon impel the segments by trying to force Teucer to give up his project.

The debate activity is highly formalized. In the first debate segment, the sequence consists of a brief prologue, Menelaus' argument, Teucer's reply, a stichomythic duel, and then a brief speech of personal abuse by each speaker. The general issue of the first debate is insubordination versus authority. In the second debate this issue is exemplified. It is not the burial of Ajax but the defiance of Teucer that infuriates Agamemnon. This second segment consists of two set speeches. Instead of the stichomythic duel, there is intervention by Odysseus. Both debates are violent in temper and impassioned, yet despite their considerable vehemence, the antagonists maintain the reserve of formal debate.

Invariably the person who has the better of the argument speaks second, as we see in each of these examples. Teucer ultimately wins only by gaining Odysseus' support. Another convention is the maintenance of equal length for each side in the argument, a curious variant of which can be found in *Ajax*. The debates, taken separately, are of uneven length (in the first, Menelaus has 39 lines, Teucer 25), but if we take the two debates as a version of one, the convention holds. Add Agamemnon's 38 lines to Menelaus' 39 and the total comes to 77, almost identical to the sum of Teucer's second speech of 50 lines and his first of 25, a total of 75.[8]

These debates are cast in a poetic form and arranged with rhetorical skill. Their delivery also requires skill in the massing of the argument and the containment of the passion. We have some reason to believe that the Greek audience valued the presentation not only mimetically but rhetorically. Pleasure and attention would arise from the double image: the characters contending with each other and the speakers building a skillful case. The debate actually may have been prismatic, operating as an expression of direct conflict as well as virtuoso display. Binding these opposing tendencies together is the fact that debate also mirrored the legal life of the populace, thereby combining nature and artifice simultaneously. In this way the actual and virtual inhere in a single activity, capable of producing both aesthetic appreciation and mimetic involvement.

In *Ajax* this activity involves the determination of Menelaus and later Agamemnon to assert their authority, even over the dead, and Teucer's determination to fulfill the familial and moral obligation to the deceased. The anger displayed by both sides, the contempt of Menelaus, and the defiance of Teucer are positive reflections of their entire beings. In one sense there is no subtext, because what the characters express overtly is what they undergo emotionally and mentally. There are, however, moral and psychological implications that go beyond the immediate issue. In the terms introduced in Chapter One, the *Ajax* debates can be characterized as a positive reflection of the inner action, the proportion of activity being narrower than the range of moral action alluded to, and deepening in a philosophical rather than psychological way.

How then shall we describe the mode of action in the entire sequence? A comprehensive description must include the temporal flow of action, the temporal manifestation of activity and the interaction between these two. The debates are active formal conflicts, constructed on assertion, counter-assertion, and a metaphor of wrestling, the stichomythic duel. The convention of the activity and the obvious skill with which it is manipulated contrast with the violence of the emotion it contains. In this we have a clue to powerful dramatic action. The very conventionality of the debate throws the seething passions of the antagonists into high relief. Not only is there contrast between the antagonists themselves, but there is also contrast between the formality of the activity and the fierceness of the action.

More removed from the formality of debate, and perhaps its very opposite, is conversation. Debate is planned speech; conversation is spontaneous speech. In plays such as *Hedda Gabler,* that is, "realistic" plays of middle-class European life, the activity tends to be conversational. Purely bodily functions (eating, sexual contact, laboring) are not ignored but, because so much of the necessary toil of "keeping the dirt of life at a distance" is vested in the servants, the activity that is proper to the characters tends to be conversational and contained in such acts as visiting, entertaining, and reporting events that have occurred offstage. But conversation dominates, and all other activities are reduced to a level of conversation. As activity, conversation has its own nature and thus determines some of the characteristics of the dramatic action. Conversation is primarily social, that is, it is intended to create an atmosphere of civilization rather than reveal inner turbulence. It also resists revelation. In conversation confidence does not readily spring forth but must be elicited by the effort of the listener. It is not a medium for conveying passion because passion is egotistical and conversation rests on an implied truce: no one is to dominate completely. The conversational basis of Hedda and Brack's tête-à-têtes depends on a balance of power. Once Brack violates that balance, he provokes a sharp burst of emotion from Hedda and destroys the possibility of conversation.

In *Streetcar* conversation is much more difficult to maintain. In fact, only Blanche and to a lesser extent Stella are capable of conversation. Thus, a larger portion of the activity of the play depends on satisfying or pursuing physical needs: drinking, dressing, bathing, going to the toilet. For entertainment, instead of conversation, the men play cards. Even the conversation, at least that involving Stanley, is a thinly disguised duel, thus making all discussion with him virtually abortive.

At its most powerful, *Streetcar* supplies incantation in place of conversation, incantation of the past (Blanche with Mitch, Scenes 6 and 9), of seduction (Scene 5, with the newsboy), of a superior culture (throughout). The truth is that conversation is not as congenial an activity for the American writer as it is for the European. Nor has the American actor mastered the skill of maintaining the tautness demanded by stage conversation. He constantly seeks to push it into revelation, argumentation, confession. The epitome of the conversational mode is the French drama, although it is also well-elaborated in English, Norwegian, Italian, and some German works.

Given the conversational activity of *Hedda Gabler,* what can be said of the mode of action? First of all, we find that inherent in this activity is negative reflection. The spoken lines only incompletely convey the underlying action. Either the depth of thought or emotion is so much greater than what is expressed or the true state is at odds with what is shown. Brack's conversations with Hedda are not masks, that is, opposites of his true thoughts, but they are more affable and less complete expressions of what really goes on within. In a play such as this, the concept of subtext is invaluable, for the activity we see communicates more by implication than explication. Occasionally the deeper state penetrates to the surface, is seen for a moment, and subsides beneath the level of conversation—for instance, when Hedda asserts that she will not endure being controlled by Brack. To produce this effect, the texture of the surface is designed to let as much of the inner action through as possible. The opacity of the activity, whether the musicality of speech, the virtuoso performance of a physical skill, or the regularity of form, is minimized. Instead, a complex tissue of sensibility is implied, requiring that the acting be transparent in order to convey the segmental rhythm analyzed previously.

By now we have slipped into a consideration of how the activity contains or reveals the action. In *Ajax* the full intensity of Teucer's passion comes to the surface so that what he expresses and what he truly feels are identical. This is an instance of positive reflection. *Hedda Gabler* illustrates negative reflection in the continuous gap between Hedda's social manner and her inner frenzy. This matter of positive or negative reflection is not a narrative but a theatrical factor. Shakespeare's art, for example, depends mainly upon positive reflection, and, except for a limited number of Machiavellian politicians and villainous characters, Iago most notably, the poetic expression mirrors exactly the inner state of an individual and of the action of a scene. Examine the heath scene again. Whatever anguish Lear experiences, he expresses. There is proportion between the force of his images and the passion he feels. Even where villainy is at work, on the part of either Edmund or Iago, Shakespeare does not stress the face-mask syndrome. Differences between the villain's mask and his true face are given facts of the narrative, but in the midst of a villain's scheming Shakespeare does not play upon the tension between what a villain says and what he feels. In *Hedda Gabler* and *Streetcar*, on the other hand, tension is frequently a product of a character's effort to hide his or her feelings or thoughts.

In *Hedda Gabler* and *Streetcar*, activity and imagined act are proportionate. In the selective process Ibsen and Williams seek to maintain due proportion among all phases of behavior. Their approach is essentially contextual, because instead of concentrating only upon climactic situations, they try to create the total pattern of low and high amplitude tension. To achieve this contextual form, they include a wide range of activities, making sure to integrate each into the entire presentation.

Samuel Beckett, who utilizes many "realistic" activities, shows in comparison how isolation of an activity from its context and concentration upon it as a purely opaque act divests the activity of its representational connotation and invests it with a symbolic potential. Every activity of *Endgame*, feeding Nagg, gazing on the "without," propping up the toy dog, has the particularity we associate with naturalism, but because each is so sharply defined, it suggests a broader range of action than a literal understanding of the activity would ordinarily denote. The activity tends to be bodily on one hand and theatrical on another. Vaudeville routines and storytelling are two such examples. A connection between stage life and actual life offstage does not seem possible, because the activity is not a mirror of the *way* people live. Yet in such an activity as Clov wheeling Hamm around the room, an analogue of action is suggested, or rather the idea of an action. Does the activity symbolize man's inescapability from his confinement in his body or on this earth? In the initial production of the play, Roger Blin arranged the setting to suggest the interior of a skull with the window-eyes looking out upon the world.[9] One is tempted to pursue such strict allegory because the link between activity and action is left so vague, so haunting, that we are continually trying to define it. Beckett, however, explicitly warns against this practice[10] and intends that we concentrate on the activity itself, making the immediate action between Clov and Hamm clear enough but the more evocative action dim, unformulated, and intentionally haunting. Activity in Beckett serves as a poetic rather than a representational image. What Shakespeare realizes through imagery and meter, Beckett puts into gestural and verbal inflections. The refrain, "I'll leave you," "You can't leave us," "Then I won't leave you," is a verbal gesture, one might say. Both playwrights create action shapes that directly arouse states of feeling in the audience without the mediation of associational images. The recognizable element in their work is not the behavioral activity but the familiar passions or sensations aroused by more or less artificial activities.

In the twentieth century, as a reaction to the extreme transparency of natural activity, with its loss of theatrical excitement as well as generalized significance, playwrights and performers have experimented with a wide variety of techniques for achieving a viable "artificiality." Genet creates his own black rituals; Brecht stresses narrative modes; Sean O'Casey develops a mixed method of "naturalism" and "expressionism." These writers also utilize song and dance to considerable effect, but it is in O'Casey's work that one can see the growth of artifice most easily. In his early plays, O'Casey employed song as natural activity, but with his turn to expressionism, commencing with *The Silver Tassie*, O'Casey employs song, dance, and scenic display as a direct expression of the action he wishes to convey. His most ambitious effort is found in *Red Roses for Me*.

Red Roses for Me portrays the aspirations of the idealistic young worker, Ayamonn. A Protestant in Catholic Ireland, a would-be artist among impoverished Dubliners, Ayamonn adheres to no single ideology but seeks to stir his fellow citizens to grasp and appreciate the joy of life. At the end of Act II, when the working men ask Ayamonn to lead a strike, he accepts although he knows that a clash with the police will be unavoidable. Act III opens in dramatic contrast with the naturalistic scenes that preceded. It displays languid and dispirited Dubliners lounging on the Liffey embankment. Before them is the bridge to the other bank (of the city? of their lives?). The women peddle fruit and flowers; the men dream of the race track.

First the police inspector and Protestant rector pass by and then Brennan. In these two segments the motif of the hopelessness of the people and their latent potential is stressed. Brennan tries to rouse their spirits with a saucy love song, but he is driven off. Coming in on the heels of Brennan, Ayamonn defends the song, much to the disgust of Roory, an old-time Irish nationalist. Roory urges Ayamonn to forget the derelicts, but Ayamonn refuses and endeavors to rouse their hopes.

O'Casey makes no attempt to show Ayamonn stirring the people and their responding to him in a realistic fashion. Instead he foreshortens the action of Ayamonn convincing the listeners and objectifies their reactions. As Ayamonn persists in invoking the promise of the future, the lights change. The buildings glow in the sunset, a surreal sunset. Three women, one aged, one mature, and one young, together representing Irish womanhood in its entirety, are transformed. Their clothes, no longer rags, seem to shimmer. The youngest springs up to dance with Ayamonn as the others sing. Through this formal activity, O'Casey seeks to evoke a paean of joy. It is Ayamonn's prefiguration of the society to be, a society of beauty and spiritual exaltation. This apocalyptic vision is the crux of the act and a climactic moment of the play. As it reaches its height, footsteps are heard and voices call Ayamonn to the strike, to the accomplishment of the vision he has aroused. With him goes the light, leaving the Dubliners to awaken from their trance.

To be artistically effective, the presentation of this segment must strike a balance between artifice and nature. O'Casey tries to establish a new convention, shifting from the photographic to the apocalyptic. He foreshadows the vision through the introduction of songs early in the play and through Ayamonn's yearning for joyful beauty. In Act III he makes that yearning palpable. The colors of the city and the sky change, ostensibly because of sunset, yet the changes go beyond sunset's changes. Ayamonn and the women sing and dance, yet the singing and dancing are more than natural joy. All changes partake of a symbolic celebration of the future. In these ways O'Casey endeavors to fashion a mode of action that, through its beauty and ebullience, can be simultaneously opaque and transparent.

As I stressed previously, there are no formulas in drama, only tendencies. Each dramatic presentation, that is, each mode of action, reconciles the divergent variables in its own manner. A mediocre work will most likely ape a mode of action achieved by others, whereas an original work will embody a unique arrangement of elements. Up to a point, the more highly articulated a form of expression is, the more easily perceived it will be, and thus the more affective. But the moment form becomes so opaque that the artificial features of activity obliterate the natural, a play loses an essential imaginative reality. Most of Shakespeare's work falls on the dividing line between formalism and realism. Like any dramatic work that concentrates its expression in one direction (in the verbal, for example), it demands greater performance skill in that respect. When that skill is forthcoming, it still must strike a balance between too obvious and too hidden a display. Actors who strive too energetically to capture the music and the imagery lose the inner life. Actors who concentrate too strongly upon the action without focusing their energies properly on the palpitation of the surface also lose the essence of the art.

The performer's ability to assess a segment accurately and then focus his performing energies properly is a prerequisite for achieving a high quality of activity. By quality I refer to the opaque texture of the activity. Part of the appeal of theater stems from the heightened sensory life that one experiences there. Unless the surface of sound and movement is abstracted from ordinary experience and articulated in a pleasurable form of some sort, theater not only loses its popular attraction but foregoes its means of penetrating the human imagination. Thrill and sensuosity are legitimate effects, as contemporary dramatists such as Samuel Beckett and Sean O'Casey well know. They have attempted to create modes of action that embody new relations between activity and action with renewed emphasis on the theatrical richness of activity, an emphasis that the contemporary theater urgently requires.

Response.

⦿ Theater is nothing if not spontaneous. It occurs. It happens. The novel can be put away, taken up, reread. Not theater. It keeps slipping between one's fingers. Stopping, it stops being theater. Its permanent features, facets of activity, such as scenery, script, stage, people, are no more theater than the two poles of a generator are electricity. Theater is what goes on between the parts.

In the preceding three chapters we have considered the ways in which the parts combine to form a segment of action, the basic building block of the drama. By varying the strength or direction of the elements, by selecting or rejecting certain features of activity, the theater artist produces distinctive modes of action. We might think of these segments as radioactive cores from which burst the potential energies that penetrate our imagination and stir our dreams. So far stress has been placed upon the internal arrangement of the segment. We can now concentrate on the relation between segment and audience.

Implied throughout our previous discussion has been the notion of a double context. First, there is the context of the segment itself, and then there is the context of segment and audience. Action and audience are welded together in strange and wonderful ways. They are simultaneously separate from each other and yet part of one another. Today there is a penchant for making activity and audience one. But a law of diminishing returns governs the mingling of the two. There is a point at which the breakdown between presentation and audience leaves no room for the imagination to operate. Physical and psychological space between audience and presentation is required. This space is usually termed "aesthetic distance." It must exist, but it must also be possible for the audience to bridge the distance, not necessarily through physical contact, but through imaginative interchange.

How a segment works upon the mind of an audience is still a mystery. Yet to be surveyed accurately is the dynamic field created by the assemblage of performers and spectators at one time in one place. The interplay of images, personal and artistic, that compose theatrical response may even appear to be inaccessible to investigation. Performers are overwhelmingly skeptical that their art can ever be known objectively and are therefore inclined to look upon the efforts of social scientists with a jaundiced eye. Yet who can tell? The continuation of artistic presentations in a society dense with sociologists and psychologists will inevitably produce studies of the theatrical process that may prove accurate and useful. Until such studies are produced, however, we must come to some understanding of the dramatic experience, even if the means be subjective and impressionistic.

THE NATURE OF
THEATRICAL RESPONSE

In examining the dramatic experience, we must distinguish between its separate phases. The experience includes both the point-to-point contact of audience and performer during presentation as well as the way the audience remembers the presentation. In general, drama critics discuss a play as a unified totality, a complete object, without distinguishing the dynamic states through which the audience passes in responding to it. Yet of all art forms, drama requires one of the longest, if not the longest period of contact between audience and artistic product. It may take more time to read a novel than to see a play, but the reader is not obliged to maintain so continuous an attention as the spectator. Only the film and an occasional musical piece depend upon so sustained a response. To assess the dramatic experience accurately, we will have to discriminate the sequence of presentational reactions from the rearrangement of those reactions into a unified response. Hereafter I shall call our reactions during production the *theatrical experience* and the remembrance of the production the *memorial experience*.

In the history of Western aesthetics, the memorial experience has received principal emphasis. Not so in Eastern thought. G. B. Mohan Thampi tells us that "Indian aesthetic thinking is primarily audience- or reader-oriented and the center of much discussion is the response of the readers." [1] Whereas the West has used the artistic object, whether play or performance, as a point of departure for discussing theme or analyzing human psychology, Indian thinking has remained closer to the aesthetic experience, being content to absorb and contemplate it. Our orientation has thus led us to habits of dramatic analysis that fail to give due consideration to the theatrical experience. Marshall McLuhan reflects the mounting rejection of those habits when he asserts that "in the arts the particular mix of our senses in the medium employed is all-important . . . A work of art has no existence or function apart from its *effects* on human observers." [2] Structural analysis, such as I have conducted in previous chapters, presupposes the centrality of the theatrical experience in dramatic art and assumes that dramatic criticism not based upon that experience is peripheral and tangential.

How can we understand the theatrical experience if the imaginative contact between presentation and audience remains a mystery? The twin weapons of social science—the questionnaire and the interview—do not seem to have produced significant insight into the experience. Some theater writers have applied findings on group psychology to the audience experience, noting the dominance of the irrational over the rational, the inclination toward conformity, and the readiness of emotional response. These general conditions do seem to exist in the group act of theater, but they do not account for the peculiar nature of the artistic experience. What seems to be lacking is not information but correct orientation toward the study of the subject.

Knowledge of the theatrical experience is not totally lacking. In fact, the performer functions daily on that knowledge. For him it is usually a result of cumulative acting experience. The skilled performer "knows" that he "knows" how to maintain and develop rapport with an audience, although he may not be able to articulate that knowledge, and may even be skeptical of others' efforts to articulate it. To paraphrase Michael Polanyi, the performer knows more than he can tell.[3] Polanyi has shown, first in *Personal Knowledge* and then in *The Tacit Dimension,* the intuitive base of knowledge, and even more, the accessibility of that intuition to comprehension. The performer's awareness of audience response is intuitive. Being intuitive, it may not be accessible to tabulation and measurement. But it is accessible to observation and sympathetic understanding. Polanyi's argument is principally directed against the supposed objectivity of scientific knowledge, which, he insists, contrary to widespread assumption, has an intuitive and passionate basis. He demonstrates the essential unity of all knowing, the artistic and scientific processes being no more than variants of a single operation of the mind. Moreover, Polanyi is not alone in this position, though, as scientist and sociologist, he has worked out the subject more thoroughly than others. Warren Weaver in "The Imperfections of Science," [4] Harold Rugg in *Imagination,* and Arthur Koestler in *The Act of Creation* adopt the same fundamental view: All knowledge depends upon intuition and an overriding conceptual framework—what Max Planck calls "a world image." [5] The world image is a structural concept of reality rather than the world of reality itself. To understand the theatrical experience accurately and profoundly, we must analyze the phenomenon within an adequate "world image." (The conception of theater presented in Chapter One is, in effect, such a "world image.") We must also be prepared to direct our attention not at the quantitative factors of audience response, but to utilize our sensibilities, kinesthetically as well as intellectually, to investigate the qualitative factors of the theatrical experience. I use the word *aware of identity as audience*

"qualitative" not in a valuative sense, that is, whether an audience does or does not like a performance, but in a descriptive sense: What is the nature of the experience through which an audience goes as it responds to a performance? *Exp. of watching*

We must begin with the obvious facts of the presentational act: The performers offer a living fiction, inviting the audience to enter the ambience of that fiction. Were the audience to do so completely, to accept the fiction as actuality, it would then have to be mad. But an audience lives within two overlapping circles of experience, that of the fiction and that of its own actuality. As J. B. Priestley, in his book *The Art of the Dramatist*, has phrased the paradox:

> Everybody and everything on the stage have [a] double character; they are seen in the strange light and shadow of belief and disbelief; they belong to a heightened reality that we know to be unreal.[6]

The paradox of belief and disbelief may be stated another way. There is the tug of the play, urging us to submerge ourselves fully in its life. There is the restraint of the larger world we inhabit. The play itself is but part of that larger world. In agreeing to believe the fiction, we invoke an unspoken convention that such belief is privileged. We must never be brought so close to our own lives that fiction becomes complete actuality. We do submit, and we do not submit, and this "double character," as Priestley terms it, sets up a field of interacting images, a complex exchange of partially uttered signals in a three-way communication: between the play, the individual and collective audience. The play projects doubly, to each member of the audience as an individual, sparking his or her private memories, and to the audience as a whole, in that distinctive configuration that it has assumed for a particular occasion.

Were we completely submerged in a play, all doors to our imagination would be ajar. We might jump up with that half-legendary cowboy who, while attending an old-fashioned melodrama, reputedly saved the heroine by shooting the villain dead, killing the actor in the process. But the impulses of a play are filtered through our imagination. To borrow a term from magnetism, the impulses "ionize" our total personality, bringing the play and our experience into imaginative harmony and producing a sense of heightened living where the paradox is resolved, where the fictional details are sublimated in the recognition that the general pattern of action satisfies real needs in our emotional and intellectual life. Such a synthesis of the fictitious and actual can flood our being so completely and with such intensity that the remembrance of that experience remains with us for decades. Moments of such high intensity—ecstasy, for instance—are relatively few in number during the course of a lifetime. Quantitatively, they are insignificant. Qualitatively, on the other hand, these few moments of high intensity may be extremely significant in adding another dimension to our memory and sense of the mystery of life. The theater, at its best, has that qualitative significance. By projecting action in an articulate form, it is capable of producing effects that remain with us long after events in our own lives are forgotten.

If, as I have intimated, the theatrical experience is a dialogue between presenter and audience, it is essential to know what constitutes the audience's side of the conversation. To what extent, for example, does audience predisposition toward theatrical experience affect its response to that experience? Because reliable answers to this question are not readily forthcoming from theater study, it is necessary to turn to parallel answers in the visual arts. Visual experiments have shown that an observer's speed in recognizing a graphic figure depends upon the degree to which he expects that particular form, and E. H. Gombrich has further demonstrated that perceptive habit, or mental set, can lead an artist to record not what he sees, but what he expects or wishes to see.[7] In theater the role that predisposition plays in speeding up or deepening audience response is necessarily far more complex. My task here is merely to show the relevance of this point and sketch some of the operative factors.

It is the folklore of the dramatic profession that the immediate circumstances of presentation affect the reception of a play. On the most basic level is the comfort factor. In the United States physical ease is a prerequisite to an audience's granting performers its attention—an auditorium that is too hot or too cold interferes with response. Modern playgoers are far removed from the Shakespearean audiences, who were prepared to sit or stand in a partially sheltered building to witness a play in mid-winter. Another circumstance of presentation is the effect that socializing may have on a play. Playgoing has always been a social activity, and it is not unusual for the performance to fall behind social prestige as a motive for attendance at the theater. These factors, it may be argued, are extraneous to the aesthetic experience. That may be so. Nonetheless, they are influential. Every culture imposes its particular social character on playgoing. It is that character with which theater must contend. In some periods and countries, the act of playgoing is conducive to audience response, making the task of the performer simpler. In other instances, the present one among them, playgoing faces substantial obstacles that the performer must overcome before he can find a favorable climate for his work.

For convenience, we can divide audiences into *random* and *communal* types. A communal audience, at its most fully formed, consists of people whose total social experience is at one with each other and with the presenters. Isolated tribes of the Plains Indians provide the few instances where "theatrical" performances were offered in a closed society. Less isolated but still communal were the audiences of ancient Greece and medieval Japan. Whether or not the values of the performers and the audience were identical, their language of thought and feeling was. They possessed what George Steiner calls a mythology, a "context of belief and convention which the artist shares with his audience." [8] Community made possible multiple communication, extending the range of the presenter's voice. All was not idyllic, however. Communal pressure imposed restrictions on the substance of the presentation, as when the Athenians prohibited Phrynichus from treating contemporary events in his plays after he criticized them for abandoning the Ionian colonies to the Persians.

At the opposite end, in contrast to the communal audience, is the random audience—a collection of individuals assembled haphazardly to witness a play. Although it is theoretically possible to have a completely random group, in practice a selective process works to give some identity to an audience. Economic factors tend to bring certain types of individuals together and discourage others; intellectual appeals will attract one type of person and repel another. Each performance thus becomes a hastily assembled community of roughly similar outlook. But exactly how similar, the theater artist seldom knows, with the result that he must treat each audience as a random sample. Unfortunately, such a random group gives him few specifics to work with. He cannot be sure that the audience will understand his language, and thus he may resort to simplified and generalized actions that are readily comprehensible without special knowledge or signals. In seeking common ground, he often exploits the sensational and the sentimental. To counteract the banality of this kind of presentation, some writers and performers rebel and, regarding the random spectators balefully, characterize them as petty bourgeois or establishment, insult or shock their political or sexual mores, and proceed by a process of alienation to weld them into a community.

A communal form must, therefore, in some way be created in the theater. The communal form of the Greek city-state can never be reestablished. The random audience, nourished by the mass media and universal education, may be evolving into a new communal type. If so, the theater artist will have to learn what its predispositions are and how to deal with them. Theater in the United States is desperately searching for its community or communities. That is why an understanding of the workings of audience predisposition is essential.

But the predisposition of an audience does not only favor negative response. It may also stimulate a positive response qualitatively, so that what might in one period be an unfavorable and superficial reaction to a play, in another can be positive and profound. The fortunes of *Troilus and Cressida* illustrate such a radical change. For two hundred years critics rejected the play as unsavory and aimless, but during the twentieth century readers and spectators have come to admire it for its "realistic" reflection of contemporary life. *The Diary of Anne Frank,* in its turn, illustrates the circumstances under which a work can exert a deeper effect in performance than its quality warrants. As Schiller remarked, "some very popular plays only touch us on account of the subject." [9] The script of *Diary* is an indifferent piece of journeyman work, competently enough written but lacking anything beyond a single dimension of sentimentality. Yet its initial presentation did arouse a penetrating response that one might call "tragic." In Germany particularly, it broke through the guilty silence of the populace and aroused intense waves of sympathy for the hapless girl. In the United States when the play was first presented in 1955, the memory of the extermination of the Jews was still vivid. People had not grasped the incredibility, the horror beyond the horror, of the Nazi destruction. The story of the young Dutch girl, Anne Frank, whose diary had been found after World War II, placed the unbelievable in human perspective. Its enactment encountered an audience already primed for deep response, its predisposition, or sensibility, ready to serve as a background for the action of the play. In effect, the juxtaposition of play and audience assumed a classic figure-ground relationship.

THE FIGURE-GROUND
RELATIONSHIP

The terms *figure* and *ground* are primarily connected with experiments in visual perception conducted by Gestalt psychologists. E. Rubin first used the words in 1915 to describe the apparent detachment of certain parts of a visual image from its surrounding field. Since the eye cannot focus upon an ambiguous image, it resolves all visual phenomena into dominant and subordinate parts of a totality. This involves what Kurt Koffka calls "double representation." [10] A circle drawn within a rectangle may be perceived either as a hole in the rectangle or a sphere on its surface. In either case a third dimension is suggested. The rectangle serves as a ground or framework in which the circle or figure is suspended. Successive experimenters have extended and refined our understanding of how this phenomenon operates, and in recent years their findings have been employed in analysis of the visual arts, most notably by Rudolf Arnheim in *Art and Visual Perception*.

But such analysis need not be confined to the visual arts. Seemingly fundamental to all artistic enterprise is reliance upon interaction between an emphasized foreground, or *figure,* and an analogous or contrasting background, or *ground,* which throws the figure into relief. Both Western and Eastern music is constructed upon the principle of a ground, or bass, and a figure, or melodic pattern. In Indian music the *Thanpura,* with its continuous, penetrating "drone" is an active *ground* out of which emerges the improvisation of the singer as *figure.*[11] In literature the ground may be imaginative rather than physical; metaphor, in particular, relies upon a double recognition of a conventional sense opposed to an original insight. Theater, no less than the other arts, builds upon figure-ground relationships, though perhaps more subtly and intricately.

In theater we cannot view the figure-ground relationship from a single perspective. There are several planes of interaction between figure and ground, each differing slightly from the other and yet all interconnected. One plane, as illustrated in *The Diary of Anne Frank,* is the audience's predisposition, or sensibility, which serves as a ground for the play as a whole. Depending upon its history, an audience is predisposed to react in certain ways, so much so that in *Diary* mention of the historical circumstances is unnecessary. Hardly a moment of the play dwells upon the Nazi holocaust. The Nazis are "offstage." The occupants of the attic must be cautious, but the danger is understated. Instead the play stresses the ordinariness of family life rather than the unusual desperation of the Franks and the Van Daans. The effectiveness of this method depends wholly on the audience's awareness of Nazi acts, of the inevitable misfortune of this family, and of the particular fact of Anne's early death in a concentration camp. When Anne discovers love, sensing the sweetness and pain and puzzlement of maturity, it is not so much her discovery that moves us as the fact that it is made in the face of our knowledge of her end. The authors relied upon that knowledge. The more sharply we sense the gap between Anne's own awareness of her growing up and our awareness of her ultimate end, the more poignant our response.

Another plane of interaction between figure and ground occurs within the context of a play. The sequence of action serves as a foreground played against a background of circumstances. In *Riders to the Sea,* this background is the hard and dangerous life of the island against which Maurya's conflict with her children is enacted. Macbeth enacts his tragedy against a background of an idealized conception of royalty. Hedda's suppressed frenzy is comprehensible only against the backdrop of a closed, bourgeois society, jealous of reputation and remorseless in persecution of its deviants. Shorthand allusions to these backgrounds occur throughout these plays: comments such as Bartley's, "It's hard set we'll be from this day with no one in it but one man to work"; the ceremonial welcome to Duncan; the periodic comment that "people don't do such things." Through such òccasional motifs, the potential background is activated in the imagination of the audience. This background is part of the original precipitating context of the play and supports the action from beginning to end.

Although the two grounds cited—audience sensibility and background of circumstance—are closely connected, they are not necessarily identical. When a playwright first constructs a play, the world of his action is usually the world of the audience—either the actual, physical world or, more likely and essentially, the social, psychological, and moral world. In these instances we may say that the two grounds of action overlap. But as a play ages and travels, its world of action encounters differing grounds of audience sensibility, which may no longer overlap the background of circumstance. When this happens there is danger that, unless the two worlds can be brought into correspondence with one another, the potential for rich theatrical response will be severely curtailed. The reasons for this are aesthetic and psychological. I have referred to a segment as a radioactive core. In order to become such a source of imaginative energy, a segment must pack into its structure a wide range of indirect associations as well as a provocative dynamic shape. A play doesn't have time to create a world of its own; it relies on signs and symbols that suggest the world. The audience fills in that world from its own experience if the signs and symbols excite its sensibility, as references to racial issues do at present. This psychological ground, linking audience world and playworld, then supports the particular response aroused by an artistically shaped action.

This process is most readily apparent in the histories of major dramatic works. For instance, the ground of audience sensibility to *Death of a Salesman* is the American success myth with its endorsement of personality marketing. Selling oneself rather than creating social value is the hallmark of that myth. The play reveals what happens to a man who lives according to its mystique. At the time of the play's first presentation in 1949, this myth was somewhat shaken, although many in the audience probably accepted its validity and everyone had an intimate acquaintance with its longstanding acceptance as an American ideal. Whether or not the audience still believed in the myth as Willy Loman did, it could share in Willy's belief. We can say that the ground of audience sensibility and the background of the play's action overlapped each other considerably. In Europe, where the same degree of overlapping did not exist, the play enjoyed a curious fortune. It was not very successful in London, where the image of the American salesman was far-removed from audience experience. On the other hand, audience sensibility in other countries furnished a different but fruitful ground for the action of the play. Arthur Miller notes that, "in Catholic Spain the play ran longer than any modern play . . . The Spanish press, thoroughly controlled by Catholic orthodoxy, regarded the play as commendable proof of the spirit's death where there is no God . . . and in the area of the Norwegian Arctic Circle fishermen whose only contact with civilization was the radio and the occasional visit of the government boat insisted on seeing it night after night—the same few people—believing it to be some kind of religious rite." [12] In these instances, congruence between the ground of audience sensibility and the background of action provided a suitable imaginative setting against which the play could unfold.

How a dramatist treats the background of action may take many forms, but, in general, we can distinguish two contradictory tendencies. The background can represent communal values with which the dramatist is in accord and which he confirms sympathetically through the working out of his action. Such a dramatist is Sophocles. In contrast, the background can represent values which the action is calculated to attack, directly or indirectly. Genet's plays rely upon the presence of a bourgeois morality in order to achieve their traumatic effects. It does not matter, as it has been charged, that the bourgeois morality Genet predicates has passed away half a century ago as long as the emotional and ideological residue of that morality remains in the marrow of the audience, an underground target for the writer's shafts.[13] In every play, the writer presumes a background which he shocks or reconfirms. Plays dealing with racial relations, such as Genet's *The Blacks* or LeRoi Jones' *The Toilet*, succeed in doing both simultaneously. They presuppose a double background, one white, the other black. From the white background, the plays arouse negative emotions of disgust and fear, except where the white person regards his own background with revulsion or guilt. From the black background and from sympathetic whites, the plays elicit positive responses through which the audience articulates its anger or frustration. Schematically speaking, we can say that dramatic action plays off the backboard of social and psychological values and customs, which, even if sketched in lightly or merely assumed, are always present.

Because the background is a shorthand expression of a social context, it is necessarily conventionalized, or schematized, in its artistic form. The nature of the convention, or scheme, shifts with historical, rather than individual, changes of outlook. In some periods the convention may be lodged principally in ceremonial decorum, as in the Elizabethan age. Scenes of procession, trials, and courtly hearings, often placed at the beginning and end of plays, and aided by the emblematic formality of the stage façade, provide the frame for the action. In other periods the convention may be summed up in the stage setting, as in the age of naturalism. The three-dimensional interior of naturalism symbolizes a cross-section of actual existence, its choice reflecting the crucial importance of a particular locale in contemporary existence. It was eminently appropriate for a materialistic society to be lodged amidst domestic possessions. The living room and kitchen of naturalism, each in its own way, epitomized the background for the action.

In general, background is expressed by social, or group, activity, treatment of stage space, and a code of behavior to which the action adheres. Although some authors utilize only one of these methods of representation, the great ones employ all three, stressing each differently, but finding a means for blending them all. The stage façade of the Elizabethan playhouse does not affect the action as intrinsically as the recessed stage of naturalism, but it does complement the ceremonial decorum of the acting. However it may be shaped, background is a mediating element between the world of the audience and the world of action.

Beyond this function, the background-foreground, or ground-figure duality has still another dimension in dramatic art. For the Dublin audience that first watched *Riders to the Sea* in 1904, the world of the Aran islands was remote and, if not exotic, at least strange. Despite the play's naturalism, it was a naturalism of the unfamiliar. The action, by contrast, being of a universal nature—the death of children and resignation of a mother—was not removed psychologically. In this way Synge achieved a resolution between the familiar and unfamiliar, a resolution that every theatrical presentation must achieve. Theater is both a mirror of life and a place of wonder. In a speech to the French Academy on the succession of Thomas Corneille to the chair of his brother Pierre, Jean Racine praised the greater brother for having "happily achieved the probable and the marvelous" ("la vraisemblance et le merveilleux") in his works.[14] The probable, the likely—or, as I would state it, the familiar and recognizable—are necessary properties of the drama. But this we now accept, because the theater of the last century has stressed these qualities. Equally necessary, though not fully appreciated in recent years, is the presence of "le merveilleux"—the marvelous, the wondrous, the unusual and exotic. The very act of presentation can be justified only if the performer can offer something otherwise unavailable, something wondrous. But, in order to appreciate the wonder, the audience must also be aware of the familiar. These two diametrically opposed properties, united in a single presentation, contribute to that psychic energy so tightly compacted in the very best of drama. In every effective presentation the duality of the familiar and unfamiliar appears, the more original the imagination of the theater artists, the more original the juxtaposition of these properties.

Figure and ground are intimately related to duality of the familiar and the unfamiliar. In contemporary drama, more often than not, the background is ordinary, that is, familiar: characters are recognizable, values are shared. Arthur Miller is the master of such background. Against this background, he often places the characters in melodramatic circumstances or at moments of extreme pressure. Yet the reverse can also occur. The background might be unfamiliar, as in *A Streetcar Named Desire*. The decay of the old South lost in the backwater of the Latin Quarter offers

a background removed from the life of the New York audience, yet nevertheless charged with romantic emotion. Against such a background, the fairly ordinary tale of a high-school teacher, alcoholic and oversexed, finding refuge at the home of her sister produces an exotic yet immediate effect. Williams' portrait of the South may or may not be accurate, but the primarily Northern audience accepted it as true because the portrait fit a conventional image of the South, an image charged with ambivalent emotions of disgust and fascination. In the past, theater tended to distance the background of narrative, placing the locale and plot in an age other than its own. Against a background of archaic wars (*Ajax*), ancient Britain (*King Lear*), or classic Greece (*Phèdre*), the performer passed through emotional and intellectual states that were perhaps more intense than the audience would experience, but at least familiar in type. Current theater, in utilizing familiar backgrounds, must compensate to some extent by introducing the perverse and clinical into the foreground.

The crucial necessity for a vital background becomes evident as soon as we deal with plays of another era. Probably one of the most important functions of the director in guiding a revival to the stage is to find the means for giving the work a background. This was the achievement of Peter Brook in his controversial production of *King Lear*. Without imitating contemporary life, he captured its spirit in setting and manner of acting. Without violating a necessary ritual in the action, he made the decorum of court direct and ruthless, like a board meeting in a big corporation.

The frequency of Shakespearean productions makes this problem of background particularly important. For example, an entire code of decorum and hierarchy is assumed in Shakespeare's history plays. Monarchy is not merely an abstract idea, but a personified idea about which the populace has strong feelings. English traditional society offered a background in depth before which Shakespeare could arrange his action. A recent study of emblem imagery[15] illustrates the overlays of association possible within that background. Of course, in witnessing *Henry IV* we cannot be moved in the same way as the Elizabethan was. When we hear of Northumberland's complicity, for example, in Hotspur's rebellion, most of us are not aware that a later Northumberland rose against Elizabeth. Nor can we completely appreciate how central ceremony was to that society, about which, as Sir Thomas Elyot put it, man knows "nothing but by outward significations . . . by some exterior sign." [16] That is why the stage ceremonies of the court—the heraldic challenge, the baptism of *Henry VIII*—appear to be decoration rather than life. In effect, the theater artist must eschew the background of the past. By studying it, he can gain an insight into what background elements are needed for the dramatic effectiveness of the play in the current theater. But, with each revival, he must find a contemporary analogue which an audience can share, yet which does not violate the central action of the work.

What is necessary for Shakespeare is even more necessary for other writers. Shakespeare's foreground is so vivid that an audience is often willing to forego the enrichment of a vivid background. Other writers depend upon the vigorous interplay of background-foreground to promote deep audience reaction. It is the province of the director to concern himself with the implementation of this factor. Analysis, however, must provide the proper reading of the text and the accurate definition of the background. We must know what background the playwright assumes and exactly how he makes use of it. How fully does he sketch it and what is its character, probable or wondrous? Naturalistic playwrights, producing case studies of lower-class life, tend to be somewhat fulsome in background and often, in fact, offer little else, as, for example, in Elmer Rice's *Street Scene* or Arnold Wesker's *The Kitchen*. We must also know what aspects of life are subsumed in the background: social values, as in Genet, social decorum, as in Shakespeare, social structure, as in Ibsen, or intellectual pretensions, as in Shaw. As we trace the action of a play, we must be aware that this action always works against a background, inherent but incomplete in the play, present but unexpressed in the audience.

THE THEATRICAL
EXPERIENCE

Thus, from the moment an audience approaches and then enters the place of presentation, the theatrical experience commences. It is, as I have remarked, an interplay—an interplay that may be imagined as essentially harmonic. It effects a congruence between theatrical emission and audience reaction. Its first step is to establish mutual attention. Interest and curiosity characterize such attention rather than complete absorption. The audience's term for such attention, and properly so, is "entertainment." Unfortunately, this word has become associated with the most superficial, most passive response of a titillating kind, that its value as a description of audience pleasure, whatever the nature of that pleasure, has been debased. Yet, from the derivation of the word comes its more appropriate meaning, namely, to designate the continuing involvement of an audience while it is in contact with a presentation. In the word is rooted the idea of interaction ("entertainment," from the French, *entretenir*, from the Latin, *inter tenere*—to hold between). Combining the notions of sustenance and interplay, the verb, "to entertain," considered etymologically, is infused with tremendously compressed energy of a vivid give-and-take. Initially, the give-and-take occurs between the physical activity of presentation and the sensitized organs of perception in an audience. Gradually the sensory response expands into the imaginative. Entertainment is thus a precondition to other specific responses. Something must be held between the presenter and the receiver. Such and such an action, being entertained, should effect entertainment in the audience.

In drama, the performer enacts a sequence of action-blocks in such a way as to project their forms to an audience. The audience, through perceiving the activity, senses the action with a mixture of belief and disbelief. It lives forward into the next moment, and the expectation may produce intense sensations of delight, thrill, suspense, in one word, entertainment. But what does the audience entertain? What is sustained between it and the performers?

Ronald Peacock writes of drama as a sequence of images. Suzanne Langer believes drama creates the illusion of the virtual future. Both stress the illusory quality of the dramatic experience, and undoubtedly it is strong. Both would agree that illusion is not delusion. For Langer the virtual life of an artistic illusion has a reality of its own although not necessarily a reality by reflection of actual life. Art being the language of feeling, the virtual image has its own syntax, depending upon the art concerned. Drama, the illusion of the immediate future, produces a virtual image of that future. Langer further indicates that the virtual existence of drama stems wholly from the artistic work itself. To allow intrusions of actual life is to distort the artistic work, to use it for ulterior purposes, she believes. This may very well be true for an art such as music, which Langer knows well. It is not true of drama, however. The materials of drama are the materials of life with a minimum of alteration. A novel's description of a man working is not at the same proximity to actuality as witnessing a man working on stage. Actuality intrudes on the dramatic experience because drama, though it does in fact abstract from life, does not *appear* to do so. Hence, the compound character of the virtual existence projected by a presentation.

The audience entertains a dynamic illusion of life. This illusion has a virtual existence: a life of its own according to its own organic nature. This first aspect of drama may be considered opaque. We see its shape, its form. But the illusion is also a reflection; it mirrors actual human situations. This second aspect may be considered transparent. We see through the action to actuality.

Although drama has this dual character, there is no such thing as an ideal balance. *The Diary of Anne Frank* is largely transparent, that is, "of its surroundings." Once the surroundings no longer supply the framework for the action, the action loses its power to grasp and sustain our attention. In allegory, too, the action is predominately transparent. The events of *Everyman,* for example, are a compressed analogue of the larger allegory of life. By contrast, the plays of Marivaux and Wilde are almost completely opaque; their reference to actuality is tenuous. Wilde's comedies are not particularly illuminating as mirrors of English society, yet as exercises in wit, as amusing charades of a topsy-turvy sort, they are delightful. Between these poles, however, fall those works whose dialectic is more nearly balanced. Is Lear's frenzied reaction to filial ingratitude an action whose formal power absorbs us in a closed world of *King Lear* or does it reflect the cruelty of a world we inhabit? Not that drama has to work by reflecting actual events or by illustrating specific theses, but the material of dramatic action is a fusion of the actual and imaginative, the observed and conceived, so that finally it is impossible to say which is which.

Is Cordelia's innocence an actual innocence? Does it have reference to a human actuality? Or is it an idealized innocence, just as Edmund's evil is an idealized evil and just as Blanche DuBois' desperation is an idealized desperation? The present vogue for realism makes the use of the term "ideal" suspect. Yet we cannot understand the working of theater without introducing it. "Art intends the ideal," Peacock asserts,[17] though he does not show fully that the "ideal" is structural, that is, action is formed into an idealized shape. I use the term "ideal" to designate that process of abstracting from the particular instance in accord with an angle of perception, an idea. In that sense every dramatic work seeks to present an ideal action.

George Lukács correctly observes that the drama like the novel seeks "to evoke a totality."[18] The drama stands for all of life. As such, it must abstract from experience more than other forms of expression. It also exists only in communal interplay and, therefore, must achieve a high level of generalization. While the abstraction and generalization may look backward to its sources— the specific instances and actual observations of life—they also look forward toward formal realization. Through the processes of selection and feedback, actuality is refined into a "pure" analogue of a larger reality. What is meant by "pure" shifts from style to style. Even naturalism, wedded to the specific case, offered a "pure" example of a type of life. The assumption was that a literal enactment of an actual experience could represent a host of similar experiences—*une tranche de vie,* after all, comes from a whole loaf. The specific plays off one's consciousness that when one sees the misery of Silesian weavers or the delinquency of the dead-end kids, one knows that each represents case after case of misery and delinquency in life. In this sense the enactment is "ideal."

So far, then, the audience entertains the presentation as a complex illusion of reality and ideality. But *how* does it entertain this illusion?

The presentation is perceived not as discrete motions but as activity, that is, coherent units of related motions. The Gestalt school of psychology has amply demonstrated that artistic response occurs through the perception of visual, auditory, or activity wholes.[19] Response "begins with the perception of a total *Gestalt* and proceeds to distinctions of ideal elements within it. Therefore its symbolism is a physical or imaginal whole whereof details are articulated, rather than a vocabulary of symbols that may be combined to present a coherent structure." [20] In the theatrical experience, the audience perceives a segment of actual, artificial activity. It is an activity that has been "idealized" structurally without loss of its concrete, sensuous quality. As the audience entertains this concrete yet "idealized" activity, it also perceives it as an illusion of human action.[21]

The illusion we have been speaking of is always in the process of change. It has been widely observed that drama yearns forward, moves, evolves, is always in a state of becoming. The illusion of stopping—what Lukács calls retardation—is merely for the purpose of heightening the forward thrust of action. In the previous chapters I examined the components of a segment in considerable detail, showing how the temporal and spatial interaction in the segment produces a rhythmic shape of action. Usually, as the tension mounts, one has the sensation of quickening that seems to be brought to a standstill at some critical moment, as when Bartley waits in the doorway. Each action-segment, thus, has its organic rhythm that parallels the shape of its interacting tensions between characters. The conclusion of one phase of an action-unit very often acts as a caesura, a cessation before the resumption of the forward thrust. The successive states of *becoming*, which characterize dramatic action, are highly varied. They cover the stops and starts, the accelerations and decelerations, which pervade an action. The rhythm of an entire play is determined by the internal rhythm of the action-blocks and the ways in which these action-blocks are linked together.

Leaning forward in one's seat, which reflects strong involvement in a presentation, mirrors the forward thrust of the dramatic action. As we follow the events of the play our interest and emotion ride upon the waves of the action. The murderer slowly searches for the hidden child and we feel "our hearts stopping"; we experience an anxious suspension that stretches to anxiety as long as the search moves toward confrontation but does not yet reach it. The same principle applies to avant-garde experiments, such as those of the Living Theatre, where direct confrontation between actor and audience produces a shape of tensions embodying provocation, resistance, and an overtly positive or negative response. But whether we deal with traditional dramatic form or with contemporary innovations, we are concerned with the same essential process. What we respond to is the *how* of the search and the *how* of the provocation. Imaginatively we follow a path that runs parallel, not to the events themselves, but to the shifts of tension either between characters or between ourselves and the performers. This process may be called *empathic parallelism:* Where the audience is engaged fully in a presentation, that is, where the interaction is sustained from beginning to end, the responsive path parallels the entire work.

I realize that what has been stated here as a simple process is really quite complex. The illusion that is entertained evokes an imaginative response. At what instant the entertainment of the illusion becomes response is a question I can only consider but not answer. Therefore, in using the term "empathic parallelism," I wish to imply that total process of interaction: the perception, the sustaining of illusion, the experiencing of sensation, and the physical and/or mental adjustment to that sensation.

Customarily, that process of interaction is considered to be wholly, or almost wholly, emotive in nature. We assume that our cognitive powers sleep during a performance and that our affective side alone remains awake. Such a view is not only popular but also learned, and is part of the philosophical assumption that our intellectual and emotional capacities operate separately and, for the most part, exclusively. But such an assumption must be seriously challenged. My own pragmatic experiences in theater support the position adopted by Rudolf Arnheim in his paper "Emotion and Feeling in Psychology and Art." He points out that "academic psychology is driven to call certain mental states 'emotions' because it is accustomed to distributing all psychological phenomena into the three compartments of cognition, motivation, and emotion, instead of realizing that every mental state has cognitive, motivational, and emotional components, and cannot be defined properly by any one of the three." [22] Paying attention to a performance is one type of mental state that contains, simultaneously, these three components of cognition, motivation, and emotion. This principle is central to our further consideration of the audience-performer interaction, for only by understanding audience response as the total response of the individual to the presentation can we adequately account for the affective as well as the cognitive aspects. At a dramatic crisis in a play we not only "feel" but "recognize"; we experience a flash of awareness as well as a sensation of empathy. The phrase "total response of the individual" does not merely mean that we respond "intensely." Polanyi, calling attention to the kinesthetic aspect of visual perception, states that "physiologists long ago established that the way we see an object is determined by our awareness of certain efforts inside our body [sic], efforts which we cannot feel in themselves. We are aware of these things going on inside our body in terms of the position, size, shape, and motion of an object, to which we are attending." [23] Although theater response seems to derive principally from visual and aural perception, in reality it relies upon a totality of perception that could be better termed kinesthetic. We are aware of a performance through varying degrees of concentration and relaxation within our bodies. From actual experience performers can sense whether or not a "house" is with them, principally because the degree of muscular tension in the audience telegraphs, before any overt sign, its level of attention. We might very well say that an audience does not see with its eyes but with its lungs, does not hear with its ears but with its skin. All of us are aware of the ionization of feeling throughout our bodies when we are absorbed in a play and the quick rush of sensation when we react to a critical moment. Nor do we have to discriminate the dramatic signals mentally in order to react. Perception includes subception, bodily response to stimuli before we are focally aware of the stimuli. In theater, this means that our bodies are already reacting to the texture and structure of action before we recognize that they are doing so.

The connecting link between dramatic structure and theatrical response may very well be what the Gestalt psychologists describe as a psychophysical parallelism, which is isomorphic in character. Derived principally from work in visual response, the concept of isomorphic response can be, and in a preliminary way has been, extended to theatrical perception.[24] Fundamentally, it supposes that there is a correspondence between physical shape and psychic reaction, that, in fact, a perceived form induces within the nervous system of the observer a psychic echo that brings the imagination of the observer in line with the form perceived. Thus, what I have termed "empathic parallelism" is actually a kinesthetic, isomorphic response to dramatic action, by means of which the patterns and rhythms of tension find their immediate echo in the imaginative response of the audience. In this context, the term "imaginative response" stands for internal activity composed of cognitive, motivational, and emotional components.

It should be increasingly apparent that the structural analysis described in the previous chapters is closely related to manner of response. Ability to perceive the possible shapes of action embedded in a text leads to understanding of possible forms of audience reaction. In order to respond to the structure, however, members of an audience need not recognize the structural patterns of an action, but they do experience the form *isomorphically* in a sympathic pattern within their bodies. This is readily seen in observing response to an active segment, for we are accustomed to recognizing the ways in which tension mounts to a direct confrontation. This may also be true in simple reactive segments, such as Electra's expression of grief, for this pattern is linear and the intensification progressive. But when we attend to more complex patterns, particularly those that are not principally temporal but also stress the spatial factor, such as the segments from *King Lear* and *The Cherry Orchard*, we may not be quite so aware of how the structural pattern induces a complex response within us. Through its aborted lines of action and spatial juxtaposition, *The Cherry Orchard* produces a multidimensional response within us, discontinuous from instant to instant, yet pervasive as we experience the linking of parts.

Hitherto I seemed to place principal emphasis upon associational factors, particularly upon the interplay between ground and figure. As previously argued, the ground gains in dramatic power to the extent that it is related to audience experience. Presently I seem to emphasize the importance of structure in inducing response. Both factors are operative: Response cannot be divorced from content, not in theater at least. Depending on the potential significance of a specific subject to a specific audience, the content has greater or lesser impact upon an audience. In general, this potential significance has a framing function and is part of the ground of action. The detailed response, however, is induced by the structure given to the material. Electra's grief for the supposedly dead Orestes is an "idealized" formulation of suffering, organized in a pattern of mounting tension through which we sense the imminent explosion of sorrow but are tantalized by its retardation until the crux is reached. That pattern, independent of the specific case, induces parallel empathy in us. Particularly when that pattern is embodied in a living performer, the universal elements come to the fore, and we respond to the action as an immediate experience. Tentatively we may say that the associational, or feedback, factors establish preconditions, which either predispose or inhibit the process of empathic parallelism.

To understand this process more precisely, let us examine its temporal manifestation. As action unfolds, levels of intensity in the audience change, kinds of responses shift, one imaginative state succeeds another. Just as the action is somewhat "idealized" so are the responses "idealized." Indian theory accounts for this by distinguishing between life emotions and aesthetic emotions. Whether or not the two are essentially distinct need not concern us beyond recognizing that all aesthetic responses are highly crystallized states of being. Our imagination is concentrated and structured by the presentation. Because the action of a play moves forward rather rapidly, we are also more conscious than we would be in life that these successive states of emotion and thought follow one another; that is, they appear to have spatial dimension. Through the process of accretion, one segment builds a ground for the next.

The build-up of imaginative response, however, does not appear to progress gradually. Even in witnessing melodrama, a form arranged to produce thrills, our excitement does not mount evenly. In fact, it seems highly unlikely that intense reactions of any sort, in life or in the theater, reach a pitch through steady increment. Instead we respond in bursts. A story, a sight, triggers a flood of felt-thought. Our attention gradually mounts in interest; we then experience a sudden leap of intensification. That is why the crux of a segment is of such psychological import in dramatic art; it is at the moment of crux that the trigger is pulled. A line or a piece of business may trigger laughter. A crisis, culminating an action, may release the tension accumulated in the spectators.

To specify this aspect of empathic parallelism, I have borrowed another term from Gestalt psychology. The Gestalt psychologist speaks of *closure* in perception when the mind completes an immanent form. Closure is "the principle that behavior or mental process tends toward as complete, stable, or 'closed' a state as circumstances permit: e.g., an asymmetrical figure tends to be perceived as symmetrical, an unfinished act to be completed, an incomplete musical chord to be resolved, a meaningless object or situation to be perceived as having meaning." [25]

A similar imaginative process seems to occur in empathic parallelism. The action itself does not contain the audience's emotion, nor do the characters undergo the identical emotions of the audience, but the evolving action gradually shapes an empathy which, when triggered, completes itself, that is, undergoes closure. The feelings of anguish we may feel for Anne Frank are a result of the gap between the facts of history and the sensitivity of the girl. Our imagination leaps across the gap, closes the switch, reconciles the conflicting elements. But this can happen only if the components of project and resistance as well as figure and ground are properly focused and related. Closure, as a central process of empathic parallelism, is the spark that vitalizes the audience's imagination periodically as a prelude to the formation of the next gap.

Closure, it is important to stress, is imaginative, that is, it embraces emotive and cognitive response so that it not only releases a rush of feeling but also provokes a flash of awareness.[26] Often, in the process of closure, we enjoy a heightened insight into human experience. Unfortunately, this heightened sense, which is experienced during performance, is difficult to experience through reading a text. Furthermore, it does not occur automatically, but only when the shape of the action is artistically managed. Two aspects of closure may illustrate this point: timing and surprise.

Effective closure is achieved by a performer's skillful timing. This is most evident in comedy. The exact rhythm of delivering a line or making a gesture determines whether or not an audience will laugh. By expert timing the performer makes it possible for closure to occur. Yet it is not fundamentally different in noncomic drama. The timing of a movement or character reaction retards or accelerates an audience's kinesthetic and imaginative state, thus making closure possible. What seems to happen is that audience reception lags slightly behind presentation. As a performer delivers a line or completes a rhythm, he opens the gap into which the audience's imagination can run. Therefore, he needs to allow time for the audience to catch up (he pauses while they laugh or experience intensification) before continuing. By subtle manipulation of rhythm, he carries the audience along, periodically bringing it to closure.

In the process of projecting the shape of action and bringing the tension to a crux, the performer must also be aware of the counter-tendencies of the familiar and the unfamiliar. Wherever the patterns of tension are trite, the audience anticipates the empathic sequence and fails to maintain attention. Particularly if the type of crux is overly familiar or unclear, closure cannot take place. On the other hand, when the crux seems appropriate to the developing action and, at the same time, contains an element of surprise, it can then produce closure of immense explosive power. Again, comedy can illustrate this concept most easily. As a comedian tells a story, we become absorbed and are maintained at a plateau of absorption. The punch line effects closure, the quality of that closure being determined by the aptness and surprise of the line. The surprise need not be sensational. In performance it may consist merely of an unexpected rhythm. But where it consists of a particularly incisive activity, one that adds dimension to the preceding events, closure produces that total impact associated with the finest drama.

From the preceding discussion it is apparent that form of response is derived from the form of the action. By form, I do not mean an easily apprehended shape or arrangement that impresses itself upon our imagination as an object. Form in drama always seems to hover on the formless if it is to exercise its powers. To maintain the illusion of life, the drama must conceal the seams between the blocks of action, suggest the spontaneous (the immediate lacking knowledge of the future), and unravel tension from organic circumstances. Hence, undue attention to form during performance is a diversion, interfering with the empathic parallelism demanded by a theatrical experience. Once the life of a scene appears as the creation of an artist rather than the give-and-take of existence, it loses the organic autonomy essential to illusion.

The intimate connection between dramatic shape and audience response affects all questions of aesthetic proportion. Once we attempt to trace the empathic pattern for an entire play, we must know the capacity of an audience to encompass a presentation. This capacity is linked to the factor that Aristotle calls "magnitude." In chapter seven of *The Poetics*, he observes the importance of magnitude as well as order of parts for the achievement of beauty. Magnitude, or length, should be in accordance with the nature of the events so that an artistic arrangement is effected. Yet Aristotle also noted that length must be limited by the spectator's capacity to encompass the entire work imaginatively. Though he avoids strict formulation, he tends to urge a fairly compressed form and thus a short duration. His stress on a single action and a crucial moment of reversal and recognition further set limits to the length of a "beautiful" work.

The magnitude of a play is a product of both theatrical practice and the playwright's vision. The theater that Aristotle knew may have referred to legends and myths of enormous scope. Yet the regulations of the tragic contests, requiring the submission of four plays by each playwright, the four plays—three tragedies and one satyr play—all to be performed during one morning, forced the writers to operate within a narrow magnitude. Why such regulations should have arisen is difficult to explain. They may have stemmed from historical necessity or they may have been the expression of national temperament, whereby habit and taste insisted on strict limitation. Such taste, acquired partly through education, partly through native traditions, led the French to follow a similar practice in limiting the scope of their dramatic works.

By contrast, medieval and Elizabethan theater enjoyed a temporal and spatial magnitude unknown in classical Greece. From the thirteenth through the fifteenth centuries, playgoers were exposed to extended cycles of plays, frequently taking two or three days for a complete performance. They were not overwhelmed by the material partly because the stories, from the Scriptures or saintly legends, were repeated. Moreover, the playgoers carried outlines of the entire story from Genesis to the Day of Judgment in their minds. Such was the heritage of a sixteenth-century Englishman. To him the plays of the Elizabethan commercial theater, so extensive in comparison to classical drama, were of more limited magnitude than the cycle plays and, therefore, I would suspect, more easily comprehended.

As Aristotle noted, the magnitude of an art work is set by the audience's capacity to embrace that work in its imagination. He assumed, however, that the limits of that capacity were fixed, and they are not. Goethe, recognizing this, ridiculed Byron for maintaining the three unities, insisting that the true measure of a drama's dimensions is its "comprehensibility" by the audience.[27] Historical habit as well as artistic need determine the variety of incidents in a drama along with its length and spatial dimension. Elizabethan taste preferred multiplicity of plots. Continental playgoers of the nineteenth century were familiar with plays of limited magnitude: a compressed action, carefully arranged in a system of rising tension. Contemporary taste is in flux. Writers have been moving in two directions. On the one hand they have increasingly narrowed the range of drama, concentrating on brief vignettes of relatively undeveloped incidents. *The Zoo Story* and *The Dumb Waiter* are sketches. On the other hand, writers have also been extending the duration of action, lengthening their plays in actual time, encompassing more varied aspects of virtual life. Brecht has been a principal advocate of this extension, his method being the epic drama. Currently, the most radical changes are in a spatial direction. Segments and activities, lacking logical connection, are arranged in contextual patterns in order to penetrate the subcognitive level of audience awareness. Peter Weiss' *Marat/Sade* and Genet's *Screens* exhibit tendencies along this line. An understanding of dramatic design must take into account the magnitude of a work as well as the magnitude of the audience's imagination, for in each age the two must be congruent.

THE MEMORIAL EXPERIENCE AND MEANING

The memorial experience is not distinct from the theatrical but merely a continuation beyond direct contact with the presentation. The form of action induces the theatrical experience directly but has an indirect effect upon the memorial experience. When unable to return to the same artistic work, the playgoer must either avail himself of a facsimile, such as a second performance of the same production, or be content to recall the initial experience. Once removed from his fellow spectators, he gains a new perspective of the work. Responses elicited in performance may seem alien in retrospect. The process of rumination alters the work. As one recalls a performance, rarely is there awareness, let alone concern, with the artistic design. In recalling a poem or a painting, the form is palpable in the memory. Even the form of a novel is retained more readily, for example, by remembering the events from the author's point of view. But where drama has impact, it is recalled as life. Fictional characters take on flesh. Regardless of the style, where the fusion of the actual and ideal is achieved, we have the illusion of life. Memory plays tricks. We think we saw actions which were merely described or remembered by the characters, and we fill in the details of the sketch of life shown to us. Consequently, analysis based on such recall, unless it is trained recall, is likely to be distorted. Both artistic experience and artistic effect are equally important if we are to appreciate a performance fully. But it is the artistic experience that we must use as the foundation for our analysis of drama.

Generally there are two aspects of the memorial experience we need to examine: one concerns the ways we reexperience a presentation, the other the meanings we draw from it. On leaving a musical comedy, it was once common, if the work were attractive and the music appealing, for members of the audience to hum the tunes they had heard. It is no longer the fashion to expect such a bounty from the musical theater. Yet that form of repetition, in which snatches of speeches, phrases, tunes, and steps are absorbed and reenacted by an audience, nourishes the well-being of the theater. The absence of such repetition reflects a lack of impact and importance that theater can hold for its spectators. Partly in fun, partly in emulation, an earlier generation—or a small part of it—fresh from a viewing of *A Streetcar Named Desire*, echoed Marlon Brando's howl of "Stell-lahhhhh!" History has it that the defeated Athenian soldiers, abandoned in Sicily after the disastrous invasion of 416–413 B.C., begged food from the peasants by singing snatches of choruses from Euripides' plays.[28] A strong and penetrating theatrical image excites the urge to reenact it. A sign of the power of a work is absorption of its key phrases and gestures into everyday experience.

Another form of repetition, which is interior rather than expressive, assumes the character of images. Strong theatrical activity may impress itself so vividly upon the mind that the original is reformed in the imagination without need for reenactment. I can vividly "see" Judith Anderson as Lady Macbeth after her visit to Duncan's death chamber. As she descended the castle steps, having summoned all her strength to place the bloody daggers next to the besmeared grooms, she retched violently, projecting in that abdominal contraction her utter revulsion at the murder. Memory of this image brings back my original empathic response to the entire scene. Nor is such a remembrance unusual. All playgoers recall similar theatrical experiences. Vivid sounds or sights or responses, preserved by the clarity of dramatic form, remain as personal memories upon which an individual can draw. This type of interior response is not sharply separated from expressive repetition. One flows into the other, arising from the store of impact a work has had upon the imagination.

Similar to the previous forms of repetition but operating at another level of behavior are the ways in which individuals often reinterpret their own lives in accordance with a dramatic style, thereby adding the new dimension alluded to earlier in this chapter. Perhaps this process may be more powerfully seen in the motion pictures although it is also a function of theater. The repetition of "Stell-lahhhhh" was symptomatic of a wider effect. Largely from the image created by Marlon Brando in that play and then given broader coverage in film, emerged the figure of "the rebel without cause." It took the form of a semiarticulate, sexually-oriented, self-contained masculine figure, brooding in behavior, alternately explosive and self-absorbed. Oddly enough the character Brando represented in *Streetcar* was a super-American type. But the image he created became associated with nonconformism, exciting emulation and imitation for a number of years. Few examples are quite so striking as this one, but other works that aroused people to reinterpret their own lives in terms defined by the theater include *Death of a Salesman, Who's Afraid of Virginia Woolf?,* and *Look Back in Anger.* The purpose of a dramatic presentation may not necessarily be to effect imitation by the audience, but a reflection of a play's (and the theater's) power will always be the degree to which it elicits repetition.

Although repetition and reinterpretation are reverberations of meaningful response, they are not usually included in any discussion of dramatic meaning. When critics speak of meaning in drama, they refer to the playwright's guiding purpose in creating the drama and a "true" interpretation of that purpose. It is against such an approach that Marshall McLuhan inveighs when he remarks that "concern with *effect* rather than *meaning* is a basic change of our electric time." [29] This may be so, and my own emphasis on the theatrical experience reflects that change. Nevertheless, we cannot totally ignore the aspect of the artistic experience concerned with "meaning," or "thought." There is no such thing as pure effect, experience, or entertainment. Every presentational activity is a sign from which a variety of meanings can be drawn.

Theatrical meaning may be divided into four levels, or perhaps more accurately, four aspects.[30] These aspects are the descriptive, participational, referential, and conceptual. The descriptive aspect most exactly parallels the literal level of medieval interpretation; it is concerned with accurate recognition of dramatic activity. The participational aspect, which covers the relation between the art being created and the auditor responding *at the moment* of creation, is not peculiar to theater or to any other performing art. But in the theater, participation is both more complex and all-encompassing, making this aspect of meaning so much more central to the total experience. The referential aspect embraces all kinds of associations between the articulated activity and non-theatrical experience. Lastly, the conceptual aspect includes all imaginative abstractions aroused by a theatrical work.

The descriptive aspect of meaning, represented by the type of analysis outlined in the previous chapter, is also the most obvious. It is the aspect of simple recognition. Normally, given a presentation that remains within the audience's frame of reference, no problem of descriptive meaning arises. As the events of a play unfold, an audience immediately perceives motion as activity. It knows what is happening in front of its eyes. To an American audience, especially a New York audience, *Death of a Salesman* is eminently lucid. The kind of man a salesman was and the kind of salesman Willy was posed no uncertainty to the playgoer and so the incidents were absorbed without conscious effort. But when the play was initially produced in England, the audience could not understand a salesman such as Willy, and so they found it difficult to respond. The problems posed by frame of reference may thus be a result of unfamiliar subject matter, as in the instance just cited, or of unfamiliar theatrical conventions. Only gradually have Chekhov's plays been accepted by playgoers, not mainly because of the subject matter, however, for the stagnancy of middle-class society in provincial Russia though unfamiliar, was not difficult to grasp. The principal impediment was the unfamiliar style, with its apparent aimlessness, its action of low amplitude, which was elusive to the uncultivated imagination, and its undefined tone of comedic tragedy that initially alienated audiences and to which they have become accustomed only gradually. *Endgame,* too, is a work that, though more readily accepted, has nevertheless puzzled audiences. Because the descriptive meaning is not familiar, the auditor is impatient with what he recognizes and wishes immediately to see the significance represented by the unfamiliar sights of Nagg in an ashcan, stiff-legged Clov scanning the without, the bi-fenestrated room, and other concrete but unexpected activities. There is a danger, however, in by-passing the descriptive meaning and rushing immediately to interpret the activity on an allegoric or anagogic plane. Because all other meanings rest ultimately on the apperception of the descriptive meaning, the first task for the spectator is to know what lies before him. How much more essential is this for a play reader, who is still further removed from the artistic experience!

The participational process in art is common to all media. A person looking at a painting or reading a book undergoes a contact with the work that is no less complex than his contact with a presentation of dance or drama. In theater, however, the importance of the participational process is much more decisive; in the first instances the individual comes into contact with a finished work, but in the theater the individual is in contact with a *nearly* finished work. How nearly finished the work may be varies with the type of presentation and the theatrical circumstances. Yet, regardless of the degree of variation, the theatrical experience consists of the simultaneity of creation and reception. I have emphasized the dependence of the audience response on the shape of action. During the run of a play, that shape of action, as illustrated in the scenes previously analyzed, retains its basic form in performance after performance. In the commercial theater, for instance, when an actor replaces the original performer of a role, he is expected to follow the format of his predecessor, a format that success has sanctified. But, even when the essential shape of a scene is repeated, the manner in which it is filled by the spontaneous energies of the performer often produces a significantly distinctive theatrical experience. All the patient care of rehearsal and planning is for the purpose of presenting a spontaneous moment, a moment that is unique to that company and that audience at a particular time.

By participational aspect of meaning, I refer to those particular features of a presentation to which an audience attaches itself and to which it can respond. The structure of action is the skeleton of that participational process. But the flesh of that skeleton, the theatrical activity, has a texture: sound, visions, physical motion. Theater involves the senses of an audience more completely than almost any other artistic form. That is both an advantage and a disadvantage. Concentration of effect can often be better achieved when an artist is working through one sense, such as the eye in reading. The advantage, if it is truly utilized, is that the theater reaches the total human being as kinesthetic stimulation. In addition to sound, sight, and physical being, there is space, that is, the space in which the audience and the performer are joined. There is also the presence and proximity of other people and the concentration of the time span. Because of this totality of involvement, the participational aspect of meaning functions even when there is a lack of understanding on the descriptive level. Whether or not we recognize the activity segments in *Endgame* for what they are, we are absorbed into the mood and rhythm of the piece. The structure of the vaudeville routine administers its little shock whether or not we know what the routine is. Obviously, the participational aspect of meaning is but weakly represented by a reading of the text; only during performance does its full weight become apparent. We cannot grasp that aspect of meaning by imagining it or reading about it, because it is accessible only to those *within* the event. When we think about a play or a theatrical experience, we are outside the event. We cannot participate in it and cannot know it. Once within it, that is, once we are participating in the presentation itself, we are no longer outsiders looking in. Thus, the participational and conceptual aspects seem mutually exclusive. Only when experienced as a flash of awareness, can conceptualization be a legitimate part of the participational process.

In tracing the workings of empathic parallelism, I have shown how the rhythm of a work triggers response, and how imagination becomes attached to differing features of the action. Though I may reiterate a bit, I should like to define the range of participation in the present context. The sequence in which we vicariously participate contains elements of the wondrous and familiar. It is this mixture that enables us to open ourselves freely to the theatrical presentation. By a happy stroke of invention, we are offered an action that is somewhat unusual (the fairy-tale world of Brecht, the sex-laden, death-laden atmosphere of the New Orleans Latin Quarter). There must always be this romantic strain in the presentation. Yet the action also contains, either in its activity or in its crises, a familiar element. It may be a wave of emotion, a social attitude, or elements of behavior. The action, composed of its wondrous and familiar parts, has the potential for becoming a metaphor of experience. The more acutely the metaphor structures unresolved imaginative (emotional, psychological, intellectual) states, the stronger the participational response is likely to be. On a superficial level of entertainment, closure occurs when there is give-and-take between performer and spectator. Closure also occurs on a more pervasive psychological and spiritual level when the metaphor of action crystallizes partially formed thoughts and emotions. Both *Death of a Salesman* and *A Streetcar Named Desire* were such apt metaphors of action, transforming the minds of playgoers in the late forties and early fifties *Marat/Sade* has had a similar archetypal response in the sixties. These metaphors fuse action and moment. With the greatest works, those of the Greeks and Shakespeare, the texts offer promise for the creation of just such pervasive metaphors. Unfortunately, we have to admit that few classical productions achieve the promise of the script. The fusion between text and moment is not easily managed. It is simply not enough to put on modern dress. To achieve the proper fusion of wondrous and familiar requires a faithfulness to the search for the essential as mirrored in the immediate. Greek tragedy has immense potential for penetrating response. The path to that potential is partly technical, partly imaginative, but few know how to walk it. Yet only when the participational aspect of meaning is part of the total meaning of a work can we really speak of meaning. Unfortunately, the thrill and joy that are indispensable features of participation are insufficiently present in current theater. Without them participation lacks substance and without that participational experience a presentation lacks meaning. A text incapable of arousing such thrill and joy is no longer a theatrical text but a literary remain. An interpretation of such a text that discounts or ignores its participational experience is a crippled interpretation.

The third aspect of meaning, the referential, overlaps both the theatrical and the memorial experience. As stated earlier, the descriptive aspect of meaning presupposes a frame of reference. Within the frame of reference, audience predisposition comes into play. That predisposition may be excited, yet confirmed, as we have seen. Or it may be challenged. Through the ages we have had example after example where the theater violated expectation, presenting a work which ran athwart the social or aesthetic preconceptions of the audience. Ibsen's career illustrates instances in which he shattered the audience's frame of reference by introducing hitherto excluded subjects. Chekhov, as we have seen, shattered aesthetic sensibilities somewhat more than the social. But whether accommodating or outraging an audience, a presentation is understood in terms of a frame of reference.

Realism and naturalism accustomed audiences to relate what they saw onstage to actuality. The stress on contemporary setting, colloquial speech, and topical problems supported such association. In this frame of reference the microcosm on stage was a fragment of a larger life that went on in the nontheatrical world. Instead of being an archetype of central features of human nature, Hedda Gabler was representative of a kind of contemporary woman. The method was clinical. The spectators were not all Heddas but did live in a world where there were Heddas. In witnessing a realistic play, we are prone to consider whether or not it is true or credible, that is, whether what we see actually could or could not happen. Such an aesthetic frame is slowly disappearing.

An alternate frame of reference may be exemplified by the Shakespearean play. Instead of being a portion of a whole, Shakespeare's plays are microcosms in themselves. *King Lear* is not part of a larger world, insofar as events are concerned. As a microcosm, the play is a model of a universe. There is only one Lear, but within him are contained the emotional states common to all men. The immediate connection between audience and action is less apparent. The events are constructions to elicit participation rather than representations to evoke associations which would in turn elicit participation. In general, the outer frame of events—plot, for instance—tends to be wondrous; the inner connection to events—the passions, for instance—tends to be familiar. A generation ago, this frame of reference seemed remote. Now, however, current taste is shifting closer to the Shakespearean view. Instead of conceiving stage life as a fragment of actual life, we are coming to see stage life as a model of universal experience. In short, we are shifting our frame of reference.

Within this context, then, the referential aspect of meaning depends on what traditional or contemporary features of existence a work relates to. In some instances the references are distinct.

Riders to the Sea is a fragment, although a highly artistic fragment, of life on the Aran Islands. *The Caucasian Chalk Circle,* though supposedly dealing with life in the Caucasus, suggests only general features of the life there, so general in fact that we regard the scenes not as images of actual life but as images of an idea of that life. Referential meaning does not emerge from the fact that we are seeing a world that exists but from the recognition of contemporary social issues in legendary form. This play avoids the allegoric, for it does not systematically illustrate a thesis but reiterates and varies the images of exploitation and sacrifice that illustrate such an outlook. In this work the references are tinged with irony.

The participational aspect of meaning, as we have seen, is wedded to the structure of the action, for the rhythm of response is a product of that structure. But how does the referential aspect relate to the action? A segment of action is a fusion of the strange and familiar. Both the strange and familiar can arouse associations, but it is the familiar that gives us a stake in the action. By presenting the unusual and, at the same time, by connecting the events to our own lives, an author simultaneously gives us something new to respond to at the same time that he relates the new to something which is already familiar. Blanche represents an alien figure of a dying aristocracy. But in her longing for culture, her search for protection, her yearning for magic, she touches a nerve in us so that part of us has a stake in her outcome, at the same time that another part of us sees her as representative of the Blanches of this world. We do not identify with her as a person, but with a common human impulse that she embodies.

Some of a play's references may become apparent as we watch a performance. Additional connections between the work and other historical and intellectual experiences become evident as we recall the performance. At the memorial level, the referential aspect begins to merge with the conceptual. As we meditate upon the performance, attempting to construct a pattern of references, we shift into interpretation. Our goal is no longer to experience but to arrive at definitive answers. A more abstract meaning emerges as we begin to connect the work with some realm of thought: philosophical, social, political, religious, and so forth.

Conceptual meaning removes us from immediate contact with

the theatrical experience. A performance or a reading provokes within us not only the imaginative experience but the desire to trace the implications of the imaginative experience to ultimate conclusions. We stand outside a work and consider what each of the parts means. Meaning here represents abstract meaning. We have shifted from a concern with imaginative and experiential possibilities to interpretive answers. We attempt to complete these sentences: This play means . . . The theme of this play is . . . These formulations, all too common, are deceptive, however. Conceptually, a play does not mean; it *provokes* meanings. If properly pursued, a presentation has sparked participational and referential meanings, which in turn provoke implications. Stirred by a play, we may detach these implications from their source and examine them in ever widening circles of application to human thought or experience. But we should not mistake the implications for the experience itself.

A play such as *Endgame* may stimulate the sensation of the timelessness with which we approach death. That is participational. When, as a consequence, we are stirred by this sensation to see in the play the analogue of the end of the world or the destruction of Christianity or the bleak darkening of man's brain, we have moved to the conceptual plane, where the rules are different and the connection with the text less certain. The structure of action does not change with time; conceptual meaning does. The end of conceptualization is philosophy, or what Eric Bentley more properly advises, "wisdom." [31] The end of presentation is experience. When that experience is powerful enough, it provokes a wide range of imaginative effects, one, but only one, of which is conceptualization.

For the most part contemporary theater criticism is conceptual. Scholars do describe the text though not necessarily the action. Some attention is given to reference, but the bulk of attention is devoted to interpretation of the conceptual sort. It is this sort of interpretation that is encouraged by schools and universities with the result that few students are capable of reading or viewing a play accurately. They all rush to results, treating the text as a puzzle to be deciphered, a riddle to be unraveled. They lack the patience and the preparation to absorb a work, and wish to define rather than experience it.

The process of analysis I am outlining is one means of becoming attuned to a dramatic work. Polanyi cites W. Dilthey and T. Lipps on the idea of in-dwelling. "Dilthey taught that the mind of a person can be understood only by reliving its workings; and Lipps represented aesthetic appreciation as an entering into a work of art and thus dwelling in the mind of its creator." Polanyi extends this concept of in-dwelling to all knowledge, scientific as well as humanistic, showing that we can master a skill, understand a process, or grasp an idea only by "interiorizing" it, that is, through "reliving its workings." [32] How important this concept is for drama!

The text is an outline for a performance. The performance, a stimulant to experience, provokes a range of meanings. How are we to move from the text to this range of meanings? Witnessing performances and by absorbing them *isomorphically* is one way. But insofar as we read the text, whether as prospective performers or not, we must learn to dwell within the material, to relive its intangible but palpable shape of action. At the center, then, lies our contact with the work. As we get further from this center a halo of memory remains, partly participational, partly conceptual. Our minds may play freely with the images that the experience has stimulated, but we should not confuse these images with the experience that provoked them. Instead we shall find that the total theatrical-memorial experience has immense range and depth. By dwelling within it, we extend ourselves.

5 Organization

Rarely in life are we ever able to encompass all segments of action within a total perception. We are aware of what happens to others or to ourselves in fragmentary sequences. Our urge to understand exceeds our imaginative grasp. Even when we gain a sense of the whole, we are unsure that new insights or fresh information may not alter our comprehension. Just when one school of historians nicely demonstrates the unity of the Renaissance, succeeding scholars discount such unity by arguing that events must be grouped in quite another way. What is true of our perception of history is equally true of our perception of daily events: We see our lives in parts; the present seems permanent, the unity with the past and future uncertain.

Drama gives an illusion of wholeness to the disorder of life. A play is an arrangement of segments of action. The arrangement is the dramatist's imprint of meaning upon man's passage through time. The purpose of analysis is to distinguish between segments and yet perceive the totality they compose. In analyzing a play in its entirety, it is necessary to discover to what extent the external context of the play affects the internal arrangement of parts, and how these parts are linked together structurally and imaginatively.

CONTEXT OF
DRAMA

A play is an abstract of a larger action—the events onstage are but a portion of all events embracing the play, and the locales presented are but fragments of a broader panorama. The action on-stage exists within more extensive dimensions of time and space, which are intimated but not directly presented. In *Riders to the Sea*, Synge makes us aware of the contiguous spatial dimension through references to the pier and people at the dock, through the presence of fishing nets, and possibly, through the distant roar of the sea. He also makes us aware of the larger temporal dimension in the report of Michael's death and Maurya's lament over a lifetime of lost men. Synge's method, one commonly followed, is to abstract the events from a time-space continuum. In this selective process the dramatist looks for a crucial period in the natural continuity of life. Structurally, this is also characteristic of Greek tragedy, where the activity presented is a crucial moment of an extensive cycle, although the selection is based upon legend rather than observable experience. In Greek tragedy, however, where the presence of the larger world is evoked through messenger speeches and choral odes, the temporal and spatial contiguity between onstage activity and offstage events is somewhat less emphasized than in the more naturalistic style of *Riders to the Sea.*

In Shakespeare's works, the offstage-onstage relationship is quite different. Rarely is there stress on an extended spatial action. Although Duncan is dining just out of earshot (*Macbeth,* I, vii), Shakespeare provides no offstage sounds or activity. He merely illustrates what is happening by having several servants cross the stage at the commencement of the scene. In his handling of time, he also rarely depends upon the suggestion of offstage duration, although his plays cover extended periods of time. He creates the sensation of passing time without giving much information as to how it passes and thus produces the effect of compactness and extensiveness simultaneously. Instead of seeking a contiguity between onstage and offstage events, he reflects the impact of the central action in subsidiary scenes. The exchange between the Old Man and Ross, for instance, demonstrates a reverberating response to Duncan's murder. This method of dramatized commentary appears even in Shakespeare's earliest works. In *Henry VI, Part III,* for example, in order to show how the breakdown of political authority leads to the destruction of all authority and humanity, Shakespeare introduces paired segments in which he presents a father who has just killed his son and a son who has just killed his father (II, v). These segments are *exempla* and the method *exemplary* in contrast to the naturalistic method, which is *contextual.*

To make a distinction between what is shown to an audience and what is suggested, it would be well to adapt two words that already imply—or nearly do—such a relationship. The word *plot* signifies the sequence of events, or incidents, in a play, but since an "event," or "incident," is merely a summary term for a segment of activity, a plot is the sequence of units of activity. By contrast, the word *story* seems to have broader significance and will be used to designate all incidents and activities that occur before, after, and during the play, onstage and offstage. Thus, the story of *Oedipus* includes the suicide of Jocasta *and* the self-inflicted blinding of Oedipus. The plot, on the other hand, includes a messenger revealing these incidents. The plot of *Oedipus* commences with the confrontation of the chorus and Oedipus, the story, with the prophecies of Apollo to Laius and Jocasta before Oedipus is born. A playwright sets preconditions for his dramatic structure by the kind of proportion he establishes between plot and story.

The ratio of plot and story is a reflection of the magnitude of the play as conceived by the artist. As previously shown, the concept of magnitude (discussed in Chapter Four, pp. 155ff.) relates both to aesthetic proportion as well as to socio-aesthetic habits. Although there are certain basic technical and artistic problems in unifying a theatrical presentation arising from the nature of the theatrical medium itself, there are also tendencies to stress different solutions depending upon the magnitude of a work. The greater the magnitude, the more difficult it is for the artist to utilize dramatic causation as a unifying element. The character of climactic action also differs considerably, depending upon whether the magnitude is compact or expansive. Through a consideration of the plot-story ratio, one gains insight into the intended scope of a work, and thereby into the problem of how the parts relate to the audience and to each other.

The history of drama makes it quite evident that *magnitude,* and therefore the plot-story ratio, has a historical character. Each dramatic period seems to stress a particular type of ratio, leaning either toward a compact or an expansive form. Whatever the ratio, it is not purely theoretical or technical in nature, but represents a deeper artistic choice of successive generations of dramatists. In effect, it places man in perspective: the narrower the magnitude, the greater the impression of man as a trapped creature; the broader the magnitude, the stronger the sense of man as wanderer. Of the previously mentioned plays, I would say that the magnitude of *Hedda Gabler* is narrower than *King Lear* and that of *King Lear* narrower than the *Caucasian Chalk Circle.*[1]

The selection of stories and the sources from which they stem establish a preliminary and significant relation of audience to action. When the source is religious myth, the story immediately establishes a communal frame of reference for the individual experience. When the source is romance and Renaissance history, as in Shakespeare's day, the story promises the audience adventure. The most revolutionary change in European theater occurred when artists went to observed life for story material. Menander and the other writers of New Comedy may have been the first to take that step, but the Romans merely adopted their stories and settings, not their practice, and therefore it was not until the seventeenth century for comedy and the eighteenth century for the rest of drama that dramatists consistently utilized contemporary life as a story source. Although it is true that until then observed experience had always found its way into the drama in some manner, it had done so within the frame of myth, legend, and romance. In the nineteenth century the practice of selecting story from life triumphed and, though frequently challenged, still remains the dominant method for the creation of plot. Audiences have come to see the stories as documentary cases subject to the test of personal credibility.

Each of these methods for selecting stories imposes conditions upon organizing plot. Myth and legend, because they are common knowledge, lend themselves to short pieces. It is not by chance that both Greek tragedy and medieval drama relied on what is, in effect, a one-act form. Renaissance drama, particularly that of the English, required lengthier pieces to encompass the more complex adventures and romances so dear to the heart of the audience. In the nineteenth century the use of natural activity as a story source led to two structural choices in the shaping of plot. Either the plot dealt with the final and crucial events of a story or it exposed three or four crucial periods. Ibsen resorted to the first procedure, his plot beginning late in the story and then continuing without interruption to the end while suggesting continuity of the story. Chekhov resorted to the second procedure. His plot also begins at a crucial point, but a less climactic one, and then proceeds in four major units to a conclusion. Both methods depend upon the careful unfolding of character relations in formal segments of twenty to forty minutes in length. Both writers, by seeking to exploit the realistic story sources, were obliged to develop compact plots.

Depending upon its story source and its plot-story ratio, a play emphasizes or minimizes the impression of continuity between life and art. Naturalism, in the main, emphasizes this continuity psychologically and aesthetically. By creating the illusion that the plot flows out of previous events into succeeding events (returning to life, as it were), naturalism reduces as much as possible the illusion of "aesthetic distance." Naturalistic play endings illustrate this intention most obviously. Life in *The Cherry Orchard*, even if it is the same life, goes on for Madame Ranevsky, for Lopahin, for all the souls, even Fiers, who waits for death in the shuttered house. Down go the cherry trees. Back to Paris and a tedious repetition of her pathetic love affair goes Madame Ranevsky. On to a more shabby service goes Varya. An era comes to an end, but life does not, and Chekhov is at pains to emphasize this.

In contrast, the structural character of most Shakespearean plays is more self-contained. The ratio of plot and story is virtually one-to-one. There is much less spatial connection between onstage and offstage life. The plays end with sharper definition. The fictional events, by being separated in time and/or place from contemporary England, seem aesthetically remote. Again, a look at conclusions will illustrate prevailing practice. Most Shakespearean plays end with some formal activity: a trial (by combat or by judicial hearing) or a discovery of a person's true identity (as a prelude to marriage). The audience is not encouraged to think beyond the events. Who, for example, wonders whether Orlando and Rosalind will have children or how Cassio will rule Cyprus?[2] If one does so, it is without the encouragement of the dramatist.

These Chekhovian and Shakespearean conclusions illustrate only two ways in which the plot-story ratio is expressed in dramatic structure. The first blurs the line between play and life, the second highlights that line. By historical practice or personal genius, a theater artist develops characteristic modes of connecting and separating his presentation from the life of the audience. The extent and quality of both connections and distinctions are initially determined by the source and magnitude of the story and by the story's relation to plot.

DETERMINING FACTORS IN DRAMATIC ARRANGEMENT

Once the magnitude of a play is decided, whether by theatrical convention or individual artistic choice, the internal arrangement of a drama—namely, the sequence of its segments and the dynamic interplay between them—is determined by the dramatist's treatment of causation, repetition, and emphasis. His handling of causation determines the extent to which one segment will depend upon another. His use of repetition creates a pattern of juxtaposition and/or intensification. How and where he places emphasis affects the overall structure of the work. By controlling these three factors, he can produce a highly complex dramatic arrangement.

Causation

One part placed after another makes a sequence. The moment the sequence has a logic, that is, the moment a guiding principle determines which part shall follow which, we have causation. Causation is not necessarily inherent in the parts themselves, but in our perception of the relationship of the parts to each other. Albert Michotte has shown in *The Perception of Causality* that "the impression of causality is dependent on specific and narrowly limited spatio-temporal features of the event observed." [3] It is self-evident that every act has a precedent and that no activity springs into existence spontaneously. But the isolation and perception of causes is quite another matter. A man rubs his jaw; another man rubs his fist. Perceiving this conjunction (these narrowly limited spatio-temporal features), we assume that the second man has struck the first. In life we continuously deduce causes from such critical conjunctions and at the same time experience uncertainty about our perceptions. As Michotte demonstrates, it is not what happens, but what we think happens that constitutes our awareness of causation.

We are particularly sensitive to this at the present time, when in every sphere of contemporary life the definition of causes is becoming increasingly elusive. Revolutionary change, with its impulsive eruptions and propagandist temperament, baffles the cause-seeker. Whether we consider psychological or social phenomena, we encounter acts the causes of which we cannot readily identify. Over the last half a century science, notably physics, has evolved a probabilistic conception of physical matter that holds that material motions cannot be isolated in specific circumstances but merely generalized. As the atomic physicist has learned, he cannot predict the path of an individual particle although he can predict the probable paths of a sample of particles. The linking of a specific cause or causes to these effects is out of the question. Only a general basis for the behavior of matter can be formulated. This difficulty in isolating causes, so great in the physical sciences, is compounded in the social sciences where human variables are not only more complex than material variables but also more resistant to detection. Naturally, this philosophy has had its effect upon contemporary treatment of dramatic causation.

Each age tends to perceive causation in a distinctive way, not necessarily alien to other points of view but organically linked to its own historical circumstance. Each author seems to work within a common conception of the causes of human activity. Each distills a special emphasis from the common outlook. Before the nineteenth century, for instance, we do not often encounter drama in which past childhood experience is the determinant of adult behavior. Only in this century does man so thoroughly venerate and investigate the stages of childhood. How has the drama responded? Either by exposing the sources of action in childhood or by presenting, over and over again, the maturation of the human being. Be it Wedekind or Strindberg, O'Neill or Williams, the playwright finds in the infant experience a vital reservoir for understanding adult activity.

In every drama we will find a pattern of causation, which is the analogue of the artist's perception of how causes work in life. It is true, of course, that the hack writer, the so-called commercial writer, adopts wholesale patterns of causation created by more imaginative dramatists. But all original writers abstract from life, consciously or not, patterns of causation for human behavior. These patterns can be distinguished according to four principal characteristics: source, compactness, specificity, and perceptibility.

SOURCE: Although the source of human action is elusive, each period acts upon the premise that such-or-such is the cause of behavior. Since Ferdinand Brunetière expounded his theory of conflict in drama, the basis of which was the human will, critics and directors and actors have explored the will of dramatic characters to discover the motive of action. Much of the language of Stanislavski centers about the words "want" and "objective," as though the human being were part of a mechanistic universe where he is set in motion by the force of will toward a specified end. But even as Stanislavski was formulating this conception of motivation, views of human behavior were shifting from a mechanistic to a more probablistic outlook.

Arthur Miller embodies a continuation of the mechanistic tradition, Tennessee Williams departs from it. Although Miller and Williams include both social dislocation and sexual desire as the sources of behavior, Miller stresses the former, Williams the latter. For Miller the true center of behavior rests in the will. He himself notes that he stresses incidents that bring man to a moment of critical decision. "I understand the symbolic meaning of a character and his career to consist of the kind of commitment he makes to life or refuses to make . . . [However differently the dramatic elements are treated, they are all formed] to the end that that moment of commitment be brought forth." [4] Either because of this preoccupation or of some artistic limitation, the sexuality of Miller's characters turns out to be synthetic. Quite the contrary for Williams. His social framework is more convincing than Miller's sexual motivations, but in his plays the true center rests within the instinct for the destructive and fulfilling release of the sexual experience.

Being of the same generation as these two playwrights, we can readily perceive the ambience from which their conceptions proceed. But we must also recognize the difficulty in perceiving sympathetically the sources of behavior in former times. Consider merely the matter of consistency. We tend to look for uniform behavior in people. We are stunned by the kindly matron who suddenly knifes her husband, expecting to find in some infantile source or domestic history a reason for her unexpected behavior. We wish to regularize the picture. This is in marked contrast to Elizabethan expectations. The Elizabethans took it for granted that individuals were quite capable of exhibiting radically inconsistent behavior, especially when possessed by passion. In accordance with modern psychological predilections, Laurence Olivier has depicted the roots of Othello's jealousy in longstanding self-deception.[5] Such an interpretation is not only stimulating but also satisfies our desire for consistency. It contradicts the Shakespearean view, however, for Othello is unmistakably transformed not because he formerly bore the seeds of rage within him but because, being a man, he has the capability of such rage once his judgment is undermined. Perhaps one of the reasons that some Shakespearean plays seem to lack unity is that the Elizabethan conception of causation differs so much from ours.[6]

COMPACTNESS: The causative link between one action and another may be either loose or tight. Ibsen, the master of tight causation, shows how each act is the immediate result of the preceding act. But not only is the effect a result of that act, but the degree of pressure exerted by one action is just the degree needed to produce the result. In the episode from *Hedda Gabler* discussed in Chapter Three, Brack exerts just so much pressure, but no more, to achieve the result he wants. By contrast, the causation of *The Caucasian Chalk Circle* is considerably looser. The Iron Shirts make Azdak a judge purely out of whim. The action does not arise from a preceding episode in a tightly linked chain of cause and effect.

SPECIFICITY: This characteristic of causation is closely related to the matter of compactness. Causes may be specific or general. They may be specific in both their source and their compactness. Othello's suspicion of Desdemona has a specific cause in Iago's slander, but the way he behaves arises from man's general potential for uncontrolled jealousy. A close look at Othello's passion in comparison to Leontes' in *The Winter's Tale* reveals great similarity, not in circumstances but in behavior. Although we are speaking only of degrees of causal specificity, we find that dramatists have a tendency to posit either particular history as the force behind events (such as Hedda's boredom, which arises from her status in a genteel, bourgeois society) or quite broad impulses, not rooted historically but inhering generally in human nature (such as Arnolphe's folly or Harpagon's miserliness) as the cause of activity.

PERCEPTIBILITY: Where causation tends to be specific and tight, it also tends to be perceptible. In Ibsen's drama, the unfolding of causes is one of the principal purposes of the action. But in drama where the causation is general and loose, as in Shakespeare's works, the causation is often taken for granted and, therefore, not expressly revealed. Yet readers and critics vainly scour the plays for hints of Iago's, Cordelia's, and Coriolanus' motivations.

During the course of my analysis of causation I have referred frequently to character traits. Recent dramatic and histrionic theory has presumed that the central element of characterization is motivation, by which is meant the exertion of will or the submission to drives. The matter is more complex, however. Character is a summary term. We do not experience character; we describe it or respond to it on the basis of appearance and act. At any one moment in a play, character is the descriptive total of what one knows of a person. The importance of causation to characterization depends upon the degree to which a society individualizes the reasons for a person's behavior. The twentieth century, at least until the present, has concentrated considerable attention upon these reasons. Earlier periods, seeing similarity of motivation rather than differences, took cause for granted and found greater interest in effect. (For a full discussion of character, see pp. 210ff.)

Juxtaposition and repetition

Along with causation, the factor that affects the connection of parts most significantly is juxtaposition. Causation implies an organic temporal connection between one thing and another. A gives direct rise to B. Juxtaposition implies relationships that are evident but not connected organically. A sees a man, fastidiously attired, with a handsome silk scarf. Later A meets another man, shabbily dressed. By chance, the second man wears a soiled duplicate of the first man's scarf. No connection exists between the two men, but through A's perception of the coincidence a connection is made. This connection may spark all sorts of thoughts or feelings within A, the similarity in the midst of diversity triggering emotional and mental reverberations.

Such juxtaposition is essentially structural. The observer recognizes similarities or contrasts in form without being able to account for them in source. In life such juxtaposition is fortuitous; in drama, it is artistically devised to stimulate a web of cognitive and affective responses. A dramatist may juxtapose characters, dialogue, activities, or all three. He may do so spatially or temporally. At the end of *The Three Sisters* Chekhov contrasts Olga's cry that there must be a reason for life with Tchebutykin's refrain that nothing matters. This is an example of oblique spatial contrast, for the two speakers, though on the stage together, are not aware of each other.

Temporal juxtaposition emerges in the form of activity repetition. Even where contrast is intended, repetition of certain similar features is introduced in order to accent the differences. *The Cherry Orchard*, otherwise causatively arranged, illustrates how Chekhov repeats fragmentary bits of action in order to reveal changes in his characters. Embedded in Acts II and IV are two analogous confrontations between the student Trofimoff and the merchant Lopahin. At one point in Act II, as Trofimoff enters with Anya and Varya, Lopahin mocks him.

LOPAHIN: Our perennial student is always strolling with the young ladies.
TROFIMOFF: It's none of your business.
LOPAHIN: He will soon be fifty and he's still a student.
TROFIMOFF: Stop your stupid jokes.
LOPAHIN: But why are you so peevish, you queer duck?
TROFIMOFF: Don't you pester me.
LOPAHIN (*laughing*): Permit me to ask you, what do you make of me?
TROFIMOFF: Yermolay Alexeevich, I make this of you: you are a rich man, you'll soon be a millionaire. Just as it is in the metabolism of

nature, a wild beast is needed to eat up everything that comes his
way; so you, too, are needed.

Everyone laughs.

In Act IV the following exchange occurs. The house is about to be
closed; Trofimoff is about to depart.

LOPAHIN: Here, drink a glass.
TROFIMOFF: I shan't.
LOPAHIN: It's to Moscow now?
TROFIMOFF: Yes. I'll see them off to town, and tomorrow to Moscow.
LOPAHIN: Yes— Maybe the professors are not giving their lectures. I
  imagine they are waiting till you arrive.
TROFIMOFF: That's none of your business.
LOPAHIN: How many years is it you've been studying at the University?
TROFIMOFF: Think of something newer. This is old and flat. (*Looking
  for his rubbers*) You know, perhaps, we shall not see each other
  again; therefore, permit me to give you one piece of advice at part-
  ing! Don't wave your arms! Cure yourself of that habit—of arm
  waving. And also of building summer cottages, figuring that the summer residents will in time become individual landowners; figuring
  like that is arm waving too— Just the same, however, I like you.
  You have delicate soft fingers like an artist, you have a delicate soft
  heart—
LOPAHIN (*embracing him*): Good-by, my dear boy.

These two segments are similar in content, but different in their
conclusions. The basic pattern consists of Lopahin teasing Trofimoff for being a "perennial student," of Trofimoff churlishly re-
sisting ("none of your business"), and then anatomizing Lopahin,
the first time at Lopahin's invitation, the second on his own initiative. Though the words are slightly different, the structure of activity in both segments is the same. The repetition of teasing and
irritated reaction highlights the change of attitude conveyed by
Trofimoff's two descriptions of Lopahin. In the second segment
Trofimoff is about to lecture Lopahin again, but then interrupts
himself to express simple affection. Through such a juxtaposition
Chekhov economically and profoundly reveals a transformation in
Trofimoff.

Shakespeare's use of juxtaposition to secure parallel or contrasting effects has been more widely recognized. Scholars and critics,

such as Caroline Spurgeon, G. Wilson Knight, and Nevill Coghill,[7] among many others, have traced recurrent patterns of imagery and structure utilized by Shakespeare. The bulk of such study, however, is devoted to language rather than action, and though the two are intimately connected, more attention must be given to action in order to provide a comprehensive understanding of Shakespeare's technique. In fact, dramatic theory as a whole has paid little attention to the techniques of juxtaposition. Most studies of dramaturgy, usually Aristotelian in approach, have stressed the importance of causation but ignored the role of repetition. This is unfortunate, for a sound appreciation of dramatic form relies upon a recognition of both causative and juxtaposed relationships.

Emphasis

A third factor that governs the connections of parts is the arrangement of emphasis. Most, but not all, plays consist of segments arranged in narrative order. Within that narrative order the segments receive varying degrees of emphasis. Normally, segments become more and more intensified as a play unfolds. Scenes previously cited from *Hedda Gabler* and *Ajax* illustrate the pattern. It is a pattern that dramatic theory has long taken for granted as the only pattern, to which it has devoted the most exhaustive analysis, and for which it has provided a special vocabulary (exposition, turning point, climax, denouement, etc.). Such a vocabulary charts a hierarchical arrangement in which subordinate segments build a foundation for the play's emphatic moments. But though this pattern is the only one that has been adequately investigated, it is not the only way to arrange segments. Medieval cyclical plays, Elizabethan dramas, Japanese plays, and, increasingly, contemporary works illustrate patterns of coemphasis. In these alternate patterns, segments may be arranged in narrative order, and some segments are indeed subordinate while others are dominant; yet even so, scenes are not generally arranged in a sequence of mounting intensification, as the two appearances of Banquo's ghost (*Macbeth*, III, iv) illustrate. In this scheme there is often narrative progression without causative development. The differences between the two types of arrangement may be most sharply discerned in the treatment of climax.

Derived initially from rhetoric, the term "climax" defined a figure of speech in which a series of ideas mounted either in intensity or expressiveness. About a hundred years ago the term became attached to the single moment of greatest intensity or significance within a series. It is in this sense that the word is used in drama. Rather than embracing a relationship of ascending parts, climax now designates a peak. That usage presupposes those astonishing *coups de théâtre* that characterized the Scribean plays of intrigue, often termed "well-made plays." That same usage also encourages the practice of climax-hunting. If, as books on dramatic construction have argued, the climax is a particular moment or segment in a play, then it must be possible to isolate it. But in order to isolate the climax, a definition is needed as a guide. Unfortunately, definitions do not always agree, with the consequence that pinpointing the moment of climax often becomes a matter of personal judgment. Moreover, when this method is applied to intractable material, such as Oriental plays or Elizabethan tragedies, the results are misleading. Seeking a conventional climax in a Shakespearean work distorts the structure of that work. The concept of a dramatic climax is invaluable, but if it is to be useful, it should be examined in light of (1) its relationship to other moments of crux in a drama, and (2) its internal dynamics.

Although Aristotle does not use the word "climax," the concept is inherent in his theory of dramatic construction. By stressing the desirability of a single action, he lays the groundwork for a mounting sequence of incidents. It is in his admiration of the instances when recognition and reversal occur simultaneously that he is in effect specifying the climax. "Recognition is most beautiful," he asserts, "when it arises at the same time as reversal." [8] Recognition is a change from ignorance to knowledge; reversal is usually a change from good fortune to bad, though it can be from bad to good. By uniting these two changes, not only does the dramatist create beauty but also an intense cathartic moment. According to Aristotle's prescription for dramatic construction, all the preceding incidents should contribute to that double moment; all succeeding moments should be a consequence of it.

The brevity of Greek tragedy facilitated compression of action and refinement of a single climactic moment. Within the usual four or five episodes, there was just enough time to develop a single line of action. It is true that not all the Greek tragedies—at least those which are extant—adhere to the Aristotelian ideal. But it is amazing that so many do. Aristotle distilled from these works the characterizing elements. Carried to their logical conclusion, they would produce a play in which all action would be concentrated in a single moment of confrontation. Contained within that moment would be every crucial factor that gave rise to it. Ideally it might be rendered as a complex symbol of the past in present action. In Euripides' plays, the token or sign whereby recognition and reversal were effected became just such a symbol. All the types of scenes that were endowed with technical names by later dramaturgy, such as obligatory scene, turning point, crisis, are inherent in the single proto-climax of Aristotle's time.

Continually associated with the concept of climax is the notion of intensity. The climax is ordinarily termed the highest, most forceful, most explosive moment in a series. At its simplest, climax is a nexus of energy. But what is the locus of this energy or intensity? Does it lie within the presentation or in the interchange between audience and presentation? This question is extremely important in dramatic analysis because, in attempting to locate a climactic moment in a play, the emotional intensity between characters is often confused with the emotional response of an audience to the action of the characters.

For purposes of analysis the double facet of climax should be kept in mind. As an element of construction, the climax is a point of reference for the rest of the action-segments of a play. As an element of presentation, it has the capacity for producing maximum reorientation in the audience's imagination. There may or may not be a correspondence between the heightened energy of the characters and the audience. This is particularly true in the plays of Ibsen and his followers. Arthur Miller and Lillian Hellman, for example, often make a moment of silence the instant of reversal and recognition. In *The Little Foxes*, this instance occurs when Horace, suffering a heart attack, knocks over his bottle of medicine as he reaches for it. He asks Regina to get another bottle. She does not move or speak. Horace and the audience realize that she will let him die, that she is prepared to go to any extreme for money and power. During the moment of realization the climax of the play is reached. For the audience this moment is more intense than the lesser crux when Regina shouts her hatred of Horace at the end of Act II. Thus, the display of intensity by a character may not be a guide to where the structural climax occurs. In order to discover that point, it is necessary to consider the play as a whole and the extent to which the work moves toward a single moment of confrontation.

The brevity of Greek tragedy, as I have already stated, readily permitted the dramatist to relate all his action to a single climactic point. As plays became longer, steps of action necessarily became more numerous and more autonomous. Racine, for instance, reduced the non-Phaedra elements of the Hippolytus legend, yet in the Phaedra story takes the audience through more clearly defined stages of psychological development than Euripides does. In addition, he added a love affair for Hippolytus to heighten Phaedra's passion. This type of amplification, both of plot features and playing time, had an inevitable effect upon the structure of the climax. Instead of remaining as concentrated as it was in Greek tragedy, the climax became diffused through the drama and divided among several moments. Thus, *Hedda Gabler* contains a series of climactic points, most significantly the moment when Hedda burns Lövborg's manuscript (at the end of Act III) and when she learns that she is in Judge Brack's power (near the end of Act IV).

With the breakdown of the three- and four-act forms and with the proliferation of multi-scened plays, such as *A Streetcar Named Desire* and *The Caucasian Chalk Circle,* the subordination of one segment to another becomes less marked. The cruxes of the various segments tend to be coemphatic. This arrangement, which characterizes Shakespearean form as well as Oriental patterns, has inspired much contemporary playwriting. Naturally, with a change of function, there is a change in the internal dynamics of the climactic moments. The ideal of recognition-reversal implies a flash of awareness, an instant of realization, and, substantially, that is what composes the climax of *Oedipus* and the last major crux of *Hedda Gabler*. The power of all previous cruxes comes to a focus at the climax. Where, however, the climactic moments are diffused, they tend to assume the reactive pattern and become moments of sustained, intense response, as in *Macbeth*. Whether or not these moments should be called climaxes is questionable.

The concept of climax, then, embraces the tendency of segments to be arranged in a series of steps leading to a single, major crux. When that tendency is realized, we can indeed locate a climax in a play. But the compactness underlying this concept is relative, because there are arrangements that can divide the concentration of climax among two or three emphatic moments. Still other dramatic arrangements may have no climax as such but rather a climactic pattern of shared intensities. In our study of drama then we should search not for the climax, but for the climactic pattern.

HISTORICAL PATTERNS IN DRAMA: INTENSIVE AND EXTENSIVE MODES

The structure of a play is the expression of the dramatist's conception of meaningful action. In part, it is a product of his imagination. It is also a product of theatrical conditions. His forms exist within the forms of his age. This is nowhere more apparent than in the plot-story ratio, a ratio usually determined by conventional practice rather than individual preference.

In the history of the theater, the line of drama from the Greeks through the French into Ibsen-oriented contemporary realism usually followed the practice of starting the plot long after the story had begun. The point of attack would be a moment of crisis, just short of the final resolution. Thus, the plot had a considerable past. Ibsen's structural skill, it has long been noted, lies in his ability to utilize the past as a scourge of the present, to introduce it as a force at crucial moments, and thus to link the characters with their own past and with that of others.

The compression and emotional power of this type of drama are well-recognized. What requires further elucidation is the assumption about human experience implied by such a form. If a particular moment of human experience can be considered the nexus of a life cycle, the most meaningful actions of life are therefore the most critical. But if critical actions are effects of the past, man is a prisoner of his past. He is caught in a highly contracted situation, his end foretold before the plot begins, for the plot is enmeshed in the toils of story.

In contrast to the practice of commencing the plot after the story is well-advanced is the practice of commencing story and plot almost simultaneously. The past is virtually nonexistent in *King Lear,* a play that is allied to traditional forms of romance and tale. "Once upon a time there was an old king who had three daughters. He determined to divide his kingdom among his daughters, and for this purpose summoned his court together. At this time the hand of the youngest daughter was being sought by the Duke of Burgundy and the King of France. Also at the court was an old lord who, having begotten a bastard son, raised him to manhood and brought him to the king's assembly with him." Here is the entire substance of the story that exists before the plot of *King Lear* commences. The full story unfolds within the duration of the plot, with the result that the characters are not victims but makers of destiny. Whatever blows fall are consequences of events we clearly see. Responsibility is evident.

Implicit in the handling of plot vis-à-vis story is an approach toward the dynamics of human experience. Fundamentally different aesthetic and philosophical assumptions about human action separate the Graeco-Franco-Ibsen line from the English Renaissance line. With detailed study of Shakespearean dramaturgy, it becomes evident that occidental drama has not only one paradigm of dramatic form, the Aristotelian, but also another, the Shakespearean.

A number of writers, Heinrich Wölfflin notably, has called attention to contrasting artistic styles arising from structural differences in the materials. In his influential work, *Principles of Art History,*[9]

Wölfflin distinguishes the closed form of painting in the sixteenth century from the open form in the seventeenth. Volker Klotz, in *Geschlossene und offene form im Drama*,[10] adopts these terms and applies them to dramatic analysis. He enumerates the contrasts between the "closed" classic tendencies of the Greeks and the French and the "open" tendencies of certain German playwrights such as Büchner and Wedekind. In brief, he also touches upon the open form of Shakespeare. Marvin Rosenberg suggests the terms "linear" and "contextual" to differentiate the two structural tendencies in drama, and Alan Downer applies the adjective "panoramic" to Shakespearean form.[11] All these proposed terms reflect a recognition of two artistic traditions, but none, in my opinion, are fully satisfactory. Whatever terms we adopt should express the central nature of drama. "Closed" and "open" may be suitable for the visual arts, but the drama needs words to define man's action in time and space.

In the Aristotelian frame of reference man is confined both in space and time. Subject to overwhelming circumstances his initiative is limited to *how* he will act not *what* he will do. As the action progresses, his range of choice is increasingly reduced, and he *discovers* that it is so reduced. The Aristotelian ideal compresses man into a moment of time when he will undergo an extreme turn of fortune (*peripeteia*) at the very instant that he undergoes an extreme shift of realization (*anagnorisis*). Because this moment of time into which man has been forced results from progressive intensification of pressures upon him, let us refer to this type of structure as *intensive*.

The Shakespearean formulation of action, on the contrary, does not rely upon forcing man into an unmaneuverable position. Indeed, there are always possibilities open for the characters, insofar as action is concerned. Temperamentally, they may be restricted, but the events do not accumulate to confine them. First, the time and space covered in the course of such a play militates against highly compressed circumstances. Second, the extensiveness of the plot inhibits a single line of mounting pressure and encourages instead a variety of intensities. As a result, the human being is not enmeshed in circumstance but passes through them. Action becomes journey rather than confrontation. Hence, it can always take a new turn. For such a paradigm the term *extensive* is appropriate.

In order to illustrate the divergent tendencies of the intensive and extensive modes, I shall concentrate upon two texts, *Hedda Gabler* and *King Lear*. Although *Oedipus the King* can be properly regarded as the model of the intensive mode, *Hedda Gabler* can reveal the typical handling of the mode in full-length form. *King Lear*, on the other hand, is to the extensive mode what *Oedipus* is to the intensive: a high refinement of the tendencies inherent in that kind of theatrical creation. The following outline schematizes the tendencies of the modes as they manifest themselves in these two plays. Again I must advise the reader that these pairings are suggestive rather than absolute, abstract guides rather than concrete formulas.

A. Causation

1. In the intensive mode the segments are the products of specific causes; in the extensive mode they tend to come from general causes. Every segment of *Hedda Gabler* arises from causes buried in the past or from antecedent segments. Hedda's restlessness stems from her status as the wife of a promising, but unspectacular historian, and that status stems from her earlier choice of the safe and mediocre Tesman rather than the dangerous but daring Lövborg. Her final entrapment is a direct outgrowth of all the preceding action. Not so with *King Lear*. The turn of events in Act V does not arise out of necessity. It is through no inherent cause either in the nature of the events or the disposition of the French forces that Cordelia loses the battle. One might attribute her defeat to the absence of the King of France, to her military inexperience, or to her distraction over Lear's condition. None of these causes are dramatized, however. The conclusion of the battle is not an accumulation of preceding events but a chance occurrence that could have turned out quite another way.

2. Another aspect of the foregoing point is the contrast between the perceptibility of causation in the intensive mode and the mere assumption in the extensive. Ibsen shows exactly how

one event leads to another. The audience sees in the very first scene, through the affectionate interchange between Tesman and Aunt Julia, the kind of intimacy that irks Hedda. Chance plays little part in the play. Even Lövborg's unlucky loss of his manuscript is not fortuitous, but a consequence of Hedda's stimulation of his immoderate nature. This nature has two aspects: a constructive one that flowers in the company of Thea, a self-destructive one that destroys itself and others in the presence of Hedda. Thea's story of the past reveals Lövborg's independent genius; the action of the play demonstrates his slavish fascination with disaster. Each step in his fall is exposed: there are no effects without causes.

But many of the causes of events in *King Lear* remain implicit. The chance outcome of the war to restore Lear is not the only example of unexplained action. Throughout the play there are others. Edmund's treachery lies in Elizabethan assumptions about bastardy and the nature of evil, and his belated effort to do some good stems from his part in common human nature. Lear's division of his kingdom is supposedly a result of his advanced age, yet nothing is revealed that substantiates a loss of authority or vigor. Why servants or masters side one way or another is not explicit. Choices merely occur without explanation. Even the reasons for Goneril's and Regan's behavior are rooted in their beings but do not seem to be provoked by antecedent events, except for the indication on Goneril's part that her father's attendants have been roisterous.

3. The parts of a play in the intensive mode are linked in a tight sequence of cause and effect. The parts in the extensive mode are linked loosely, often abbreviating the causes. Only in an extensive drama would a character say to another, as Iago does to Roderigo (*Othello*, IV, iii), "Come, stand not amaz'd at it, but go along with me. I will show you such a necessity [for you to murder Cassio] that you will think yourself bound to put it on him." In such a manner the propellant causes are cut short, and the resultant effects receive more attention. This is in contrast with the intensive mode wherein the building of one pressure upon another brings about the crux. Throughout, the amount of pressure exerted to effect an end is just enough to match but not exceed the result. In *Othello* an audience more familiar with the intensive

mode may be disturbed by the inadequacy of the causes that provoke Othello's jealousy, particularly the loss of the handkerchief.
Between the motive and the effect in this play there is a gap not
frequently found in the intensive mode. In *King Lear* this gap is
apparent in Cordelia's reply to her father and her consequent dis-
inheritance. Both lack root in earlier behavior, but arise instead
from temperament. To repeat, the theatrical effect of the intensive
mode is achieved by the gradual mounting of overt pressure, of
the extensive mode by the abrupt appearance of action that has a
general rather than specific connection with what happens. Thus
in the intensive mode, inevitability is possible. In the extensive, it
is not.

B. Repetition and juxtaposition of segments

1. The intensive mode contains relatively few formally defined
segments, the extensive mode many. *Hedda Gabler* is divided into
four, *King Lear* into twenty-six. Within the four acts of *Hedda
Gabler* there are, of course, many subordinate segments, but Ibsen
maintains a continuous flow between them. In several instances
he overlaps the end of one segment and the beginning of another
in order to conceal the seam. Examples of the desire to maintain
that flow can be found in a comparison of segments as they appear in his preliminary draft and as they were revised. For instance, in the segment cited in Chapter Three, note the transition
after Hedda cries out that she cannot endure the thought of being
subject to Brack. In the finished version, Brack asserts that she
will accept the inevitable. She closes that subsegment with a cryp-
tic "Yes, perhaps," and then turns her attention in two rhythms,
first to Tesman, whom she mocks, and secondly to Thea. The transitions that give an impression of flow from one point of focus to
another are omitted in the early version. Below is reproduced that
version with all the additions of the later version in bold type.

HEDDA: I am in your power none the less. **Subject to your will and
your demands.** A slave! a slave then! Oh, that intolerable thought. I
cannot endure it! Never! (*Rises.*) [12]

BRACK (*looks half-mockingly at her*): People generally get used to the inevitable.

HEDDA (*returns his look*): Yes, perhaps. (*She crosses to the writing-table. Suppressing an involuntary smile, she imitates* TESMAN's *intonations.*) Well, are you getting on, Tesman? [13] Eh?

TESMAN: Heaven knows, dear. In any case it will be the work of months.

HEDDA (*as before*): Fancy that! (*Passes her hands softly through Mrs. Elvsted's hair.*) Doesn't it seem strange to you, Thea? Here you are sitting with Tesman, just as you used to sit with Eilert Lövborg.

This type of flow reduces the definition between parts and gives the impression of continuity. In *King Lear*, however, the many scenes are defined not only by the clearing of the stage at the end of each one, but by the concluding couplets and the shift from a scene dealing with one plot to a scene dealing with another. Influenced by the cinema, contemporary producers have emphasized overlapping continuity from scene to scene in Shakespearean drama, although actual Elizabethan stage practice may very well have emphasized the separation of scenes.

2. The segments of the intensive mode are largely *active*, of the extensive mode, *reactive*. Repeatedly, intensive action moves toward moments of confrontation, one character exerting pressure upon another to bring about the confrontation. In the Greek tragedies the active segments propel events to a climax, which is then followed by a compressed segment of reaction. Extensive form usually emphasizes response in the early scenes. Shakespeare, in particular, foreshortens the impellant, or active, element in a scene and extends the reactive. This is evident throughout *King Lear*. The precipitating context leading Lear to divest himself of his kingdom is undeveloped. So is the abrasion that produces the clash between him and Goneril (I, iii). Action is instead concentrated upon his passionate response to Goneril's and later Regan's "ingratitude." We have seen the same pattern at work in the banquet scene of *Macbeth* and can find it in all of Shakespeare's work.

3. In the intensive mode the segments tend to be uniform, in the extensive mode, diverse. All segments in *Hedda Gabler* are concerned with domestic life; they all arise from the basic assumptions of provincial middle-class existence; they all maintain a

uniform tone, in this case, serious, whatever humor there is arising naturally out of the temperament of the characters. The segments are variations of a primary form of action: Hedda's avid feeding upon the goings, comings, and doings of the other characters. They all rely upon conversation as the mode of activity. A similar uniformity guides the choice of story materials. During most of his career as a dramatist Ibsen treated a narrow range of domestic conflict. In this he paralleled classical practice. From the days when Phrynichus was fined and admonished for dramatizing a touchy topical event, the dramatists were encouraged or pressured into treating relatively few of the legendary or mythical stories. By the time of Aristotle, it seemed advisable to confine the drama to the events concerned with a few legendary families.

In the intensive mode, it is true, the degree of uniformity is relative. Greek tragedy, for instance, is structurally more diverse than Ibsenite drama. The alternation of ode and episode emphasizes one type of mixture. In addition, the conventional forms provide some variety: the debate, the stichomythic confrontation, the arias of suffering, the messenger's report. But, despite the variety of segments, each type of segment is formalized and repeated so that, within a traditional framework, the action is limited.

In *King Lear*, on the other hand, the activities are both natural (quarrel between children and parent) and artificial (various disguises of Edgar). There are scenes of narrative illustrations, of dramatic developments, and of choral comment. Some segments are of high seriousness, others of sheer melodramatic horror, tragedy and grand guignol side by side. Others are intimate and personal, or formal and ceremonial. Though Shakespeare does not, in this play, introduce a formal song, he does interweave musical elements through the Fool. As for story materials, the entire range of romance and history, of ancient and near-contemporary subject matter provides a source for his imagination, and generally, writers in the extensive mode tend to draw from more varied sources than do writers in the intensive mode.

4. The intensive mode relies upon temporal and spatial unity, the extensive mode upon temporal and spatial multiplicity. This difference is readily apparent. The intensive mode avoids, wherever possible, shifts of locale, giving the few locales used as complete a sense of wholeness as possible. Thus, effort is made to

suggest the continuum of Hedda and Tesman's rooms with other rooms, the hallway, the garden, the street, and the town. Space always has one character: three-dimensionality congruent with actual space. The size of the rooms in *Hedda Gabler* should be, or give the impression of being, about the size in any home of that class and character. Differentiation between stage time and actual time is minimized. When someone enters a room, time must be given to the little amenities of welcome in order to maintain the illusion that actual time is not being distorted. Time is also continuous. It arises from the past and, despite Hedda's death, moves into the future—we know that Tesman and Thea will work over Lövborg's notes for months, and perhaps years, to come.

In contrast, temporal and spatial multiplicity is apparent in *King Lear*. The play moves over a significant geographical area of England not by easy flow but by leaping from one area to another within the general outline of Lear's travel to Gloucester's castle and then to Dover. In addition, the character of space is diverse. In *Shakespeare at the Globe,* three types of locales are identified: localized, unlocalized, and generalized.[14] One localized scene occurs at the door to Gloucester's castle (II, iv). An unlocalized choral scene occurs in the exchange between Kent and a Gentleman as the French and English forces are assembling (IV, iii). Most scenes are generalized: Gloucester's castle (but no specific part of it), the moor, Dover. None of these have any particular character as space beyond the mere identification. They *present* the idea of locale rather than *represent* its nature. By mixing these different spatial types, Shakespeare achieves an impression of multiple worlds.

Time, too, undergoes a similar treatment. Not only does Shakespeare leave the duration of the action vague, he manipulates it so that in one portion of the play considerable time seems to elapse while in other portions very little. This is most evident in the use of double time. Lear's stay with Goneril suggests that some time has passed since Act I, Scene i, for Goneril asserts that "day and night he wrongs me" (I, iii). But the events of the subplot, Edmund's scheme against his brother and its success, seem to be continuous. In one day the letter is shown to Gloucester, a trial made of Edgar, and Edgar driven from the castle. Between I, ii and II, iii, the Edmund plot requires less than twenty-four hours. During the same portion of the play the Lear plot requires several weeks at least. Both plots arrive simultaneously at Act II, Scene iv. The purpose of this comparison is not to stress the relative times involved, whether one week or three, but rather to emphasize the diversity of impressions of time and encourage a consideration of the relation between this temporal multiplicity and the total dramatic impact of the play.

5. The intensive mode depends upon the *accumulation* of parts, the extensive upon the *juxtaposition* of parts. Because the parts are uniform in intensive drama, the theatrical force comes from adding one part to another in a continuous and cumulative sequence. Extensive drama relates parts to each other in some form of significant repetition. The outrages against Lear are counterpointed by the more violent outrages against Gloucester. Lear's rising madness (II, iv) is balanced by his subsiding frenzy (IV, vi–vii). In this juxtaposition, the previously discussed diversity of segments is important, for one scene parallels or contrasts with others throughout the play.

Naturally, accumulation and juxtaposition are not exclusive to one mode or the other. Tesman is certainly juxtaposed with Lövborg, and *King Lear* does contain a progressive sequence of events. Nevertheless, the inclination toward one or the other manner of relating parts is strong enough to dominate each mode. The treatment of time and space, as discussed in point 4, reinforces this inclination. Because the intensive mode relies on continuous time, it reinforces the sense of one part emerging from another. The presence of distinct breaks in time and space characteristic of the extensive mode isolates each part, therefore making it considerably easier to juxtapose one to another imaginatively and presentationally.

6. As is evident from the previous points, the intensive mode leads to a sustained rhythm and the extensive mode to a dispersed rhythm. In *Hedda Gabler* the "natural" rhythm of domestic life is maintained throughout the work. The large blocks of action (the four acts) contain a constant coming and going that reduces the abrupt and the staccato. Thus, events seem to swell, accumulate, and rise to crucial moments. Quite different are the shifting

rhythms of *King Lear*. Action bursts, subsides, meanders, as in the Edgar and Gloucester scenes of Act IV. One of the reasons the audience experiences contrasting feelings of compression in *Hedda Gabler* and of ebb and flow in *King Lear* is because of the rhythms produced by the segmental arrangement. Neither subject matter nor characterization is as instrumental to the participational experience as the rhythmic effect resulting from the differentiation of parts, the length of each, the total number, and the way they are related temporally and spatially.

C. Arrangement of emphasis

1. From the preceding analysis we can begin to draw conclusions about the contrasting ways in which the parts of a play may be arranged for emphasis. In order to treat causation adequately and maintain uniformity, the intensive mode must limit the number of its dramatis personae. The opposite is true of the extensive mode, which tends to introduce characters freely. Only by confining itself to a handful of persons can the former trace each stage of the causative process. The original impulse leading the Greeks to limit the number of actors first to two and then to three persons is lost in antiquity. But the principle established then was imitated by the entire line of intensive drama. In Latin, French, and later realistic plays exemplified by Ibsen, the cast is normally limited to fewer than a dozen. That there was any relation between availability of performers and number of roles must be discounted. Both the English troupes of the early sixteenth and the French troupes, notably Molière's, of the late sixteenth century were composed of eight to ten leading players. The English, however, presented plays with dozens of characters, whose representation could be achieved either by additional actors or, more likely, by considerable doubling of roles. The French, with a core of the same size, relied very little, if at all, on doubling and presented plays with no more than the number of roles that could be managed by a troupe of less than a dozen. *King Lear* contains more than eighteen speaking roles in addition to supporting servants, soldiers, and other attendants. *Hedda Gabler* contains seven roles. Whether the size of cast produces concentrated causation or such causation

leads to limited casts, the two go together. In general, the greater the number of characters the looser the causative links. The Chekhovian plays fall somewhere between the extremes: *The Cherry Orchard* has fifteen speaking roles plus visitors and servants; *The Sea Gull, Uncle Vanya,* and *The Three Sisters* require from eight to fourteen actors. As a result the impulses behind some of the characters remain implicit and simplified as, for example, with Tchebutykin in *The Three Sisters* and Epihodov in *The Cherry Orchard.*

2. The concentration of action and limitation of numbers also contribute to the projective nature of the intensive mode. A single line of action pointing toward an ultimate resolution characterizes this mode. Furthermore, the unfolding of the story and the mounting of the plot are combined so that all elements tend to cohere about moments of crux. Through either the project of the characters or the given circumstances, an ultimate point of issue is projected into the future. The pursuit of that future is the action of the play.

This type of singleminded pursuit is not representative of the extensive mode. Instead we find a presentation of an explosive incident that provokes a chain reaction. The reaction, like expanding sound waves, reverberates from the catalytic incident until it reaches its ultimate intensity. Then it appears to contract, to compress the antecedent pressures into a narrative issue. This is quite evident in *King Lear*. The shock, first of Cordelia's response and then of Goneril's restraints, propels Lear into a state of hysteria. Though he fights the madness which threatens to overwhelm him, he cannot accept rejection and plunges into alternating stages of frenzy and anger. The heath scenes depict successive waves of unreasonableness until his body succumbs to the frailties of age and he falls into sleep. The reaction to the catalytic incident has reached its ultimate extension. What follows is a concentration of pressures in the struggle between evil and the remnants of good, finding theatrical expression in the battles and the trial-by-combat of Edgar and Edmund.

The Caucasian Chalk Circle, a modern example of the extensive mode, also depends upon an explosive catalytic incident, the abandonment of the child and its acceptance by Grusha. This incident produces an ultimate impact upon Grusha at the end of the first part when she loses both the child and Simon. New narrative material, dealing with Azdak, continues the action until the two threads of the plot are united in the trial scene.

3. The intensive mode tends to be architectonic, linear, melodic, temporal; the extensive mode tends to be organic, tentacular, harmonic, spatial. Hitherto I have dealt with *aspects* of these two modes. *Hedda Gabler* and *King Lear* will now be considered in detail. *Hedda Gabler* is divided into four formal blocks of action, the four acts, a division both conventional and yet congenial to Ibsen. Act I, in turn, is subdivided into four major segments: Aunt Julia's visit, Mrs. Elvsted's visit, Judge Brack's visit, and Hedda's adjustment. Tension levels are low, as is customary at the commencement of a realistic drama. Moreover, a veil of propriety lies over the activity of the characters so that whatever tension is introduced by an incoming character is not readily evident. Both Mrs. Elvsted and Judge Brack have more than casual purposes for their visits, yet the revelation of their individual concerns comes slowly and rather diffidently. Each visit intensifies the action by bringing crucial issues nearer and nearer to Tesman and Hedda. The issue of the act is: Will Hedda become involved in the concerns of others? In the first segment Tesman makes an effort to involve Hedda in his family. The crux occurs when Aunt Julia "takes Hedda's head between both hands, draws it downward, and kisses her hair." Hedda pulls away, unable to stand such familiar contact. The crux of the next segment occurs as Hedda learns of Thea's involvement with Lövborg. This provokes a reference to the mystery woman who threatened to shoot him. Though Thea is unaware, Hedda becomes exceptionally tense as she queries Thea on the identity of the woman. A danger has passed, a change has occurred, for Hedda is assured of her continuing power over Lövborg. In the third segment, as the delay in his appointment is revealed, Tesman's anxiety is contrasted with Hedda's composure. A third attempt by Tesman to involve Hedda in his concerns meets rebuff. It is Brack who advises her to curtail spending for the present. Hedda's remark, "This can make no difference," casual though it may seem, is a critical point. It certifies her alienation from family. But in the last segment, we finally see her interest aroused. Tesman eliminates the immediate possibility of securing certain trifles she had in mind, such as a footman

or a horse. She turns to the one thing that helps her pass time: her father's pistols. This revelation reaches a crux, first, because it shows Hedda's only genuine interest, and second, because it confirms what we have already suspected, that Hedda is the mystery woman in Lövborg's life. The actress must convey the first point. A shift from cool detachment to avid excitement must occur so that a window into her destructive nature is opened. The second point is built into the script, so that if the actress projects the first point well, she will also reveal the nature that so possesses Lövborg's imagination.

The pace of Act I is leisurely. Most of the tensions are oblique. Only now and again, and even then without great force, does a confrontation emerge: Aunt Julia and Hedda over the bonnet or the kiss, Judge Brack and Hedda over her expenditures. Such a handling of tensions, however, is a natural outcome of the forces at work in the play. Hedda and the Judge are the most strong-willed people, but they are obliged to mask that will in a middle-class environment. Hedda casts an especially austere cloak about her to conceal fierce destructive impulses. Consequently, Hedda must exert her force indirectly. For the most part, the activity is domestic and apparently trivial. But through such activity (Hedda's reaction to Tesman's slippers, for instance), the underlying impulses are revealed.

Characteristic of this type of drama, as suggested before, is the reliance upon revelation of the past for dramatic effect. Of the four segments we have been considering, two lead to crises of revelation, two to crises of choice. All of them are active. In the first segment Tesman and Aunt Julia endeavor to bring Hedda fully into the family, that is, they are trying to create a new field of action. The direction is forward. In the second segment, Tesman and Hedda at first, then Hedda alone, question Thea Elvsted about the past. As the questioning proceeds, the involvement of both Tesman and Hedda increases. Hedda seduces Thea into revealing more and more of the intimate details of her affairs until her past points toward a link with Hedda's past. This direction is backward, or inward, a type of revelatory action that Ibsen shares with ancient Greek tragedians. The activities usually associated with such action are inquiry and discovery of tokens.

Act II has three major segments, the first extending from the beginning of the act to Tesman's reappearance in evening dress for the Judge's party; the second, from this point to Hedda's warning to Lövborg not to believe in a special intimacy; the third, from Mrs. Elvsted's entrance to the end of the act. Each of these major segments has subordinate segments. In the first, for example, the exchange between Hedda and Judge Brack composes one subdivision, that among Hedda, Brack, and Tesman a second, and then another between Hedda and Brack, a third. A careful scrutiny of each subsegment discloses the changes effected by each. Through the activity of relating her wedding trip, Hedda reveals her boredom. This unit can be called "Making a Bargain." Hedda reveals her restlessness; Brack seeks to establish entree to the house. They arrive at an understanding. Through the analogy of railway travel, Hedda imposes conditions upon the kind of intimacy she will allow—above all, she refuses to mingle with others. We must remember that she and Brack are not referring to railway coach cars but to carriages in which the passenger or passengers are isolated from other travelers. The crux, I suggest, comes when Hedda acquiesces with the remark, "Yes, that would be a relief indeed."

Tesman's intrusion is merely a brief transitional unit. Tesman's enthusiasm for someone else's work is in marked contrast to Hedda's disinterestedness. In offering Lövborg's book for Hedda's perusal, he repeats the pattern of attempting to engage Hedda in his interests. She at first refuses, but then equivocates. The third subsegment returns again to the past, to the time when Tesman wooed Hedda. In the first half she reveals the insubstantial foundation upon which her marriage to Tesman was established. In the second half she yearns for some activity to engage her energies. She thinks of manipulating Tesman, but the idea is futile both because of the man and his modest position. Brack prods her into facing the possibility of motherhood. To this, with its thoroughgoing subservience of mother to child, she reacts violently.

HEDDA (*angrily*): Be quiet! Nothing of that sort will ever happen!

This reaction is the crux of the first major segment. In the course of the action, Hedda has faced different approaches toward her involvement with other human beings. Even the suggestion of an affair with Brack is circumscribed by her reservations. The sequence of cruxes shows a pattern of augmentation. The first one with Brack shows conjunction but not confrontation. The second with Tesman is oblique and relatively relaxed. The third is more direct and certainly the most explosive.

This type of augmentation can be found in the other two major segments. The second one proceeds from correct behavior toward Lövborg to his attempt to elicit a sign of empathy from Hedda. Her rejection of his overture is a variation of the type of rejection we have seen before in the act. In the third major segment she undertakes an active, though covert role. She has been stimulated to engage in another's life, but in an extremely detached and safe manner. She enacts the role she briefly imagined for herself as the power behind Tesman. Her manipulation produces a sequence of crises in Lövborg's behavior leading to his decision to accompany the Judge and Tesman. To Thea's remark, "Oh, Hedda, Hedda— how could you do this?" Hedda replies, "*I* do it? *I?* Are you crazy?" The final crux occurs near the end of the act when Hedda reveals her motive to Thea and then (*Clasps her passionately in her arms.*) "I think I must burn your hair off, after all." This impulse reveals once again that fierce destructive energy which seethes in Hedda. It is the second time that we see this aspect of her nature. The first is in the opening act when she turned to her father's pistols. The second time her impulse is more intense and more direct. The third time occurs at the end of Act III when she burns Lövborg's manuscript; the fourth, when she turns her destructiveness upon herself and commits suicide. Thus, the entire play is built on the augmentation of these critical moments, and the dramatic gap lies between the extended periods when she maintains her cool detachment and those brief but fiery flurries of destructiveness.

Act III is divided into six major segments: revelation of the long night of waiting, Tesman's disclosures, Brack's warning, Lövborg's false information to Thea and Hedda, Lövborg's revelation to Hedda, and Hedda's destruction of the manuscript. Except for the first and last segments, the act is constructed on a pattern of revelation of the previous night's events. The primal activity is Hedda's reception of information. The facts that we as the audience learn hold our interest, but the true focus of attention is upon Hedda's response. This action is symbolic of Hedda's entire life action. Loathe to participate directly in the sordidness of life, she feeds parasitically upon what others do. In the past her desire to share vicariously and securely Lövborg's bohemian existence drew the two young people together. The image of a deliciously secret exchange between the two in the presence of her father, the General, is evoked in Act II. In Act III she also feeds upon the somewhat wild events which she would never join but in which she finds a morbid attraction. During the course of the act variations of the previous crises occur. At the end of the Tesman segment, he asks her to visit the dying Aunt Rina. Of course, Hedda refuses. The main crux of this unit, however, centers about Lövborg's manuscript, which Tesman has found. The crisis builds in four steps: Tesman reveals the manuscript; Hedda responds strongly against his intention to return it to Lövborg immediately; she responds equivocally to the idea that the work could not be rewritten; she assures Tesman she will hold onto the manuscript. In terms of shape, there is an ascension of intensity in Hedda's response through the first three crises and then an in-gathering, a resolving of the intensity, as she is satisfied to absorb the script. The principal crux of the Brack segment occurs when Brack reveals his proprietary interest in the Tesman household. He means to hold Hedda to their bargain of Act II. The action prefigures the segment of Act IV that is discussed in Chapter Three (see p. 96). The form of the next segment is far more important than the content. In it we find the archetypal action of Hedda's life: overhearing or witnessing the living experience of others. In this segment of fifty-two speeches, Hedda has nine brief lines as Thea and Lövborg play their scene of revelation and farewell. In all but three instances her expression consists of no more than one to four words. Yet the action is built upon her response. In the beginning she offers to leave the two together, possibly sensing that Lövborg does not wish to be left alone with Thea. Most of her responses are choral and draw no response from the other two. In other words, she undergoes her own private action as a parallel to the scene she is witnessing. Only once does she nearly give herself away. When Lövborg claims to have destroyed the manuscript, she starts to protest that this is not true. At that moment the three are wedded together through Lövborg's self-accusation and both

Thea's and Hedda's responses. Hedda's recovery without the necessity of explaining that she has the manuscript is one crux. It occurs during Ibsen's stage direction (*collecting herself*). The second crux occurs in the different reactions of Thea and Hedda to Lövborg's admission that the destruction of his writing was akin to infanticide. Hedda's enigmatic but powerful, "Ah, the child—," peaks the segment, for the exclamation serves both as actuality and sign. The manuscript did serve the purpose of uniting Lövborg and Thea as a child might and of divorcing Hedda from human concerns, for she has already reacted violently, as seen in Act II, to the idea of motherhood. In Ibsen's early draft this portion of the text is substantially the same as the final version. Ibsen, however, made one crucial addition. Whereas he at first had Hedda respond merely with "Ah" to the confession of infanticide, in the final polishing he added the important words, "the child," to indicate what Hedda's sigh expressed.

The next unit consists once again of Hedda's receiving information, this time the true meaning of Lövborg's loss. She acts coolly and non-committally. As Lövborg displays his full despondence, Hedda takes the initiative—one of the few times she does—by giving Lövborg the pistol. This act energizes the image of Hedda and the pistol in Act I. It is also a logical development of her previous positive actions: the remark about Aunt Julia's bonnet, the breakdown of Lövborg's continence, and the teasing threat to burn Thea's hair. It is certainly one of the main cruxes of the act. The final segment, when Hedda burns Lövborg's manuscript, though very brief, is in its totality the principal crux of the act: it brings to a high pitch the pattern of the previous acts, that is, the full display of Hedda's destructive impulses. (For a discussion of the second half of Act IV, see pp. 87ff.)

From this analysis it should be apparent that a recurrent shape of action pervades the work. For the most part this shape relies upon Hedda absorbing, watching, witnessing. At first she does so in a desultory manner. But, as the play proceeds, the intensity of her observation mounts. Periodically, the observation turns to activity of a mildly then a fiercely destructive nature. How such an analysis of the action can be utilized by directors and actors in the process of production will be discussed in Chapter Six. But it may be appropriate to mention at this point that such a structure requires an actress who can communicate a range of inner responses through such neutral remarks as "Yes, the manuscript—?" and "Yes, so I understand." Unless the actress can radiate fire through a cool and correct manner, the performance will be a rather tedious exposition of not very intriguing events. In Act III particularly, the focus of the action is not on the revelation of events but on Hedda's response to the revelation.

It should also be apparent that the play as a whole is built architectonically upon a pattern of crises, which move from minor to major, from specific domestic matters to more generalized moments with wider ramifications. If we attempt to locate the climax, we find that the choice lies between the destruction of the manuscript at the end of Act III and the realization by Hedda that she is trapped in Act IV. But it is unnecessary to make this choice and far more important to distinguish the connection between the two cruxes. The first is an intense release as a culmination of all preceding events. It is a moment of augmentation. Structurally the presentation must reach a point of intensity at the end of Act III sufficient to propel Hedda into an euphoric state. Throughout the early part of Act IV Hedda feeds upon the exhilaration that such a release has brought her. Only as the action progresses is this exhilaration drained by Brack's revelations and finally by his threats. The second crux, when Hedda realizes she is in Brack's power, is a moment of reversal. Thus, we find repeated in the entire play the pattern we find in each act and in subsegments within each act: witnessing, release, and contraction.

This detailed description of the intensive structure of *Hedda Gabler* is illustrative not paradigmatic. Not every intensive play follows exactly the same pattern. Yet they all share some of these features. They have patterns of augmented crises. They move forward either from apparent release to contraction (*Hedda Gabler* and *The School for Wives*) or from apparent entrapment to release (*The Little Foxes*). They repeat shapes of action, and, except for some shorter plays, such as *Oedipus*, moments of reversal and moments of reaction (a form of recognition) are diffused in the last third of the play. A fairly common method in the three- and four-act forms is to place a moment of reversal or augmentation at the end of the penultimate act. It often involves violent activity, such as burning a manuscript, a son striking a father (*All My Sons*), or a vituperative attack (*The Little Foxes*). In the last act comes reaction or recognition, the facing of consequences.

The foregoing analysis of *Hedda Gabler* draws upon centuries of Aristotelian criticism. The following analysis of *King Lear,* as an example of the extensive mode, does not have so ancient a heritage. It has taken readers and auditors a long time to appreciate fully the harmony of *King Lear,* because it violates so many of the expectations of a more contained response characteristic of Western art. But in it Shakespeare achieved a synthesis of the various tendencies he explored in his own work and shared with writers of his age.

At the end of the nineteenth century Richard G. Moulton proposed a theory of the five-act form in *Shakespeare as a Dramatic Artist.* Describing Shakespeare's plays as pyramidal structures, Moulton showed how the action rose to a peak of intensity in the center of the play and then descended to the finale. More recently, T. W. Baldwin and Clifford Leech have stressed the importance of the five-act tradition as a foundation for Elizabethan, and particularly Shakespearean, dramaturgy.[15] In his monumental work, *Shakespere's Five-Act Structure,* Baldwin traces the historical growth of Latin forms and then argues that Elizabethan writers used these forms consciously. Unfortunately, the multiplicity of the Shakespearean play does not quite accord with the theory, for though a writer such as Terence used the double plot, the fundamental rhythm of his plays is intensive. In his plays the action, normally the outcome of a young man's romance with a supposed courtesan, becomes progressively entangled. It appears that the fellow is caught in an inescapable trap. Only at the last moment, is it revealed that the beloved is the long lost daughter of a citizen and, therefore, entitled to wed the young man after all.

Yet, despite the limited utility of earlier concepts of Shakespearean form, the essential rhythm discerned by Moulton does pulsate in Shakespeare. There is a central intensification of action and a realignment after that point. But Moulton's conception of a *point* of intensity and of a falling action is too simple and does not reveal the full richness of a play such as *King Lear.* In citing the center of intensity, Moulton recognizes, in Aristotelian terms, the presence of a split structure. A rapid overview of *King Lear* will reveal its principal characteristics.

The split structure exhibits two successive sweeps of action. First, a catalytic incident precipitates a sequence of repercussions. These repercussions reach their most extreme limits, that is, the most far-reaching effects or possibilities of the initial act are explored and revealed. Second, the adjustment to the consequences is explored. Thus, in the first half Lear insists upon absolute identification with himself. This demand is rejected by Cordelia, and so the unnatural division between father and daughter is precipitated (I, i). The effects are immediately apparent, but the next crucial act occurs when the two elder daughters close ranks against the father and strip him of everything that has hitherto given him dignity: authority, ceremony, devotion. This segment (II, iv) serves as a springboard into the intensified atmosphere of the heath scenes. In rage and madness, Lear fully expresses his reaction to the circumstances he precipitated, finding in his companionship with Mad Tom the ultimate expression of this reaction. He can go no further in his consciousness of rejection and passionate response to it.

Paralleling this major rhythm is the mirror rhythm of Gloucester's betrayal by his bastard son. In bringing about his father's ouster and blinding, Edmund carries the action against his father to its extreme possibility. Thus, both the Lear thread and the Gloucester thread reach similar levels of intensity in Act III. But, whereas the Gloucester thread (III, iii, v, and vii) consists of active scenes leading to the discovery by Gloucester that Edmund has betrayed him, the Lear scenes (III, ii, iv, and vi) are reactive. In them Lear's passionate hysteria is fully elaborated. In a previous work, I have characterized Act III as a climactic plateau, that is, a sequence of coemphatic scenes of heightened intensity.[16] Unlike the intensive mode, where one crux is either superior or inferior to another in a hierarchical arrangement, the extensive mode relies on a sequence in which each crux is another aspect of the state precipitated by the initial catalytic action.

In Shakespeare one of the clearest indications of the split structure is the disappearance of the central character after the climactic plateau. At this point subsidiary aspects of the narrative receive attention. In *King Lear* it is the adjustment of Gloucester to his blindness and the rapid development of the liaison between Edmund and Goneril together with Regan's jealousy. Lear's own adjustment to the turmoil of his soul is no longer a godlike madness but a muted oddness of manner and outlook. Is it too much to say that he seems to have become a bitter fool, half adjusted to the facts of life? Perhaps that is why the old Fool is no longer needed. Lear's resurrection comes when he awakens in Cordelia's presence (IV, vii). In the finale, as in the finales of most Elizabethan plays, a judgment is effected. In *King Lear* it is effected by means of trial-by-combat. Usually, as in *Hamlet* and *Macbeth*, such a judgment encompasses the principal figures, not necessarily rescuing them from destruction, but putting their actions into perspective and consequently restoring order. Not so here, where Shakespeare varies his customary finale by showing that the triumph over Edmund is irrelevant to the rescue of Lear and that the remaining figures, Albany and Edgar, are unsure of themselves and the world they are to rule. Albany's offer to split his rule with Kent and Edgar, recalling the disastrous trisected rule intended by Lear, betrays the superficiality of the reestablished order.

As we have seen earlier, the shape of Shakespearean action is not toward a point of crisis but away from a point of explosion. This is clearly revealed in *King Lear*. The first scene is just such an explosion. Acts II and III contain the extreme effects of that explosion, Act IV, the readjustment to the events (a new beginning), and Act V, the nexus, not of intensity, but of the moral and spiritual forces that have been coursing through the work.

This pattern does not depend upon the emergence of one scene out of another. What links the scenes is not a causal relationship. The dramatist inherited a traditional narrative, which he shaped and altered but retained in whole. Retrospective action is ignored for the most part. By encompassing an extensive magnitude of action, he was forced to leap ahead, not move step by step. His answer was the rhythmic structure that I have described. Further investigation, beyond the scope of this book, should be undertaken to discover the relationship between the Elizabethan conception of human action and the archetypal form that resulted.

Within the framework I have outlined, other features of this type of drama can be explored. As previously noted, the extensive mode mixes types of action. Shakespeare used choral scenes repeatedly, as in the exchange between the two Lords in *All's Well that Ends Well* (IV, iii) and in the scenes between Kent and a Gentleman in *King Lear* (III, i and IV, iii). These scenes have several purposes. They provide narrative links, and they echo a neutral but not unfeeling reaction to events. In the first of these scenes from *King Lear* (III, i), the Gentleman describes the old king in the storm, but describes the situation chorally, painting a picture of the weather and Lear's rage in order to prepare us for the events on the heath. In the second half of the scene the narrative is advanced through Kent's report of the coming of an army from France. This pattern, chorus followed by narrative, is identical with that found in *Macbeth* (II, iv) and is as formal as the musical pattern of prelude and fugue.

Throughout, artificial devices of disguise and observation mingle with more natural expressions of behavior. In *King Lear* Shakespeare carefully varied his forms to achieve expressiveness. The first scene is a ceremonial prologue. Its function is to illustrate the immediate situation provoking the narrative. Rather than the commencement of the play's history, it is a capsule scheme of the precipitating forces. A ceremonial beginning is characteristic of Shakespeare though he often varies his method by inserting a brief mood scene first. In *Macbeth, Hamlet,* and *Julius Caesar,* an initial scene of wonder and atmosphere is followed by the ceremonial. In *Antony and Cleopatra* as in *King Lear,* a ceremony illustrative of the central issue comes first.

Ceremonial finales normally complete the play. Spaced throughout the work are scenes of differing dimension: individual, duets, and public ceremony. Although Shakespeare's patterns have that Gothic irregularity of which Ruskin wrote, the overview nevertheless reveals a narrative rhythm of some consistency. It is this narrative rhythm that binds the works together. In the intensive mode causation gives a play an organic and internal unity. In the extensive mode the unity is achieved partly by the finality of the story.

To fill the ample magnitude of this mode, there is a constant interplay of parallelisms. Eschewing tight causation, Shakespeare and other extensive writers depend upon the theatrical sparks that can be struck by the juxtaposition of segments. The two plots of

King Lear contain an elaborate pattern of parallelism, exemplified in the similar invocations Lear and Edmund address to "Nature." "Thou, Nature, art my goddess," exclaims Edmund (I, ii). "Hear, Nature, hear! dear Goddess, hear!" cries Lear (I, iv). This type of verbal juxtaposition has been mentioned earlier in this chapter. As noted then, the juxtaposition of action, which has supported the juxtaposition of word, has received less attention than it deserves. Not only in the comparative situations of Lear and Gloucester, but in many lesser details Shakespeare fills his narrative of *King Lear* with dramatic parallels. Cornwall's compliance with Regan is set against Albany's resistance to Goneril. Oswald's ready participation in his mistress' evil is opposed to the attempt of Cornwall's servant to thwart the Duke (III, vii). Imaginatively and physically the action of stripping oneself naked is enacted. These interactions are all bound within the powerful flow of the play from its precipitating thrust through the climactic plateau and its contraction in a narrative finale.

Although all plays incline toward the intensive or extensive mode, all plays cannot be so neatly divided between these modes as *Hedda Gabler* and *King Lear*. Many plays combine features from each of these paradigmatic structures. Among them fall Chekhov's works. For example, *The Cherry Orchard* contains a simple line of action of the intensive type: the impending and, finally, actual loss of the orchard by Lyuboff and Gayeff. Built about that simple line is a spatial elaboration that produces a variation of the extensive mode. Parallel to the main issue, Chekhov juxtaposes a number of autonomous segments. They dramatize differing types of ties between one person and another as opposed to ties between people with either the house or the orchard. Petya and Anya, Varya and Lopahin, Yasha and Dunyasha, but above all Lyuboff and her lover in Paris experience different kinds of affection. These parallel segments give the effect of a richly textured community of feeling. But, because the individuals do not actually confront each other to bring their relationships to fulfillment, we have the effect of abortive confrontation. Chekhov thus creates the illusion of a closely knit family with feeling but without spine. In essence, his method has affinities both with Shakespeare's and Ibsen's.

CHARACTER

Implicit in the discussion of dramatic modes is the recognition that drama primarily treats the human beings who generate the action as forms of energy. They communicate force and response first. Only secondarily do they emerge as entities, independent of the action they undergo. In tracing the shape of *Hedda Gabler* and *King Lear,* attention has been directed to the interplay of energies that support our empathy.

Eric Bentley and J. L. Styan, in their studies of dramatic form, have clarified considerably the nature of dramatic character.[17] They have pointed out that the illusion of three-dimensional existence aside from the events of a play is misleading. Bentley emphasizes the primacy of the archetypal character who contains large movements of energy rather than specific behavioral patterns. Styan distinguishes between the dramatis personae, that is, the dramatic agent, and the character, which, after all, is the impression left by the actions of the dramatis personae. Once again it is essential to examine the temporal element. Like the word "plot," the word "character" denotes a summarized perception. We can speak of the character of Hedda only after Ibsen has supplied us with enough information to provide a set of given characteristics. Although the full image of the character does not appear until the play is over, there are intermediate stages. Each segment of action reinforces or modifies our impression. But during each segment we do not, and cannot, separate entity and action. Moreover, it is very important that we do not. Only by responding to the flow of action do we participate in that flow. Too much stress upon idiosyncrasies separates us from the experience. Throughout a dramatic presentation, character grows by accretion. The initial image of personality, which is a fusion of actor and role, is amplified and modified by successive actions. Predictable patterns of behavior begin to emerge and condition our expectations. For the most part this occurs in leaps, as we witness the consequences of events. The impression of character results from the accumulation of responses to action.

Where does character reside? Does it inhere in the individual? Is it a property of his behavior? Or is it a property of our perception of his behavior? These questions are equally applicable to actual persons as well as to fictitious characters, and though they are general and all-encompassing, too much so to allow for thoroughly satisfactory answers, some attempt to deal with the central nature of character is essential.

Again I should like to return to fundamentals. Theater is man presenting himself through the medium of activity. As we watch the rope walker or the acrobat, do we have any sense of what we call character? There is some slight impression derived from the physique of the performer, but, because a minimal litheness is common to all circus people, the impression we gain is suggestive rather than definitive. Watching a group of tumblers at work, it is often difficult to distinguish among the performers unless one is featured in the various acts. Even then little sense of distinguishing personality results. In these presentations the emphasis concentrates so much upon the feat that other factors are normally subordinated. Normally but not wholly. For, though there is considerable similarity between such performers, here and there distinguishing traits appear. This is particularly evident in the way a person takes a bow. Conventional though the bow may be, a little flourish or a change of timing will produce a distinct image, which in turn produces a sense of character. In the highly trained atmosphere of the circus, the slight variations of behavior often communicate character to an audience.

On a more subtle level, the same sort of condition exists in the drama. Perhaps this can be most easily seen through an examination of similar dramatic figures, such as Cordelia and Grusha of *The Caucasian Chalk Circle*. What are the given facts about these two? They are both young, but their social circumstances are quite different, and this may lead us immediately to imagine a difference of character. Such an assumption, however, depends upon extradramatic assumptions rather than textual evidence. Their physical appearance is not specified. In general, they have much the same honesty and human sympathy. Were both plays in repertory, the same actress could very well play both roles. But if she did, how would she distinguish between the two characters?

Grusha is a much longer role than Cordelia, and therefore we learn more about Grusha than about Cordelia. Yet what differentiates one from the other is not the amount of information we have but how we see them. If we were to imagine Cordelia in the Brecht play, we could very well see her taking up the abandoned child, caring for it at her own cost, truly loving the young soldier, and certainly incapable of tearing out the child's arm to pull it from the circle. Thus, the events themselves do not necessarily produce an impression of character.

From what does the sense of Cordelia's character come? Initially, it arises from the slight conflict between her pain at hearing her sister's words and her own sense of integrity. The curt reply to Lear is open and unhesitating. Throughout the first scene, she is straightforward and correct. Except for the two asides, her manner is aggressively open. Grusha's manner is also direct, but with a difference. At the end of the first scene we see an extended inner conflict as she tries to decide whether or not to rescue the child. In essence, it is similar to the one Cordelia faced. Should she act to gain advantage or uphold what she knows is right (Cordelia) or decent (Grusha)? But Grusha does not articulate her conflict. That is left to the narrator, with the result that the conflict in Grusha emerges as inchoate feeling and in Cordelia as a conscious issue of principle. When we first meet Grusha, she is accosted by the soldier, Simon. Her attitude is direct and open, but couched in indirect phraseology. Instead of asking, "Won't you say what you mean?" she says, "Won't the soldier say what he means?" This indirect style of address gives a formal and provincial elegance to their encounter. It also tempers Grusha's earthiness, imparting a delicacy to her activity and contact with other people. And, although it is true that Grusha could be more robust and peasant-like than Cordelia, such differences are neither central' nor required by the script. At the end of the first scenes of these two plays, our impression of character will be determined partly by social circumstances (merely because we associate certain kinds of people with royalty or service), but principally by the form of behavior. Social assumptions change, and an earthy Cordelia would be quite acceptable in the present day. But the real difference between the two characters lies in the way each consciously asserts herself: Cordelia's clear-cut conflict and defiant candor differs quite markedly from Grusha's indirect directness and inarticulate turmoil. As we can see, our perception of each character comes not merely from what each does, but perhaps more importantly from the form of her behavior. In these two plays the writers supply the actors with clues as to *how* they should behave, knowing that the manner is the true content of character. As we perceive the manner, that is, the characteristic activity, we assume the character, for *character is the interpretation we attach to an individual's activity.*

In order to come to grips with the idea of character, we must distinguish between character-made and character-in-the-making. The character-made is an afterimage, "a product" in Styan's phrase, which can be handled imaginatively or critically after the play is over. It is this afterimage that is often detached from the circumstances of the drama for the purpose of either contemplation or explication. As long as we realize that the entity we discuss is not identical with the character-in-the-making, no real harm is done. Only when we burden the character-made with extradramatic ideas and then impose those ideas upon a production or a reading do we distort the play.

The character-in-the-making, with which analysis is concerned, can never be considered an entity. Instead it is a series of behavioral possibilities. Although the actor is concerned with the impression he produces, he cannot achieve character impression directly but must leave to the spectator the coalescing of an image from presented activity. As we have seen, the coherence of activity arises from the interaction of project and resistance. In examining the character-in-the-making, I shall extend the specific features of the dramatic segment to a play as a whole.

Close study of a dramatic segment has revealed the inseparability of activity, action, and agent. In seeking an overview of an entire play, however, it is necessary to isolate the element of character *temporarily* for the purposes of examination, being careful at all times to envisage the repetitions and shifts that compose the rhythm of the character. Dramatic figures have three dimensions: *width, length,* and *depth.* From an investigation of each of these dimensions, we can approach an understanding of the distinguishing features of a particular character.

By *width* is meant the range of possibilities inherent in the dramatic figure at the commencement of the presentation. This dimension corresponds to the precipitating circumstances of the dramatic segment. First of all, there is the physical being. The specificity of that physical being varies from play to play. Cordelia and Grusha do not necessarily differ in this dimension. They are both young, their mode of speech is neither affected nor coarse; they may be either plain or pretty. Hedda, on the other hand, must be an attractive woman with a compelling presence. As we respond to a play, a physical image of each character is suggested to us. We must always be sure, however, that this suggested image is actually required by the text. Too often it is produced by conventional expectations or by a sort of aesthetic prejudice. In fact, textual limitation upon the physical appearance of a character tends to be generalized, and only occasionally does a playwright specify the exact features of a character.

More complex than the physical features are the social and temperamental features. The initial circumstances may or may not include modes of behavior that override the individual case. Thus all members of the nobility supposedly adhere to certain elements of decorum that distinguish them from the peasant class. Though such a distinction is fast disappearing in productions of Renaissance drama, new ones arise. For example, in expressionistic theater a mode of distorted, mechanical behavior often serves as the underpinning for individual activity. Such background behavior belongs to the world view of the theater artists. The individual character's place in the background scheme serves as part of the width, or range of behavior, open to the character. Lear is a king and shares with all rulers that special place in the social sphere. That aspect of his character is hardly developed in the play because it is taken for granted. But it is one of the premises for the man. How to give that premise sufficient weight today, when kingship is no longer venerated, is the director's and actor's problem, one not easily solved.

When the social and temperamental features become so firmly fixed that they lead to traditional behavior, stock character types emerge. These types usually divide along lines of rank or age. In commedia dell'arte the Bolognese doctor and Spanish captain unite professional and personal qualities in fairly rigid forms. The young *amoroso* and the old Pantaloon embody temperaments that result from age rather than position. Tradition in these cases prescribes the boundary within which a character functions. Obviously, the popularity of such types testifies to their effective representation of central human qualities.

The width thus embraces two starting points of character: the initial being (physique and state of mind) and the range of possibilities (the permissible modes of behavior). Proper analysis of width is a prerequisite to envisioning effective performance. In *Riders to the Sea*, for example, Bartley's age is not given by the author. Bartley is merely the youngest son. But the impact of his encounter with his mother will vary considerably depending upon whether or not he is an adolescent or a young man. If a young man, he comes to his responsibility in due course. If an adolescent, he is pushed into responsibility before his time by the death of Michael. Whatever physical statement is made affects the entire tonality of the scene. The same is true of the range of possibilities.

The text of *Endgame* permits the actor playing Hamm considerable latitude. But, regardless of his interpretation, the actor must fulfill certain energy demands. Hamm, shackled though he is to a wheel chair, exerts a psychic dominance for most of the play. Whatever variations an actor may attempt, he must be able to achieve that dominance merely through his presence and voice.

By *length* of character I refer to the passage of the individual through the play. This dimension corresponds to the shape of the action. The project, as we have seen, is the image of the future in the mind of the individual. That image may be projected into the far future, as a character with a strong will and great determination might project it. Such a character is Edmund. The image may be generalized and projected no more than a moment or two into the future. Such a character is Hedda at the beginning of the play. As a character pursues the project, his image becomes sharper or vaguer, more distant or near. It may actually change, as Lear's does. His first project is one of release from care. He envisions himself in all the trappings of kingship, but without its burdens, with the eager servitude of Cordelia always at hand. When he comes upon stage, that image of the future is strong within him. But it is soon shattered. In its place, he tries to substitute the same image in another environment, that of his other daughters. That image, too, is shattered, and Lear is left with the project of madness. He imagines himself in a disordered state, and recoils from that image with horror. "Let me not go mad," he cries. When he does lose rationality, he envisions a cosmic leveling and a forlorn justice.

The project, then, may evolve and shift from segment to segment as in the case of Lear. It may expand continuously as in the case of Hedda. Or, as in the case of Edmund, it may be directed at some long-range achievement and so contain a sequence of intermediate steps. Whatever the form, the project in passing through successive segments of action produces a pattern of behavior that I shall call the *development* of the character.

Character development falls into three broad patterns. Initially, in a play, the given characteristics (width) of a figure emerge. Subsequently, these characteristics may undergo change or become intensified. In addition, new features may be revealed. Thus, we can speak of development through change, through intensification, or through revelation. It is possible that a single individual may exhibit all of these kinds of development although one will tend to be accentuated. In *Hedda Gabler* none of the characters develops through change, because none alters fundamentally in the course of the action. Instead, their development occurs through intensification and revelation. Thea's anxieties, evident from the beginning, are revealed in increasingly intense states. What she is, is revealed at the beginning of the play but is not further augmented. Brack, on the other hand, exhibits a sinister side to his urbanity, but this side is developed by revelation. As the action becomes more crucial, he reveals the extent of his ruthlessness. This quality he always possessed; he merely did not need to show it early in the action. Hedda develops both by intensification and revelation. Her variant states of boredom and interest are intensified in the course of the action. Revealed, increasingly, is her passionate thirst for destruction. This potential for meddling lies within her from the beginning. It is revealed to us, not gradually but in moments of daring. This development by revelation parallels the climactic pattern of the play. Even parallels is not a good word. The revelation is the stuff out of which the climactic moments are made. Moreover, the revelations themselves become more intense as the play progresses.

In *Endgame* Clov develops somewhat by intensification but principally by revelation. He and Hamm go through their routines, routines which are endlessly repetitious. Toward the end Clov's irritation with Hamm gets the better of him and at last he strikes Hamm with the toy dog. But it is principally when Hamm insists that Clov speak from the heart that the private world of Clov is exposed to us. Clov starts the play by announcing that "it is finished . . . almost nearly finished." Once or twice he alludes to the inner impulses behind his threat to leave. But not until the moment of departure, when he speaks of all that was promised him, of his instructions to himself to suffer better, of his resignation, and finally of his awareness that he can depart, does he fully reveal the dream of his inner experience. It parallels the revelation Hamm has uttered earlier and like Hamm's revelation passes from the past through the present and into the future. The music of his thoughts has a different timbre from that we heard before in this play, yet these thoughts lay within him from the very beginning. A climactic moment of the play consists of this revelation and, because it is a new sound, evokes from the audience an empathy never quite realized in the play before.

Each character combines segments of intensification, revelation, and change in its own way. By studying these patterns rather than character qualities, the reader and the performer can appreciate the unity of action and character rather than treat each as a separate entity. From any segment, an impression of distinctive qualities will emerge, that is, the sense of a character-made. But by perceiving whether a character in a segment proceeds by revealing himself, or by undergoing intensification, or by actually changing in some fundamental way, the reader and performer can adhere closely to the dynamic states of character-in-the-making.

By *depth* of character, I refer to the relation between a character's activity and his inner life. This dimension corresponds to the activity of a segment and its action. The variant ways in which activity and action relate to one another, as explored in Chapters One and Two, are identical here. In simplest terms depth is concerned with how the inner life of a character continues or counterpoints the outer. For instance, all figures in *King Lear,* except the outright villains, exhibit continuity between these two levels. At whatever point in the play we consider Lear himself, his expressed state reveals a depth of feeling that pervades his entire being. There are no contradictory impulses which he hides from us and which lurk beneath the surface. Quite the contrary. What he shows is what he feels. In *Hedda Gabler,* however, the opposite is true. Both Hedda and Brack mask impulses and attitudes in different ways. But lest they be thought of as villains and the distinction seem to be between good and evil rather than between modes of dramatization, we can consider Thea and Tesman. At the very beginning we see Thea masking her true feelings for Lövborg, and, though she partly reveals her commitment to Lövborg, she does so only to Hedda, and continues to mask her feelings from the others as well as from Lövborg himself. Thus, the character alternately hides and reveals an inner life that is in contradiction to the behavior she exhibits on the surface. In her case the inner feelings keep breaking through. Tesman, in a somewhat more subtle fashion, has the potential for envy and tolerance of deception, which he is ashamed to exhibit and which arouse guilt within him. The line between his social behavior and those moments of inner contradiction are not distinct, yet if an actor were to explore the counterpoint he would discover a complexity not immediately apparent.

In general, the modern temper inclines toward characters whose dimension of depth tends toward counterpoint. O'Neill and Genet schematized this counterpoint, the first through the use of masks and/or soliloquy, the second through the use of role playing. Yet in contemporary drama we also encounter figures in which counterpoint plays a lesser role. Hamm and Clov do not lack depth of experience, as their climactic speeches reveal, but for the most part their activity does not convey inner experience so much as it suggests wider significance. Despite Beckett's warnings to the contrary, critics cannot resist allegorizing the activity. In terms of character, however, what an individual does and says seems to sum up his entire state at that particular moment. Clov, for instance, becomes more and more irritated by the constant orders he receives from Hamm. But, as he feels the irritation, he expresses it. Early in the play, his threat to leave and his reversal, "then I won't leave," does not suggest inner turmoil but acceptance of fact.

In analyzing this dimension of character, therefore, we need to locate the distance from the surface where the true inner life of a character resides. In *King Lear* and *Endgame*, though the activity is continuous with the subsurface, there is a difference of emphasis. In *King Lear* the surface passions penetrate deeply into the fiber of the individual. In *Endgame* the characters lack a commensurate depth. There is greater opacity in the activity and thus greater concentration upon it by the characters. Just so with the plays in which there is counterpoint. Tesman contains inner contradictions not fully explored or resolved. Chekhov's characters reveal not contradiction so much as incompleteness. So much more lies within them than is revealed that one gets the sense of seeing fragments of a total life, clues toward a totality that must be completed in the spectator's imagination. It is the task of analysis to explore and define the mode that each playwright follows in structuring the dimension of depth.

As we consider these various dimensions, we should identify those features of energy that a dramatist regards as crucial. Character is formed through a selective process, a process that is only partly conscious. Conceptions of human behavior inherent in a societal imagination are reshaped by the dramatist into character dimensions of width, length, and depth in order to provide a vehicle for the actor to realize the "character" that exists in the dramatist's imagination. Ibsen sets up a dialectic between social constraint and inner impulse. The inner impulse has sexual overtones although it is not primarily sexual. The energy of the impulse does not seem to arise from the libido but from the imagination. It is essentially conceptual. Hedda imagines a state of freedom and knowledge void of all restraint. One might call it a "bourgeois Faustianism." The operation of an imagination tinged with but not subservient to sexuality may be seen most clearly in Solness. The Master Builder is stimulated by a latent sexual attachment to Hilda, but his fulfillment lies principally on the imaginative plane.

An analysis of a character's dimensions such as I have outlined should lead us to identify a *center of being* in a character. The meaning of this phrase can be clearly shown in a comparison of Arthur Miller's and Tennessee Williams' characters. Both writers touch upon sexual and social matters, but the center of a Miller character lies in the will. He pursues and is confronted by decisions. Willy's extramarital escapade arises from social rather than sexual causes. Willy's life springs not from the delight in physical pleasure but from the pursuit of social success. The center of a Williams character, by contrast, lies in the instincts, primarily the sexual instincts. He is a physical being first, a social being second. In Stanley that core of sexual life is on the surface, or very close to it. In Blanche it lies close to the surface, but is usually masked by gentility. In Mitch it lies deep within, only once bursting into the open, but at a climactic moment. Thus, the actors of Miller's and Williams' characters must concentrate their attentions at different points and build within themselves a reservoir of appropriate experience from these separate centers of being. Since, as I have said, the image of character is completed in the minds of the audience, the actor must make the correct selection of elements out of which such an image can be formed. The final questions we are left with are: What aspects of experience does a dramatist choose to dramatize? What is our connection with those aspects?

I use the word "choose" in a loose sense, for the dramatist's choice is not necessarily or perhaps even primarily conscious and decisive, but rather an evolutionary revelation of a distinctive attitude. Miller's concern with self-confrontation on social issues and Williams' salvation through sexual fulfillment emerge as resolutions of a series of creative acts, acts which combined conscious, imaginative, and nonconscious efforts. As we receive the texts, they embody a distinctive formulation of experience. In probing the characters, we find that each writer has "chosen" to concentrate upon one or another aspect of human behavior. Communicating it to the audience is relatively simple when a dramatist's conception of humanity is part of an audience's background. But when time has dissolved that background, it is necessary for the performer to build a bridge between text and audience. Contemporary conception of evil, for instance, is radically different from the late medieval conception so prevalent in Elizabethan drama. Without ignoring either the contemporary or medieval conceptions, a modern performer must find ways of communicating the character's *center of being* to spectators. Only by deeply understanding the particular aspects of humanity realized by the text can the performer provide the links. It is easy enough to leap at superficial similarities between contemporary thought and classic expression. But a far richer and infinitely more difficult task is to give due weight to the central elements of classic figures when we seek to reconstruct them as contemporaries.

THE RELATION OF ARTISTIC CONCEPT TO DRAMATIC ARRANGEMENT: MEANING

In Chapter Four, I defined four types of meaning that cluster about a text: the descriptive, the participational, the referential, and the conceptual. My observations at this point extend the previous discussion to dramatic form as a whole.

In creating a theatrical work, the theater artist is caught between two contradictory impulses: to include everything relevant to the full story and to exclude all but the essential points. Metaphorically and mimetically, he strives to relate his activity to the world as a whole. The magnitude of his work, the dimensions of his characters, and the symbolic quality of his activity are all means of representing a totality far beyond the limits of stage and actors. Of course, if he includes too much, he defines nothing. Thus, he must organize his material into a limited structure, thereby excluding possibilities. To create viable characters, he must concentrate on circumscribed aspects of behavior. What is excluded, however, is not necessarily ignored. It is suggested, often obliquely. By creating a configuration of activity capable of producing a forceful closure the theater artist resolves the dialectic of the inclusive and exclusive.

The Greek chorus fulfilled that purpose for a time. In Aeschylus and Sophocles the choruses, for the most part, share in the events and at the same time point outward to the implications of the events. For Molière the *raisonneur* supplies the same function. By and large, however, the nature of the dramatic structure resolves the contradiction of inclusion and exclusion. Generally, the intensive mode with its insistence upon a linear and climactic form and upon a causative sequence does not allow for independent devices to suggest links with the larger world of experience. The convention of the chorus and the prevalence of rhetorical debate provide some means for such reference. But, with the elimination of the chorus in later intensive structure, the task of extending meaning depended wholly upon the fictional activity.

In the extensive mode, however, with its looser structure, opportunity is provided for actions other than the pursuit of a confrontation. Frequently, tension is reduced in order to permit opportunity for less vigorous activities, such as reflection and meditation. This pattern occurs in Shakespearean comedy and tragedy alike. Viola's musing over the character of Feste or Edgar's over Lear raises the specific event to general observation. Not that either one enunciates a philosophy but each expresses a way of thinking about events or people. With Shakespeare, the refraction of each passion through the prism of metaphor extends the implications of a dramatic event beyond the limits of a play. The overriding structure provides the narrative thread that maintains a sense of wholeness and brings the expansive tendencies into focus. That structure has the quality of a journey, one that is both earthly and spiritual. The philosophical foundation that invests the journey is often exposed in what may seem to be digression but is merely one of the independent parts of that mode. The consequence, it is important to note, is not a systematic expression of a moral, political, or social philosophy but a highly varied impression of existence.

Brecht's work, which appears to be firmly based upon an active political philosophy, would seem to belie this point. Nevertheless, his plays are not doctrinaire. They embrace a manifold suggestiveness. In *The Caucasion Chalk Circle* this is particularly so because of the ambiguous character of Azdak. Whether in the songs of

Brecht or the reflections of Shakespeare, a complex of thought is provoked by event and comment, but the reduction of that complex to a coherent statement is almost impossible. This is patently evident in Shakespeare's works, less apparent though nonetheless true in Brecht's. There is more to *The Caucasian Chalk Circle* than the idea that "the land goes to those who can use it." The audience witnesses naiveté triumphant. By yielding to humane impulse, man thwarts fate.

A last word must be said about the notion of dramatic unity. For the most part playwrights and performers no longer observe the unity of time, action, place. Until quite recently, they strove for unity of effect, particularly in performance. Yet even this unity is disappearing. Unity is partly a product of convention. Yesterday's acclaim establishes today's standard of unity. Even this is not the whole story, for dramatic periods seem to have arrived at structural patterns that set, in a wholly organic manner, models of unity. The present age is atypical. Models of unity are hardly established before they are smashed. Yet this contemporary iconoclasm is far more desirable than the imitation of outworn formula. It releases a fresh, if crude, excitement in the theater, and by reducing drama to basic, and perhaps primitive, essentials, creates a groundwork for the future.

Eventually a new sense of structural unity will have to be cultivated. This unity, as all unity, will emerge from complexity. A unity, or harmony of parts, that is too conventional reads as cliché. Artists are, and always have been, on the frontiers of chaos. In creating dramatic work, they provide the audience with an object about which and in relation to which its imagination can cluster. Inchoate states find objectivity and form in communion with appropriate activity.

Dramatic unity results from interrelationship of parts and sustainment of effect. Both depend upon the governing structure of a play, and that structure in turn emerges from either a conventional or original treatment of traditional forms. Because of the high degree of both abstraction and simplicity required by drama, the theater artist must rely on established patterns or devise new symbolic activity to contain the interplay of forces he senses in life. Yet so organic is the process of creation that only a person steeped in a world view which complements the world of actuality can create an individual variant of dramatic form. By successfully structuring the quintessential elements of existence as he perceives them, the theater artist compresses into the limited time and space of the theater the expansiveness of life.

Presentation

6

◉ Aristotle initiated an unfortunate precedent in first compart-
mentalizing the six parts of tragedy and then rating them in
degrees of importance. He considered spectacle, the physical realization of costume and setting, to be the least vital aspect of presentation. Whether or not he included the physical expression of
the actor in spectacle is not clear, for although he related vocal
melody to verbal expression, Aristotle did not provide a place for
gesture in his hierarchy of the theatrical act. The unfortunate aspect of this compartmentalization is that by relegating spectacle
to a lower rank, he encouraged generations of critics to discriminate against the visual and kinesthetic aspects of theater and to
neglect the study of the interrelationship between the internal and
external features of presentation. But plot and spectacle cannot be

measured one against the other. Spectacle is an aspect of activity; plot is the end result of the arrangement of action and is manifested through activity of which spectacle is a part. Thus, rather than being coextensive, spectacle and plot are inextricably bound so that one is merely another face of the other. Spectacle is not subservient to plot, for plot cannot exist without spectacle. Instead one can distinguish between an expressive spectacle wed creatively to an action or a superficial spectacle in which the inner content is stale or unrealized.

An appreciation of the external forms of theater, namely activity, is both necessary and artistically healthy. When this appreciation is not constantly related to imaginative purposes, it encourages mere formalism. But when the imaginative purposes constantly seek the richest yet simplest expression, theatrical work can be of the highest artistic order. In the present chapter I shall deal with the two sides of activity, the physical act of presentation and the physical environment of that presentation. For each side I shall examine the factors that determine or influence the external expression of action.

THE PHYSICAL QUALITY OF PRESENTATION

The physical act of presentation depends upon the kinds of sensuous contact that can be established between performer and receiver. More than any other art, the theater relies on the engagement of several senses in the presentational process. The two most prevalent terms for the receiver—spectator and auditor—give precedence to the senses of sight and hearing. Efforts to reach the other senses—touch, taste, smell—have usually been indirect, largely by means of the sense of sight or hearing. The sense of touch, or an extension of it, the kinesthetic sensation, is easily and frequently induced by the visual sense. The sight of a violent act, for example, is often experienced sympathically throughout the entire body. Moreover, avant-garde theatrical troupes have experimented with tactile contact between performer and audience. Actors have clasped hands with audiences, patted them, and even embraced individuals.[1] The extension of theatrical communication to the tactile level is unusual but not necessarily untheatrical. Whether or not the sense of touch can be a significant externalization of a dramatic action, however, depends on the logistics of audience arrangement as well as the communicative potential of the sense of touch.

Because theater has traditionally relied upon visual and auditory communication, the bulk of this discussion will be confined to those two kinds of expression. What is a visual signal to the spectator, however, is a muscular activity for the performer. This overlapping of sensory impressions somehow produces a comprehensive imaginative signal that unites all the physical resources of performer and audience.

Underlying all theatrical activity is the energy of the performer, which is highly focused and sharply projected. By directing his energies into limited channels, the performer creates the illusion of heightened intensity. He also tends to direct the energies at persons or objects outside of himself. Instead of diffusing that energy in random gesture and sound, he fixes it upon a real or imagined target. Such energy manipulation not only commands attention but also enables the performer to create the necessary illusion of life. In fact, without that focus and projection, illusion would be impossible.

The performer's manner of projecting his energy may be direct or indirect. He projects his energy directly when he focuses his attention upon the audience itself. He projects his energy indirectly when he focuses his energies upon another actor or upon real or imagined objects. But whether working directly or indirectly, he actually addresses himself to the audience. His means are nothing more than his voice and his gesture.

By definition I include all bodily expression, even mere presence, in the word "gesture." Therefore, sitting in a chair or standing at attention is a gestural act. The first thing to note about gesture is its continuity. Whereas vocal expression is intermittent, sound alternating with silence, gesture must maintain a continuous flow of energy from performer to receiver. Levels of energy may change, but a minimal level must be sustained by each performer while he or she is on stage. The state of becoming, previously described, is a product of that sustained flow of energy. Naturally, such a flow cannot be projected abstractly. It achieves expression through some bodily form. That form I shall call *silhouette*, a term borrowed from costume design.

The silhouette is the organic expression of bodily adjustment to social circumstance. Each historical period and each social class within each period seems to have a characteristic stance, a stance that is a product of some prevailing image of man in the world. The mid-twentieth century middle-class silhouette of contained informality, stressing the head and a moderately relaxed spine, is quite distinct from the loose, concave-chested, hip-thrusting stance of the young nonconformists of the sixties. Each theatrical tradition also has its silhouette. Partly a consequence of theatrical practice, partly a response to the fashions of the day, the theatrical silhouette serves as a basis for the performer as he searches for the silhouette of the individual character.

As an element of characterization, the silhouette is the outward expression of what I have called the width of the character. The silhouette is the form appropriate to the figure within the social milieu of the drama. Its source is both the play and the period. For a contemporary production of a historical play, this source partially reflects the artifacts of the period but principally the dramatic background contained in the play itself. The background of each play, not the time when each was written, causes the silhouettes of Hedda Gabler and Blanche DuBois to differ. In comparing each play, it is immediately apparent that Tesman's house conforms to a social and domestic code and that Stanley's stresses physical presence. In Tesman's house, mind governs; in Stanley's, bowels and skin. Hedda strives to maintain social appearance; Blanche strives to impose not merely social but cultural behavior upon the premises. Hedda's silhouette is one that she shares with others in her stratum of society, and is thus expressed through bearing. The head and shoulders, the set of the spine, the maintenance of physical position, all are aspects of this bearing. An initial channel for energy is through assertion of this silhouette.

Blanche's silhouette, a personal memory of a vanished society, may once have had roots in a social bearing, but now remains as more of a mantle than a spine. She contains a dream spirit that occasionally seems to ooze through her skin (in the scene with the newsboy). In comparison to Hedda, her silhouette is more shell than vertebrae, more skin than skeleton. This type of silhouette was realized by Jessica Tandy in the initial production of *Streetcar*.

The background of dramatic action allows alternative silhouettes, yet imposes limitations upon the performer's freedom of choice. Feedback is again a factor, for the possibilities of gesture in a play are defined by what an audience associates with certain distinguishing traits. Lear, for instance, must project the silhouette of a king. But what does that mean for a modern actor? During the first scene of Peter Brook's production of *King Lear,* Paul Scofield sat huddled in his throne, not erect but somewhat askew. He found a silhouette that conveyed both contemporary informality (or naturalism) with a thrust of his head which asserted the necessary authority. Concurrently, Morris Carnovsky, in his portrayal of the same character, adopted or was given quite another silhouette for the same scene. It was erect, squarish, almost monolithic. Its solidity was reinforced with an opening arm movement. Pointing the fingers of his right hand, he seemed to dip his right arm and then raise it in a supposed ritualistic sign. This opaque gesture was purely formal. It was not linked to other artistic forms nor was it an abstraction of a recognized life form, that is, it was neither grounded artifice nor observed naturalness. Consequently, it could be judged only on purely formal terms, and on these terms it failed because the forms were too plain and brief to excite a solely aesthetic response.

A performer's silhouette is the starting premise of any presentation. Aside from the setting, it is the form that the audience first encounters, and it has the most immediate impact. Whatever its shape, it fuses the structure of the action, the experience of the performer, and the expectations of the audience. It can be traditional and reflective of previous artistic images, as the Kabuki silhouette, or it can be current and thus reflect contemporary observation.

Against the background of a prevailing silhouette, the particular gestures of the performers are presented. Under this heading fall both the idiosyncratic motions of the performer and the sustained activity called "stage business." For both categories choice of gesture is, for the most part, historical and theoretical although performers would be the last to admit this. In traditional theater, particularly, historical gestures, including stage business, were handed down from one generation of actors to another. The *mie,* a traditional pose in Kabuki, is such a gesture. From the fifteenth to the seventeenth century the Italian comedian relied upon an accumulated tradition of comic business. André Antoine and Constantin Stanislavski rejected this type of tradition, believing it to be arid and false. Stanislavski systematically trained his actors to observe life and draw their gestures and silhouettes from actual experience. This change of attitude toward a performer's source of inspiration accompanied the playwright's exploitation of contemporary situations.

Though gesture can assume a highly articulate form that is true language, examples are almost wholly confined to the Orient, where even those few examples, such as the Nō, are dying. Because of the breakdown of traditional society and the diffusion of populations, gesture as a specific means of communication is slowly disappearing. In the West the communicative character of gesture has always been more general. Perhaps the better word would be contextual. Attempts to establish or identify a language of gesture have never proven fruitful so that even where ritual, particularly Christian ritual, has provided source material for gesture, such as making the sign of the cross, an alphabet of gesture that would afford sustained communication has never been established. Some students of Elizabethan acting have endeavored to demonstrate the existence of gestural conventions, but the proof is not very convincing, and the existence of such conventions may be discounted. On the other hand, the theater has and continues to display certain typical practices in connection with gesture, and these can be profitably explored.

The range of gesture reflects the range of all activity: from the natural to the artificial. Patterns of movement involving stage crossing and grouping are artificial because they must conform to the space of presentation and are fundamentally a product of the theater. Stage business tends either toward the artificial or the natural. Facial response such as the double-take, for instance, may occur in life but what is presented on stage is usually a product of stage experience itself. In general, naturalistic convention depends upon a multitude of small gestures, most of which are related to physical objects. Instead of encouraging the performer to utilize his body autonomously, naturalism sublimates the gesture by projecting it through props of various sorts: glasses, dishes, chairs, trunks, and so forth. In Greek and Elizabethan drama, gesture tends to be direct. A stage property, at the rare times that it is central to the action, may be symbolized; Philoctetes' bow and arrows and Desdemona's handkerchief are examples. By contrast, *Streetcar* abounds in objects either as foci of conflict (Blanche's letters) or as instruments of everyday life (the liquor and beer bottles). Through the manipulation of and contact with these objects, the performer expresses not only the verisimilitude of stage to life but also, indirectly, his emotional state. As Blanche says, Stanley bangs things. The properties thus externalize social and emotional states.

Because gesture is only suggested by most scripts, its choice and execution become a major responsibility of the performer. An analysis of a play should lead one to an understanding of what gesture is needed to express the action. In *Hedda Gabler,* the dramatic structure is so arranged that Hedda is constantly receiving information, listening to conversations, feeding upon others. Act III particularly builds upon successive waves of her response. Gesture is the principal means by which the actress can convey her reactions. They must be "natural" reactions, that is, gestural responses that seem plausible to an audience. On one level of artistry, the actress can merely seek variety. Through expressiveness of face, hands, and shoulders, handling of objects or clothing, and shifts in timing, she can provide a spectrum of responses. An imaginative actress can extend and enrich such reactions by finding ways to surprise us in her choices. At a more advanced level of artistry, she could relate, group, and accent types of responses in order to reveal successive stages of excitement. A still higher order of artistry would be for her to make and execute gestures that tend to assume the double character of symbol and reality. At that level, her activity becomes metaphorical—she creates an image of a respectable voyeur—enjoying her peculiar pleasure of vicarious living. The actress might explore the artful ways in which Hedda observes without being observed, in which she experiences without losing restraint. Thus, even so-called natural activity, when properly pursued, leads to the creation of expressive form.

Purely abstract gesture is rare in the theater. Tied as it is to the human body, gesture cannot readily be divorced from behavior without becoming dance. In Happenings and certain experimental presentations such as those of the Open Theatre, however, activity moves toward gestural abstraction. Inner content is minimized and a purity of group movement is stressed. From it may very well come fresh discoveries of artistic presentation though these efforts are not wholly novel. William Butler Yeats' borrowings from the Oriental theater, Harley Granville-Barker's Shakespearean innovations at the Savoy in 1912–1913, and the surrealist innovations in the twenties also had the effect of exploring such gestural abstraction. In theater there is always an impulse pushing in the direction of dance. The reluctance of stage movement to become dance arises not from aesthetic chauvinism but from awareness that too much stress on pure movement diverts the audience from the mimetic aspect of behavior. Nevertheless, every gestural pattern does have an abstract quality and a potential form buried in the most concrete behavior. The performer must seek this form.

From a consideration of gesture, I turn to a consideration of the oral element in presentation. The spoken word is both a more precise and, in the European tradition, a more significant instrument in the theater than gesture. There are, however, two qualifications that should be mentioned. First, present trends seem to be moving toward a balance of emphasis between oral and gestural expression. Second, though it is generally accurate to point out the dominance of the spoken word in European dramatic history, it is equally important to note that the exact proportion of emphasis between word and gesture varies from age to age. Commedia dell'arte relied less upon the spoken word than did French neo-classical tragedy, and Jonsonian comedy was less exclusively verbal than Restoration comedy. These distinctions arise, not necessarily from differences in literary quality, but from differences in dramatic structure and the relation of word to structure.

It is apparent that good dramatic dialogue and literary speech are not identical. Within the past hundred years some of the finest literary figures have endeavored to create drama only to find that, whatever their gifts, they lacked the histrionic touch. The obvious examples are Henry James, James Joyce, Thomas Hardy, William Faulkner, André Gide, as well as many lesser figures. No single explanation can account for these valiant efforts yet meager results. There are, nevertheless, some general propositions that may illustrate the difference between literary and stage writing.

First, stage speech contains a gestural element. By that, I mean that transitions between sentences and thoughts imply an action of the mind that affects the physical stance of the individual and so requires a change of tone or emphasis. A speech from *King Lear*, Goneril's fulminations against her father, will serve as an example:

> By day and night, he wrongs me; every hour
> He flashes into one gross crime or other,
> That sets us all at odds: I'll not endure it:
> His knights grow riotous, and himself upbraids us
> On every trifle. When he returns from hunting
> I will not speak with him; say I am sick:
> If you come slack of former services,
> You shall do well; the fault of it I'll answer.   (I, iii)

Note the action of mind and, therefore, its rhythm. Willful as she claims Lear to have been, Goneril feels justified in her anger. His manner and the manners of his entourage are insupportable. Her first words express her reaction to the precipitating circumstances. Between "all at odds" and "I'll not endure it," she caps her reaction with decision. In the next line, "His knights grow riotous, and himself upbraids us/ On every trifle," her anger continues to build, culminating in her exasperation that the slightest thing arouses his remonstrance. At the end of this line, a mental and physical transition occurs as she determines her course. The shift is from mounting anger to giving provocative instructions. After she asserts that she will not speak with her father, there is an apparent hesitation. She appears to retreat by suggesting an excuse, "say I am sick." But then there appears to be a countershift. Perhaps annoyed with her irresolution, she directs Oswald to go from passive to active resistance in order to provoke Lear deliberately.

A speech such as this is more loosely written than speech in a more literary medium, for it leaves gaps to be filled in by the mental and gestural expression of the actor. To provide the transition, the performer must make both an internal and external adjustment. Vocally, the adjustment may emerge in shifts of timbre, rhythm, force; gesturally, through shifts in degrees of energy, a turn of the head, a change of visual focus, or any other number of ways in which the performer conveys the inner action of the imagination.

Shakespeare is a master of the gestural in speech. Because he is so precise in his verbal expression, he sharply defines the unspoken transitions between words. More realistic dramatists write an even looser dialogue so that the gestural possibilities between words are greater or, more significantly, the gestural implication may carry a larger part of the action. However defined or broad the transitions, though, all dramatic language has the characteristic I have noted. It is written with elasticity so that a performer's imagination has room to expand into action. The performer does not merely *render* the word or express the literal meaning. He *encounters* the thought. Thus, when Goneril says, "say I am sick," she is emotionally facing the consequences of her own audacity. Critics have noted the vitality of Shakespeare's verbs. They convey tension and power to an extent rarely matched by other dramatists. How does Goneril encounter the word "flashes" in the phrase "every hour/He *flashes* into one gross crime or other"? This verb, because of its forcefulness, provokes a vigorous response from Goneril, more intense and specific than if Shakespeare had used a more neutral or passive term.

This observation on the confrontation of character with language leads us to the second feature of stage speech, the vocal element. Stage speech is theatrical activity and, like any activity, is constantly interacting with action. Previously I separated action into two broad types: the active and reactive. Speech broadly parallels these types of action. In active segments, stage speech is directed at bringing about changes, in effecting internal shifts, in forcing confrontations. Brack's apparent casual conversation with Hedda in Act IV illustrates this function of dialogue. The gestural element of speech is exceptionally important in these segments, for the lines reflect forces of pressure and resistance. Reactive segments, on the other hand, pose a special problem for playwrights. When they write in a poetic form, delineation of emotional response seems to be a natural extension of the reactive tensions. The poetic context makes it perfectly plausible for the characters to articulate grief or joy, outrage or dismay. In colloquial speech, on the contrary, verbalization of deep emotional states seems inappropriate, and rhetorical elaboration strikes the audience as false. That is why plays in realistic prose often come to points of confrontation where gesture is substituted for vocal expression. When Hedda is faced by the realization of Brack's power, she can merely cry, "I am in your power none the less. Subject to your will and your demands. *A slave, a slave then!*" The words I have italicized contain the crux of her reaction. To a modern ear, it is true, the word "slave" in this context might seem overly histrionic and slightly comic. Nevertheless, its melodramatic quality is faithful to Hedda's passionate response.[2] Far more important than these words, however, are her gestures, for through them she conveys the horror of her condition. In intensive, prose drama, action normally builds to a confrontation, which is then expressed through gestural response. Modern attempts to transcend the limitations of colloquial speech may be found in *The Caucasian Chalk Circle* and *Red Roses for Me* where song and/or dance express heightened reactions.

At this point one might wonder why, if the poetic form is so expressive of dramatic reaction, it is no longer the prevailing mode. The verbal dryness of realistic reaction is reason enough to justify the endless efforts to revive poetic drama. But these efforts repeatedly founder on the third factor of stage speech: the ear. The role played by selection and feedback in creating an illusion of actuality is noted in Chapter One. Auditory response is governed by these same factors. Every audience brings an expectant ear to a performance. That ear limits what will be accepted as true or false. If one of the essential aspects of dramatic activity is its adequacy as a truthful structure, then the ear of the audience helps discern this truthfulness. Synge recognized the crucial role of the ear in his famous introduction to *The Playboy of the Western World,* when he observed that "in countries where the imagination of the people, and the language they use, is rich and living, it is possible for a writer to be rich and copious in his words, and at the same time to give the reality, which is the root of all poetry, in a comprehensive and natural form." In Ireland the writer was fortunate because he could draw upon "a popular imagination that is fiery and magnificent, and tender." The rhythmic richness and rhetorical power of Tennessee Williams has a double source. From Southern speech Williams draws a language that is both natural and heightened. Because it is Southern, its rhetoric is more readily acceptable to audiences, whose ears, attuned to the flamboyant language of southern politicians and citizens, accept such stage speech as "true" as well as beautiful. By comparison, Arthur Miller's efforts at rhetoric strike one as self-conscious, more an affair of the mind than the ear.

In the twentieth century the ear has been principally tuned to colloquial speech. Williams succeeds because he blends the colloquial and the rhetorical. Sean O'Casey also sought the same combination though he often stretches the limits of the colloquial to achieve the rhetorical and emotive. Whether his exile from Ireland encouraged a forced rhythm, or whether he sought a heightening beyond the possibilities of prose, O'Casey was driven to find in the scenic and gestural an analogue of universal passion. Act III of *Red Roses for Me* attempts to shift from verbal to gestural and scenic activity and thus effect an apocalyptic leap into a vision of future joy. Such attempts to stretch the limits of speech are common in this century, for the urban ear is dry and flat. Harold Pinter has tried to deal with these conditions by concentrating upon the very dryness of contemporary rhythms. Other writers such as Samuel Beckett have sought in metaphors of gesture (such as scanning the horizon outside the room of *Endgame*) the evocative potential formerly associated with verbal expression. These trends have both a negative and positive motivation. The negative motivation arises from the fact that the contemporary ear is accustomed to colloquial and superficial expression; the positive motivation is that audiences, trained by photography, films, and television, have a greater visual than auditory acuity.

Auditory expectation defines not only the boundaries of writing but the characteristics of delivery. The contemporary ear suspects the overly-resonant voice, the ornamented phrase, the orotund tone. Flatter, plainer speech seems to be in demand, not merely or even principally in terms of commercial acceptability, but in light of truth. Audiences seem to recognize the flatter delivery as natural and true, the orotund delivery as manufactured and false. Again the mass media may have conditioned them to this acceptance. It is interesting to note the vocal characteristics of world figures, particularly American figures. Even wealthy and highly educated public figures from established families retain regionalisms and a colloquial manner in order to remain acceptable to their constituencies, whereas the urbanity of too cultivated a delivery tends to alienate large segments of the population. Sociologically, the expectant ear reflects widespread taste within which the actor and writer are bound.

What is true of the present is true historically. Although it limits the possibilities of delivery in any given period, the expectant ear is, nevertheless, continually changing, sometimes rapidly, as in sixteenth-century England, sometimes slowly, as in late seventeenth- and eighteenth-century France. The playwrights reflect and sometimes promote these changes. From the vantage of the present day, Shakespeare's poetry is formal. In speaking the lines, modern performers often seek a balance between the regularity of the original and the colloquial orientation of the twentieth century. In Shakespeare's day, however, his poetry must have produced the contrary impression of growing informality.

Behind the poetic style of the Elizabethan play lay a heritage of the medieval stage play and the Renaissance love lyric. Medieval stage speech consisted of a highly complicated verbal structure. The mystery plays often employed rigid septets and octets, intricately rhymed. Moralities such as Bale's *King John* observed a strict pattern of rhymed hexameter. As late as the third quarter of the sixteenth century, the popular play *Cambises* employed the florid rhythms of the meter jocularly known as the "galloping fourteener." The king, Cambises, opens the play with these rolling lines:

> My council grave and sapient, with lords of legal train,
> Attentive ears towards me bend, and mark what shall be sain.

These portentous accents were on the wane, however, by the 1580s. Courtly influences, represented by sonnet sequences and the brilliance of Lyly's prose, encouraged the more colloquial melody of the iambic pentameter. At first, Shakespeare used this meter with strict regularity and considerable rhyme, but his form gradually became looser and more complex. Lines of irregular length began to appear in his work with increasing frequency and became so prevalent in *King Lear* that the resulting rhythm is almost colloquial. One difference exists, however, between the colloquial quality in *King Lear* as heard by a sixteenth-century Elizabethan and by a twentieth-century cosmopolite. For half a century the Elizabethan had been exposed to highly structured meters so that he became accustomed to a variety of conventional melodic patterns. As anyone who is conversant with Shakespearean production knows, the beat of iambic pentameter is penetrating and rapidly instills an aural memory in the listener. In departing from strict metrical form, Shakespeare could treat the aural memory of the audience as a silent bass against which his melodic variation would sound all the more daring. For the twentieth-century cosmopolite, on the other hand, colloquial expression is the norm. He hears Shakespeare's lines not as a departure from a regular pattern but as a structuring of colloquial conversation. Moreover, he associates such colloquial conversation with truth and sincerity.

As a writer, Shakespeare moved from formality to informality. Contemporary writers must move in the opposite direction, from informality to formality. To do so successfully, they must proceed slowly, for audiences distrust overly-structured speech. Yet, in order to create a texture that will have sufficient theatrical excitement, performers need a more formal expression. Pinter succeeds in moving in that direction on the rhythmic plane alone. O'Casey and Brecht to a lesser extent abstracted regional qualities to produce a poetic prose. Reliance on song is a means of achieving structure and truth, once the frame for song is conventionalized. This raises once again the question of the duality of opacity and transparency.

Colloquial speech tends toward the transparent; poetic speech, toward the opaque. Sensitivity to the surface of poetry, to the meter and imagery, stresses the opacity of dramatic language. Sensitivity to its mimetic character, to the immediacy of experience, stresses the transparency of dialogue. Each age finds its own balance between the two tendencies, a balance that will satisfy the expectant ear. As I have noted, opaque speech is suspect today. Only where there is regional justification (as with Williams) or sufficient emotive force (as with Osborne) is there convincing use of opaque elements. The greatest degree of opacity at present can be found in the laconic rhythms of Pinter and Beckett.

For purposes of illustration I have discussed voice and gesture separately. But, of course, the performer endeavors to suit "the word to the action, the action to the word." Dramatic art does not consist solely of gestural activity, because it would then be dance or mime. It does not consist solely of vocal activity, because it would then be song or oration. It embraces both forms of activity, and subsumes them in another level of activity that has very distinctive features. The performer treats the activity, be it natural, artificial, or a mixture of both, as a segment of highly concentrated and simplified existence. It does not matter whether the performer speaks to an audience, mimes an animal, drinks a cup of coffee, or converses with another actor. All of these activities are reduced to their simplest shape and invested with heightened energy. Yet simplification is relative, for no matter how simplified activity is, it must continue to express the inherent contrasts of the action.

In his grief and anger, Lear endeavors to curse his ungrateful daughters at the very instance he senses his impotence:

> No, you unnatural hags,
> I will have such revenges on you both
> That all the world shall—I will do such things,
> What they are, yet I know not, but they shall be
> The terrors of the earth. You think I'll weep;
> No, I'll not weep:
> I have full cause of weeping, but this heart
> Shall break into a hundred thousand flaws
> Or ere I'll weep. O Fool! I shall go mad.   (II, iv)

This segment contains nothing but Lear's rising drive to retaliate against the unbending fact of his powerlessness and the resolution of this conflict in his refusal to show weakness in tears. Because it so simply yet absolutely captures those mutually contradictory energies, and because those energies embody fundamental human experience, the segment can stir widely differing audiences. It is not that an audience necessarily recognizes its own experience in Lear's, but it undergoes a parallel action empathically, an action that is analogous, and penetrating even though synthetic. The audience's empathy is paradoxical, being objective and subjective simultaneously. If the shape of the activity is indeed concentrated and simplified without losing the inner complexity of the action, then the audience can enjoy that double sensation of submitting itself to the "life" of the action and of responding to the form of the presentation. A great dramatic work is composed of segments that, capturing as they do the essences of human situations, can be activated to produce this double response.

The dramatic contrast in a script may be apparent to the reader, but as art it is only potential. The performer invests that potential with three qualities. First, he makes the action sensuous. The action underlying the phrase "they shall be/ The terrors of the earth" demands a vocal quality that will carry the preceding speech to its culmination in a striking way. The sound of the word "terrors" must vibrate with Lear's frustrated rage. Second, the performer exploits the action inventively. He transforms the outline of the action by imparting something of the unexpected to the activity. He may understate the climactic moments of the speech, make a gesture, or alter the phrasing in such a way that an original impression is created. Third, the performer makes the action resonant. By intimating that his energies are greater than what he expends and by controlling the direction and intensity of his concentration, he suggests that events echo more deeply within him than they appear to do. Invention and resonance must fill the moment when Lear finishes the phrase, "the terrors of the earth." His next line is, "you think I'll weep." Is the "you" singular or plural? Is it preceded by a glance? At one daughter? At both? What does the glance, if the actor employs it, portend? Its manner of fulfillment, its sensuousness and implications, when highly concentrated, produce an activity that is simultaneously opaque and transparent and that projects an idealized human action. Activity of that quality deserves the adjective *elegant*.

Elegant in this sense does not mean opulent but simple rightness. Mathematicians use the word in much the same way. They call a theory that accounts for complex factors in the most economical way, "elegant." By the term they are extolling the utter simplicity of the theory, a simplicity of enormous skill, a simplicity of form that is totally satisfying. Elegant is also the word acrobats apply to superior performance.[3] The same idea, though not the same word, is expressed by Rudolf Arnheim in his study of visual perception in the arts. He writes that "when a work is praised for 'having simplicity,' it is understood to organize a wealth of meaning and form in an over-all structure that clearly defines the place and function of every detail in the whole." [4] When a dramatic activity is elegant, it has the transparency of life and the opacity of art. The most casual word or gesture is seen as an integral part of the entire mosaic of action.

To achieve the simple rightness of elegance is not easy. It comes only with great experience and ability. It is a result of testing many alternatives in order to distill those motions and contacts that communicate the most with the least energy. The act of distillation leads to the creation of ambiguous activity shapes. They are both natural, yet artfully contrived, interesting as entertainment, yet highly evocative. In order to illustrate these shapes, it is not possible to cite texts, for the script merely provides the opportunities for such activity to occur. It is only in the work of exceptional productions and performers that these shapes are fully crystallized. *A Streetcar Named Desire*, *West Side Story*, and *Marat/Sade* exercised so pervasive an influence on the theater because they achieved this elegance. Eva LeGallienne as Katherine in *Henry VIII*, Louis Jouvet as Arnolphe in *L'Ecole des Femmes*, Laurence Olivier as Shaw's Caesar, Mary Martin in *South Pacific*, to name but a few, are elegant performers because they created fleeting images that are memorable for a lifetime.

THE ENVIRONMENT OF
THE PRESENTATION

Aristotle dealt with the temporal and spatial frame within which presentation occurs under the rubric of spectacle. For him spectacle was a decorative addition, which bore little or no organic connection with the action. In that sense spectacle does exist in the theater. But my concern is with the total environment of action, an environment Aristotle took for granted since the form of his stage and auditorium was fixed and could be varied only slightly. Presently, when the very existence of a theater building is in question, the fundamental nature of the performance's relationship to the audience within the presentational environment must undergo examination.

The environment of theatrical presentation is both spatial and temporal. Though one usually thinks of environment as spatial, the variation of lighting and sound in the course of a performance gives a temporal character to spatial environment. Under the heading of the purely spatial environment I include the theater building and the stage setting. By stage I refer to any portion of theater space isolated for presentation. The necessity for such isolated space has been questioned, explicitly by Richard Schechner and by those who advocate the Happening as a basis for drama, and implicitly by those groups, such as street theaters, that seek to break down completely the barriers between audience and presentation. But, as I showed in Chapter One, an audience could not exercise its imagination if there were not some measure of isolation.

Three spatial relationships govern the theatrical process. The first is the relationship of audience to the theater building and to the event as a whole. By circumstances of its location and by manner of receiving audiences, the theater initially determines the psychological and physical state that an audience brings to the presentation. Festival theaters, whether at Stratford, Ontario, or Epidaurus, enjoy the tremendous advantage that proper spatial preparation affords dramatic production. When a theater is structured like a department store, its goods are regarded suspiciously and treated as a commodity. When a theater, and that includes the adjacent grounds or streets, holds special significance, because it falls either within a park or exotic urban area, then the presentations are likely to be approached more eagerly. A concomitant factor is the physical proportion of theater to the individual spectator. An intimate auditorium induces quite a different psychological set than a large one does. Exactly how size affects audiences needs some study.

The second relationship involves the audience and the presentation. This relationship embraces both spatial pattern and decorative background. The spatial pattern is determined by the degree and manner of contact between presentation and audience. That contact can be divided into the following categories: (a) *face-to-face*, where a performer may face the audience without pivoting more than 180° (proscenium form); (b) *modified face-to-face*, where the performer must pivot as much as 270° to address the audience (thrust stage, open stage, amphitheater in part); (c) *face-to-back*, where the performer must pivot a full 360° in order to address the complete audience (arena, center or circus form); (d) *face-to-side*, in which the audience must pivot 180° or more to maintain contact with the performers (wrap around stages with actors playing at the sides of the audience); and (e) *multi-face*, which utilizes the previous patterns in rapid succession within a single presentation (some circus forms, environmental form). Most theaters employ one layout consistently although that layout may be a variant of the preceding patterns. For example, the disposition of skene and orchestra in the Greek theater required the chorus to observe a modified face-to-face pattern, while it permitted the characters to alternate from a face-to-face pattern to a modified face-to-face pattern.

Despite the long life of theatrical art, there have been relatively few variations of the stage-audience pattern. In each age one dominant arrangement recurs in work after work. Part of the reason for this uniformity lies in the nature of the art itself. Once a city, sovereign, or entrepreneur erects a theater, the form of the building shapes production for generations. This, however, accounts for the persistence of a pattern, but does not explain the reason why one pattern or another evolves. Alan M. G. Little has traced the evolution of the Greek stage from the earliest times to the Hellenistic period. C. Walter Hodges has attempted to show how the Elizabethan stage evolved from booth stages.[5] Both men demonstrate that organic social and aesthetic processes refined the physical plan of the respective theaters over a period of decades and finally produced a representative type. In the case of the Greek theater, these processes produced a type that remained vital for centuries and has been revived in the twentieth century.

To pursue the subject further leads to the third relationship, that between performer and setting. Considering the permanence of architecture and matters of economy, it is not surprising to find that a single spatial pattern between audience and performer dominates an age. It is surprising, however, to find that for each of these ages a single type of setting also tends to prevail. In the history of the proscenium stage the perspective setting dominated the sixteenth and seventeenth centuries, wing and drop, the eighteenth and nineteenth, and three-dimensional domestic interiors, the late nineteenth and twentieth. Over the entire period there was also a gradual shift from exterior palaces and forests to middle-class interiors.

The prevalence of one type of locale over a considerable span of years is the rule rather than the exception. Greek tragedy, except in very few cases such as *Ajax* and *Philoctetes*, unfolds before a palace and about an altar. Modern drama, until recently, occurred in parlors and then spread, in some instances, to other parts of middle-class homes. In general, the intensive drama has relied upon a setting congruent with actuality. The dimensions of stage space and of fictive space have been kept nearly equal. That tendency may have contributed to the shrinking of theater buildings in the nineteenth century. As the dramatic locale became fixed in the private, middle-class home, the setting was reduced in size in order to retain the congruence of the fictive and actual parlors; this necessitated a corresponding reduction in proscenium width and height, and thus in the theater itself. On quite a different scale, this congruence is characteristic of Greek, Roman, and French theaters. In fact, unity of place demanded congruence between fiction and actuality.

Extensive drama does not make that assumption, for the magnitude of action is greater than can be physically accommodated on a stage. Shakespearean battles and Grusha's journey through the mountains illustrate that greater magnitude. Since the stage cannot be congruent with reality, it must somehow conventionalize a fictional place. The form of the setting must be abstracted from actuality in order to serve as a sign or symbol capable of conveying dramatic truth. Elizabethan popular drama was enacted before a conventional façade that did not represent any particular locale but presented an emblem of the universe. Brecht utilized narrative techniques of story-teller or scene announcements to emphasize the illustrative quality of his presentation. Apparently each age and each theatrical tradition evolves an archetypal environment for its dramatic action, an environment where the essential action of life occurs, for continual placement of dramatic action in a recurrent setting must reflect not merely aesthetic conventions but evidently satisfies a deep identification of locale and existence. The aura of the sacred dancing circle hovers about all stage space. That space is not merely an imitation of a probable or actual locale but the central focus for the human action of an age, and though decorative and aesthetic factors influence considerably the form that that space assumes, the cultural and psychological factors are probably more significant. Thus, the environmental equivalent of activity, the setting, also has its inner content and is originally allied to the action.

Of the plays treated in this book, *Hedda Gabler, Riders to the Sea, A Streetcar Named Desire,* and *The Cherry Orchard,* all rely on the modern domestic setting. These settings reproduce a fragment of locale as completely as possible. From the audience viewpoint, the dramatic presentation is embedded within the setting so that both activity and space are viewed as a totality. The characters have a personal connection with the space and the objects located within the space. Often relations to objects and physical locale substitute for relations with other characters. Hedda's pistol and Blanche's Chinese lantern are personal expressions of each woman. In these instances, however, the relation goes beyond the psychological into the poetic. The metaphorical dimension, inappropriate for colloquial speech, is realized through contact between person and thing, and in many instances besides the two already cited such a poetic extension emerges.

As a totality, the setting becomes part of the dialectic interplay of pressure and resistance. The stage becomes one performer in the action. Normally, it serves as background, and as background reinforces or counterpoints the action. The Tesman home reinforces all the inclinations of Tesman, Aunt Julia, even Judge Brack. For Thea it is a sanctuary where she can find help. For Lövborg it is one of the few homes in which he can find welcome, though it does impose a stiffness on his behavior. Only for Hedda is it stifling. Her relation to it is ambivalent: she encloses herself within it for protection, while, at the same time, she longs to break out of it. In a broader sense the Tesman household symbolizes the entire genteel bourgeois life within which Hedda hides and yet which bores her to distraction.

The Latin Quarter and the Kowalski home within it are reflections of Stanley's spirit and the one to which Stella has become accustomed. Williams immediately describes its easy going, unpretentious, vivid personality. In the original production, Jo Mielziner, by using a scrim for the rear wall, created an evanescent but insubstantial atmosphere. Yet the Kowalski world is not insubstantial. It is bawdy, it is tawdry, it is lower class without being impoverished, it is colorful without being odd. For Blanche it is a battlefield in which she must show her superiority. Throughout the play Blanche struggles against the environment. When she moves in, she dominates: her trunk fills the kitchen, she requisitions the bath tub, she changes the lighting, and adds her own bedspread. Embedded in this environment, she squirms and kicks against it, only to have her efforts destroyed successively: Stanley ripping off the table cloth and dumping the birthday dinner on the floor, Mitch tearing down the colored lampshade, and Stanley raping her in the bedroom she has tried so hard to decorate.

The Cherry Orchard reveals a more complex use of environment. Every connection with locale reflects an aspect of loss of control, of decay, and, essentially, of alienation from the land and one's birthright. There is no simple pattern of reinforcement or counterpoint. Each character relates differently to the environment. For the older people, Lyuboff and Gayeff, there is sentimental attachment. Even for Lopahin this is true, though he is not so sentimental that his business sense fails. For Varya the estate is a trust to which she is dedicated.

As the play progresses, the locale shifts from the nursery to the orchard, to the ballroom, and back to the empty nursery. Each choice is of psychological and symbolic significance. Lyuboff returns to the nursery, to the memory of her dead son. Within the nursery are objects that recall the past. The characters are essentially in harmony with their surroundings, but in that harmony lies the dramatic issue, for the principal impelling force, the imminent loss of the orchard, summed up in Lopahin, is directed against the family and the environment of which they are a part. The alienation is illustrated at the beginning of Act II. The servants loll on the fringes of the orchard, taking over the grounds in a parody of a *fête champêtre*. Yasha smokes a cigar—and the masters go to town for lunch. They return to their grounds but are ill at ease. An echo of disaster is heard, a stranger intrudes, and the land, with which they should be at one, is already detached. Perhaps there are one or two moments when they still possess it, but these pass away. At the end the young people are left in the fading light. This setting, though still having all the external marks of "realism," is already a metaphor of the entire play.

The referential meanings of these domestic settings are readily apparent. The audience is expected to accept the artificial image of the stage as an accurate document of a group of homes that exist or have existed in actuality. Through the actual, it is expected to perceive the workings of general principles. For such a purpose the proscenium frame is exceptionally important because some sharp limit must define where the document ends and theater begins. In truth, that kind of documentation need not be confined to the proscenium if another method were available to establish the limits. One might readily turn an entire theater into a courtroom, and thus achieve the same sort of documentation. Whatever the limits, within them the details are proportionate to each other as they would appear in the source. The audience then associates the entire presentation with actuality, and through that association experiences the drama.

This approach is quite at odds with the one found in the Elizabethan theater. It is immediately apparent to the reader of *King Lear* or of any other Shakespearean play that the action is fluid and thus the stage must provide means for rapid movement from scene to scene. Since the last quarter of the nineteenth century, producers have restored Shakespeare's text to its original sequence and devised new methods of staging his works in order to provide the necessary fluidity. In the course of time two approaches have come to prevail. One, represented by the theater in Stratford, Ontario, relies upon a neutral platform which permits performers to enter from any point and which can represent any place or no particular place. It is noncommittal in background and distinguished merely by a small portico at the rear of the stage. The second approach is to devise a simple decorative scheme, either of expanding and contracting porticos or of rising and falling scenery, by which the producer can enlarge or contract the stage space. Often such a method is followed at Stratford, Connecticut, and sometimes at Stratford-upon-Avon. Both approaches are successful, insofar as success is determined by the ease with which the activity moves from scene to scene. The Ontario stage, moreover, has the added advantage of bringing the actor close to the audience and, when utilized effectively, of allowing stirring processions. Yet neither really comes to grips with the social and psychological importance of stage space.

For the Elizabethan the public stage presented a fixed façade. Yet this façade was anything but neutral. On the sheerly sensuous level, it was a "gorgeous playing place." Decorated with columns and statuary, brightly painted, it must have made a dazzling spectacle. Simply on a theatrical level the stage radiated wonder. What its referential meanings were must be inferred from the plays which appeared upon it and from its origin. Several things seem likely. Its sumptuousness gave it a courtly air. In form and design the stage seems allied to the pageants used by the burghers to celebrate the annual Lord Mayor's installation. Some scholars have argued that the stage façade echoed the rood screens erected in the great halls of religious institutions and private nobility.[6] Others see it as an analogue of the astonishing triumphal arches erected in the streets of London to welcome the new King James in 1603.[7] Beyond these associations arising from similarity of design, there seems to have been a more abstract association. In no way did the façade *look like* the universe yet the nomenclature of its parts indicates that it *stood as a sign* of the universe. To what extent the terms "hell" for the area beneath the stage and "heaven" for the area above the protruding shadow were vestigial reminders of the medieval stage, it is difficult to tell. But these areas were utilized in a practical way to represent these antithetical ends of man's universe. Devils would leap from the hell and gods would drop from the heavens. Between the two world events occurred, and however much the symbolism was taken for granted, it was a symbolism upon which the theater artist could draw. It is precisely a psychological and philosophical equivalent of this symbolism that most modern methods of Shakespearean staging fail to supply.

Like all aspects of theater, space too has a double character. It is *presentational* space. The actual space is acknowledged as theater by audience and performer. It is also fictional or *representational* space. Representational space should not be confused with the depiction of actuality. In intensive drama, it may represent photographic reality. In extensive drama, it may represent the idea of a locale, as in the Elizabethan drama. Presentational space is opaque. It offers the sensuousness of line, color, mass, sound, proportion. It induces wonder and enlarges life. Representational space is transparent: it suggests realms, stirs memories, deepens life. Every theatrical setting must serve a double function as the space of presentation and representation if it is to assume a symbolic character and so lead to metaphorical truth.

The text of a play gives only meager information about the setting. Yet the setting creates the initial psychological and social conditions which initiate audience response. In studying the stage text, we need to discover the essence of the world in which the action occurs and then the relation of the various performers to that world. This essence and these relationships must be seen in the external forms that they assume. And finally, these forms must be understood as parts of the total world that the image theater presents to our minds.

For Brecht the theater is a teaching platform. His presentations are exempla, and so he adopts projected announcements, teaching songs, and other methods to create the kind of stage he advocates. He also adopts many features of Oriental theater, for its use of narrative, brief segments, masks, and other devices lend themselves to didactic purposes. He does not treat his stage as an analogue of actuality, but as an analogue of social education, and in his insistence upon having his works performed elsewhere as they were first presented at the Theater am Shiffbauerdamm, he endeavors to establish a chain of such stages. Unless *The Caucasian Chalk Circle* is understood as occurring within a philosophical framework, it is in danger of being treated decoratively.

But though the theater was Brecht's teaching platform, the world of his plays is more than lesson. The use of the narrator and the placement of the action in the context of the argument between Russian collectives emphasize the play as a social exemplum. At the same time the naiveté of Grusha and the picaresque quality of the narrative link the play to the satiric line of Simplicissimus, the innocent fool who somehow survives the misadventures of this world. The action does not occur in the actual world, nor does it occur in a psychological world or a philosophic world of hell-to-heaven hierarchy. It occurs in a world of romantic social ethics. The elements of this world are not hell and heaven, but exploitation and the canny efforts to avoid or thwart exploitation through circumspect goodness. The prologue suggests that this world is an actual one, and it certainly does refer to actual circumstances, but Brecht was inclined to turn to historical and theatrical materials (*Good Woman of Setzuan, Mother Courage, Coriolanus*), knowing that the distancing he achieved would permit him to deal more intimately with that area of concern which he regarded as central. He thus created works possessing the double quality of romance background and social foreground, which in juxtaposition produce a complex, theatrical effect.

Proper analysis of the theatrical environment is of equal importance to the reader, the performer, and the designer. It leads the reader to examine the nature of the world in which a play's action occurs. It makes the actor more aware of the presentational and representational elements of the action and how they are reconciled. It forces the stage designer to go beyond the manipulation of purely aesthetic elements in design. In the United States stage design has long been dominated by the ideas of Robert Edmond Jones which, however liberating and stimulating they were in the twenties, are fundamentally psychological and appropriate for a world of dreams. The contemporary designer, in seeking to create a new theater world, cannot create imaginatively without creating philosophically. New techniques and excitations are not enough; new perceptions of our world leading to new conceptions of its form may come from anywhere: director, writer, actor, but certainly the designer cannot abdicate that search. That a search is underway is evident from many experimental theatrical efforts. It is intriguing, and perhaps significant, that as the actual world becomes more heavily dominated by machines and electronics, the theater turns human beings into scenery, as the Open Theatre tends to do, or creates voids without definition, as the thrust stages tend to do. Are these the analogues of our universe? Or have we not yet found the most fruitful one?

In this chapter I have dealt with the shapes of activity and the factors that influence the shapes. To investigate each of these factors as thoroughly as it deserves requires a much longer work than this. I have merely attempted to supply an analytic basis from which such an investigation might proceed. The widespread tendency of theater artists in the United States, particularly actors and designers, to avoid consideration of the external elements of presentation reflects their fear of superficiality and falseness. But superficiality and falseness can be overcome not by neglecting technical matters, but by linking vision and craftsmanship. We must correlate attention to external factors with focus upon inner forces. Simultaneously, we must see how a hand moves and sense the energy that flows through it. Whether we are actors and directors striving to learn our craft or audiences seeking to understand the theater, we need to search for the presentation that unites outward activity and inward action.

AFTERWORD

My purposes, as stated in the Foreword, are theoretical and practical. Though not wholly novel, the theory that I have presented does offer a systematic and comprehensive approach to dramatic form. It begins by clarifying the relationship between theater and drama, and then investigates the fundamental building block of drama, the segment of imagined activity. Throughout, I have concentrated on the segment as the central element of drama, examining how it is structured, how it can be modified and varied, how it exerts its power in the presence of an audience, and how it can be organized into different modes. Basic to the theory and repeatedly implied throughout the book is my conviction that we lack knowledge about how theater truly functions and that in the present state of social and artistic turmoil, we require such knowledge if the theater is to flourish. To gain that knowledge we must develop a sound method of structural analysis.

First, we must recognize that between reading a play and interpreting it, there is an analytic step. That step is preliminary to any appreciation or evaluation of a work.

Second, analysis depends upon theoretical tools that can properly direct our attention to the substance of dramatic art. These tools exist only in part. I have tried to supplement our meager resources, but considerably more work is necessary in order to refine the instruments we have and to devise new ones.

Third, analysis must be creative. We must "live into" a production or a text, letting interpretation impress itself upon our imagination rather than permitting our willfulness to force interpretation upon the text. To cultivate analysis of that temper, we need a correct conception of analysis itself. Theater research in audience responses, for example, has had the unhappy tendency of aping the social sciences by imposing an inappropriate pseudo-objectivity upon research. But the social sciences and even the natural sciences are coming to recognize that complete objectivity is a myth. Where so individual and emotive a field as drama is concerned, "objectivity" can lead only, and has so far led only, to irrelevancy. In order to investigate the artistic heart of drama, we need to nurture what Erik Erikson calls a "disciplined subjectivity," [1] a phrase he uses to describe the clinical methodology of psychiatry. Though paradoxical, "disciplined subjectivity" connotes an actual mental discipline in which trained intelligence is focused upon the examination of internal, elusive processes. It is just such a discipline that is required by those who work in theater as well as by those who would truly understand and appreciate its artistry. Armed with such discipline, the student of theater can engage in that fruitful description, which, pursued through re-reading and rewitnessing, merges into deep and ever renewing interpretation.

Last, analysis must be practical. On the surface, reading plays seems to require no special preparation, but, in fact, it is as complex a process as reading a musical score and requires as much training. The validity of the theory in this book rests finally upon the usefulness of its methods for the analysis of specific plays and theatrical periods. These methods, however, require concentrated practice. As we find whenever we take up an unfamiliar tool, our first efforts in handling it always prove awkward. Only with perseverence and repetition do our painfully conscious motions yield to autonomous command.

The United States is undergoing an unprecedented expansion in theater education. It is exceptionally important that the teachers and performers who engineer this expansion be properly equipped with the intellectual tools to deal with the drama. The continuing investigation of the entire field of theater, conducted in close collaboration with living performance, can ultimately provide the aesthetic and sociological knowledge upon which this expansion can be firmly based.

NOTES

Chapter One

1. See my essay, "Dramatic Theory and Stage Practice," David M. Knauf (ed.), *Papers in Dramatic Theory and Criticism* (Iowa City: University of Iowa Press, 1968), pp. 24–36.
2. Kenneth Burke, *A Grammar of Motives* (New York: Prentice-Hall, 1945); Francis Fergusson, *The Idea of a Theater* (Princeton: Princeton University Press, 1949); Suzanne Langer, *Feeling and Form* (New York: Scribner, 1953) and *Problems of Art* (New York: Scribner, 1957); Ronald Peacock, *The Art of Drama* (London: Routledge & Kegan Paul, 1957); J. L. Styan, *The Elements of Drama* (Cambridge, England: Cambridge University Press, 1960); Elder Olson, *Tragedy and the Theory of Drama* (Detroit: Wayne State University Press, 1961); Eric Bentley, *The Life of the Drama* (New York: Atheneum, 1964).
3. Richard Schechner, "Comment," *Tulane Drama Review*, 9 (Spring 1965), 13–24.
4. In *The Drama Review*, 12 (Spring 1968), Richard Schechner enumerates six axioms of environmental theater, that is, a theater that seeks to end the separation of actor from audience both tactilely and spatially (pp. 41–64). Whether or not such a breakdown in isolation occurs in practice remains to be seen. Experiments in environmental theater are still too recent to provide conclusive answers. My own experience as a spectator of environmental theater (including Schechner's own production, *Dionysus in '69*) indicates that isolation, though recharacterized, still exists, and is, in fact, heightened by the very attempts to eliminate it. Occasionally, when members of an audience become involved as participants, isolation is eliminated *for them*, but then, so is theater.
5. See in particular, Rudolf Arnheim, *Art and Visual Perception* (Berkeley and Los Angeles: University of California Press, 1954)

and E. H. Gombrich, *Art and Illusion* (New York: Pantheon Books, 1960).

6. Burke, p. 108.

7. In a recent history, *Le Théâtre: Des Origines à nos Jours* (Paris: Flammarion, 1966), Léon Moussinac envisages the first theatrical act to be primitive man, before the tribe assembled about a fire, imitating the animal that he is to kill (p. 5). This picture of theater's origin in mimetic play (*jeu mimétique*) has wide currency but is largely suppositional.

8. Elder Olson (pp. 18–23) also distinguishes between natural and artificial behavior in drama, but stresses signs rather than activity and links the artificial signs to convention rather than presentation, as I do. Thus, he treats both the social convention of laying funeral wreaths and the artistic convention of passing "the hand before the eyes" in Nō drama as artificial signs, while I would call the first natural to a given culture and the second a natural gesture made artificial.

9. Jean-Paul Sartre, "Beyond Bourgeois Theatre," *Tulane Drama Review*, 5 (March 1961), 4.

10. Langer, *Feeling and Form*, pp. 47–48.

11. Allardyce Nicoll, *The Theatre and Dramatic Theory* (New York: Barnes & Noble, 1962), p. 11.

12. Northrop Frye, *Anatomy of Criticism* (New York: Atheneum, 1966; first published, 1957), p. 269.

13. Langer, *Feeling and Form*, p. 314.

14. Olson, p. 8.

15. Fergusson, p. 8.

16. Bentley, pp. 9–14.

17. *Ibid.*, p. 15.

18. John Howard Lawson, *The Theory and Technique of Playwriting and Screenwriting* (New York: Putnam, 1936), p. 171.

19. Bernard Beckerman, *Shakespeare at the Globe* (New York: Macmillan, 1962), pp. 35 ff.

20. Fergusson, p. 11.

21. Robert H. Hethmon (ed.), *Strasberg at the Actors Studio* (New York: Viking, 1965), p. 290.

22. Langer, *Feeling and Form*, pp. 59–60. In *Problems of Art*, pp. 5–6, Langer explicitly argues that actuality disappears in the performing process, and that we perceive only "virtual entities."

Chapter Two

1. Erving Goffman, *The Presentation of Self in Everyday Life* (Garden City, New York: Doubleday, 1959); Eric Berne, *Transactional Analysis in Psychotherapy* (New York: Grove Press, 1961).
2. Ruth Manning-Sanders, *The English Circus* (London: Werner Laurie, 1952), p. 260.
3. Henry Thétard, *La Merveilleuse Histoire du Cirque* (Paris: Prisma, 1947), Vol. II, p. 126. My own translation.
4. Michael Polanyi, *Personal Knowledge* (Chicago: The University of Chicago Press, 1958), p. 56.
5. Michael Polanyi, *The Tacit Dimension* (Garden City, New York: Doubleday, 1966), p. 11.
6. Jean-Paul Sartre, *In Search of a Method* (New York: Knopf, 1963), p. 91.
7. Manning-Sanders, p. 258.
8. John Howard Lawson, *The Theory and Technique of Playwriting and Screenwriting* (New York: Putnam, 1936), p. 167.
9. Henri Bergson as quoted by Harold Rugg in *Imagination* (New York: Harper & Row, 1963), p. 209.
10. Louis De Broglie, *The Revolution in Physics* (New York: Noonday Press, 1953), p. 218.
11. Michael Kirby, "The New Theatre," *Tulane Drama Review*, 10 (Winter 1965), 25.
12. Allardyce Nicoll, *The Theatre and Dramatic Theory* (New York: Barnes & Noble, 1962), p. 11.
13. Jan Kott, "Theatre and Literature," David M. Knauf (ed.), *Papers in Dramatic Theory and Criticism* (Iowa City: University of Iowa Press, 1968), p. 43.
14. John Millington Synge, *The Aran Islands*, in *The Complete Works of John M. Synge* (New York: Random House, 1935), p. 363.
15. J. M. Synge, *Collected Works*, Ann Saddlemyer (ed.) (London: Oxford University Press, 1968), Vol. III.
16. *Ibid.*, p. 235.
17. *Ibid.*, pp. 243 ff.
18. *Ibid.*, p. 236.
19. *Ibid.*, p. 245.
20. *Ibid.*, pp. 8–11.

Chapter Three

1. Sophocles, *Electra,* David Grene (tr.), *Complete Greek Tragedies,* Vol. II David Grene and Richard Latimore (eds.). Copyright 1957 by The University of Chicago Press. Reprinted by permission of The University of Chicago Press.

2. Bernard Beckerman, Chapter Two, "The Dramaturgy," *Shakespeare at the Globe* (New York: Macmillan, 1962).

3. For my translation I purposely selected the more dated one by William Archer (*Ibsen's Prose Dramas,* London and New York: The Walter Scott Publishing Co., Ltd., and Scribner, 1903, Vol. V), with a few slight changes: "Assessor" to "Judge," "Jörgen" to "George," and "cock on the fowl-roost" to "cock of the roost." A comparison of this translation with one of the latest, for example, J. W. McFarlane (ed.), *Hedda Gabler* in *The Oxford Ibsen* (London: Oxford University Press, 1966), Vol. VII, pp. 261–268, will demonstrate that the shape of the dramatic action is virtually identical in both versions. For some readings the Oxford text is more colloquial than the Archer, but insofar as perception of structure is concerned, the older translation conveys the interplay of project and resistance more distinctly.

4. E. H. Gombrich, *Art and Illusion* (New York: Pantheon Books, 1960), p. 50.

5. Anton Chekhov, *The Cherry Orchard,* in *Best Plays of Chekhov,* Stark Young (tr.) (New York: Random House, 1956). Reprinted by permission of The Estate of Stark Young. Copyright 1939, 1941, 1947, and 1950 by Stark Young. Copyright © 1956 by Stark Young.

6. Albin Lesky, *Greek Tragedy* (London: Ernest Benn Ltd., 1965), p. 139.

7. J. C. Kamerbeek, *The Plays of Sophocles* (Leiden: E. J. Brill, 1963), p. 13.

8. Line count follows lineation of the Greek text in the Loeb Classical Library edition of *Ajax,* F. Starr (tr.) (Cambridge, Mass., and London: Harvard University Press and William Heinemann Ltd., 1951).

9. Ruby Cohn, *Samuel Beckett: The Comic Gamut* (New Brunswick, N. J.: Rutgers University Press, 1962), p. 325n.

10. Hugh Kenner, *Samuel Beckett, A Critical Study* (New York: Grove Press, 1961), p. 10.

Chapter Four

1. G. B. Mohan Thampi, " 'Rasa' as Aesthetic Experience," *Journal of Aesthetics and Art Criticism*, 24 (1965), 75.
2. Marshall McLuhan, *Understanding Media* (New York: McGraw-Hill, 1965), p. 242.
3. Michael Polanyi, *The Tacit Dimension* (Garden City, New York: Doubleday, 1966), p. 4.
4. Warren Weaver, "The Imperfections of Science," Samuel and Helen Wright Rapport (eds.), *Science: Method and Meaning* (New York: New York University Press, 1963).
5. Max Planck, *The Philosophy of Physics* (New York: W. W. Norton & Co., 1936), pp. 54 ff.
6. J. B. Priestley, *The Art of the Dramatist* (London: Heinemann, 1957), p. 5.
7. Rudolf Arnheim, *Art and Visual Perception* (Berkeley and Los Angeles: University of California Press, 1954), p. 51; E. H. Gombrich, *Art and Illusion* (New York: Pantheon Books, 1960), pp. 68 ff.
8. George Steiner, *The Death of Tragedy* (New York: Knopf, 1961), p. 318.
9. Friedrich von Schiller, *On Tragic Art* (1792), as quoted in Barrett H. Clark, *European Theories of the Drama*, rev. ed. (New York: Crown, 1947), p. 322.
10. Kurt Koffka, *Principles of Gestalt Psychology* (New York: Harcourt, Brace & World, 1935), p. 191.
11. R. R. Menon, "Indian Music and its American Audience," *Saturday Review* (January 27, 1968), 50. Life situations themselves contain the duality of figure and ground, as Kenneth Burke emphasizes in *A Grammar of Motives*, p. 12.
12. Arthur Miller, *Collected Plays* (New York: Viking, 1957), p. 28.
13. *Times Literary Supplement* (April 8, 1965), 266.
14. Jean Racine, "Discours Prononcé a l'Académie Française à la Réception de Mm. Corneille et Bergeret" (le 2 janvier 1685), *Oeuvres Complètes* (New York: Macmillan, 1962), p. 414.
15. Russell A. Fraser, *Shakespeare's Poetics* (London: Routledge & Kegan Paul, Ltd., 1962).
16. Sir Thomas Elyot, *The Book named The Governor* (London: Everyman's Library, 1962), p. 163.

17. Ronald Peacock, *The Art of Drama* (London: Routledge & Kegan Paul, 1957), p. 82.
18. George Lukács, *The Historical Novel* (Boston: Beacon Press, 1963), p. 139.
19. Rudolf Arnheim, "Emotion and Feeling in Psychology and Art," Mary Henle (ed.), *Documents of Gestalt Psychology* (Berkeley: University of California Press, 1961), p. 349.
20. Suzanne Langer, *Problems of Art*, p. 166.
21. Harold Rugg, *Imagination* (New York: Harper & Row, 1963), pp. 78–79.
22. Arnheim, "Emotion and Feeling in Psychology and Art," p. 377.
23. Polanyi, *The Tacit Dimension*, p. 13.
24. Rudolf Arnheim, "Gestalt Theory and Expression," Mary Henle (ed.), *Documents of Gestalt Psychology* (Berkeley: University of California Press, 1961), pp. 308 ff.; Rugg, p. 268.
25. Horace B. and Ava C. English, *A Comprehensive Dictionary of Psychological & Psychoanalytical Terms* (New York: Longmans, Green & Co., 1958).
26. Rugg, p. 10.
27. Johann Wolfgang Goethe, as quoted in *Goethe on the Theater*, John Oxenford (tr.) (New York: Dramatic Museum, Columbia University, 1919), p. 34.
28. In *Nicias*, Plutarch reports the story that the soldiers "received food and drink for singing some of [Euripides'] choral hymns." See *Plutarch's Lives*, The Loeb Classical Library (London: William Heinemann, 1916).
29. McLuhan, p. 26.
30. My division of theatrical meaning into four aspects parallels roughly the categories of meaning characteristic of medieval scriptural exegesis. Biblical commentators usually adopted a three- or four-fold interpretation of text conducted on literal, tropological, allegorical, and anagogic levels. The literal level was mainly descriptive, concerned with the immediate perceptions of a work. The tropological dealt with the moral implications of a passage. The allegoric interpretation referred to the larger world of experience of which the particular work was a reflection. Lastly, anagogic interpretation was concerned with the mystical experience intended by the work. All four levels together composed the total meaning.
31. Eric Bentley, *The Life of the Drama* (New York: Atheneum, 1964), p. 108.
32. Polanyi, *The Tacit Dimension*, pp. 16–17.

Chapter Five

1. *The Cherry Orchard* falls between *Hedda Gabler* and *King Lear*, combining the impression of a trapped family and multiple effects.
2. The conclusions of *King Lear* and *Troilus and Cressida* are exceptions. Shakespeare emphasizes the desolation of Lear's death by showing the irresolution of the two victors. Neither Albany, the victor in battle, nor Edgar, the victor in the trial-by-combat, asserts effective authority. The foreshadowing of Troy's fall in *Troilus and Cressida*, pointing the action of the play toward the future, is extremely unusual and has led one scholar to suggest that the play may have been planned as the first part of a two-part play. T. W. Baldwin in H. N. Hillebrand (ed.), *A New Variorum Edition of Troilus and Cressida* (Philadelphia: Lippincott, 1953), p. 452.
3. R. C. Oldfield, Introduction to Albert Michotte, *The Perception of Causality* (London: Methuen & Co., Ltd., 1963), p. vii.
4. Arthur Miller, *Collected Works* (New York: Viking, 1957), p. 7.
5. Laurence Olivier and Kenneth Tynan, "The Actor: An Interview," *Tulane Drama Review*, 11 (Winter 1966), 93.
6. See Hardin Craig, *The Enchanted Glass* (New York: Oxford University Press, 1952); Ruth Anderson, *Elizabethan Psychology and Shakespeare's Plays* in *University of Iowa Studies*, III (March 15, 1927); E. M. W. Tillyard, *The Elizabethan World Picture* (London: Chatto & Windus, 1948).
7. Caroline Spurgeon, *Shakespeare's Imagery* (Cambridge, England: The University Press, 1935); G. Wilson Knight, *The Wheel of Fire* (New York: Oxford University Press, 1949); Nevill Coghill, *Shakespeare's Professional Skills* (Cambridge, England: Cambridge University Press, 1964). Coghill (pp. 72–76) has a perceptive discussion on the repetitive use of the name Eros in *Antony and Cleopatra*, excellently combining theatrical and literary analysis.
8. Aristotle, *Poetics*, Kenneth A. Telford (tr.) (Chicago: Henry Regnery Co., 1961), p. 20.
9. Heinrich Wölfflin, *Principles of Art History*, M. D. Hottinger (tr.) (New York: Dover, n.d., first published in German, 1915; first English translation published, 1932).
10. Volker Klotz, *Geschlossene und offene form im Drama* (München: Carl Hanser Verlag, 1960).
11. Marvin Rosenberg, "A Metaphor for Dramatic Form," *Journal of*

Aesthetics and Art Criticism, 17 (1958), 174–180; Alan Downer, *The Art of the Play* (New York: Henry Holt and Co., 1955), pp. 174–175.

12. Instead of "Oh, that intolerable thought. I cannot endure it!" the final version has, "No, I can't endure the thought of that!"

13. "George" in the final version.

14. Bernard Beckerman, *Shakespeare at the Globe* (New York: Macmillan, 1962), pp. 64–69.

15. T. W. Baldwin, *Shakespere's Five-Act Structure* (Urbana: University of Illinois Press, 1947); Clifford Leech, "Shakespeare's Use of a Five-Act Structure," *Die Neueren Sprachen,* 6 (January 1957), 249–263.

16. Beckerman, *Shakespeare at the Globe,* pp. 40–45. Here I give a fuller description of the split structure and the aesthetic conceptions underlying Shakespeare's techniques.

17. Eric Bentley, *The Life of the Drama* (New York: Atheneum, 1964), pp. 34 ff.; J. L. Styan, *The Elements of Drama* (Cambridge, England: Cambridge University Press, 1960), pp. 163 ff.

Chapter Six

1. At the conclusion of *Viet Rock* the actors went through the audience, clasping hands with those people they could reach. In *Dionysus in '69* the chorus selected people from the audience during one of the choral odes and freely caressed them.

2. In *The Oxford Ibsen,* the lines, "I am in your power none the less. Subject to your will and your demands. A slave, a slave then!" are rendered as, "In your power, all the same. Subject to your will and your demands. No longer free!" (p. 266). In Norwegian, the final phrase is, "Ufri. Ufri altså!" Neither Archer nor the Oxford text fully convey the finality of the phrase. "Altså" means "therefore, accordingly, consequently." The literal translation would be "Unfree. Unfree therefore!" expressing not that Hedda is free no longer but that the consequence of Brack's blackmail is that she is now "unfree" or "a slave."

3. Henry Thétard, *La Merveilleuse Histoire du Cirque* (Paris: Prisma, 1947), Vol. II, p. 121.

4. Rudolf Arnheim, *Art and Visual Perception* (Berkeley and Los Angeles: University of California Press, 1954), p. 45.

5. Alan M. G. Little, *Myth and Society in Attic Drama* (New York:

Columbia University Press, 1942); C. Walter Hodges, *The Globe Restored*, 2nd ed. (London: Oxford University Press, 1968).

6. Glynne Wickham, *Early English Stages* (New York and London: Columbia University Press and Routledge & Kegan Paul, 1963), Vol. II, p. 203.

7. George R. Kernodle, *From Art to Theatre* (Chicago: University of Chicago Press, 1944), pp. 150–151.

Afterword

1. Erik H. Erikson, "On the Nature of Psycho-Historical Evidence: In Search of Ghandhi," *Daedalus*, 97 (Summer 1968), 695.

INDEX

Note: *The index may also serve as a glossary. Numerals in boldface refer to pages on which a term is examined in detail.*

Théatre

performers: posi'r of

dominance

audience: vulnerable

possibility of

interaction - requiring
alternative attitude.

audience: passive

(TV+) during perf.